Text Production with Microsoft Word

SECOND EDITION

Geoffrey Foy

Gill & Macmillan

Gill & Macmillan Ltd
Hume Avenue
Park West
Dublin 12
with associated companies throughout the world
www.gillmacmillan.ie

© Geoffrey Foy 2005

978 0717 3845 6

Index compiled by Grainne Farren
Print origination by Carrigboy Typesetting Services, Co. Cork

Screen shots reprinted by kind permission of the Microsoft Corporation.

CONTENTS

INDEX

Page numbers in italics refer to illustrations.

PREFACE

So here we are, four years after the publication of the previous edition. Though Microsoft Word has not changed a great deal, it was considered appropriate to make a number of changes to the earlier text. These include the following:

- Additional exercises on topics such as macros, mail merge and graphics.
- Updated Letters, Memos and Forms sections, with exercises that require the rearrangement and layout of text, rather than straightforward copy typing.
- Additional typed, as opposed to manuscript, exercises to reflect the fact that text processing operators are now more likely to find themselves editing work that has already been keyed in, rather than poring over handwritten material.
- Suggested model answers to certain exercises.

As to that much-heralded day when voice-recognition systems may render keyboarding obsolete, it seems as far away as ever. For this reason the Keyboard section has been retained, notwithstanding the wide use of keyboarding packages. No doubt such packages have their place, but the author has found that traditional speed development exercises are probably more effective in preparing students for examinations, which for the most part are still in hard copy format.

ACKNOWLEDGEMENTS

This text would not have been possible without the help and encouragement of many colleagues and acquaintances. Special thanks must go to the following:

- Ailbhe O'Reilly, formerly of Gill & Macmillan, who did the progress chasing for the original edition.
- All at Gill & Macmillan, in particular Marion O'Brien, publishing executive, and Aoileann O'Donnell, managing editor.
- All those who reviewed the original text, in particular Joan Gallagher and Dawn Mulholland.
- Mary Collins and other colleagues at the Athlone Institute of Technology, including Assumpta Byrne, Brigid Delamere, Eimear Kelly, Rosaleen Lohan, James McNamara, Dermot O'Rourke and Dr Patrick Walsh.
- Dr Eliathamby Ambikairajah, University of New South Wales, Paul Breen, Temple Printing Company, Athlone, Anne Foy, Dermot Foy and Valerie Byrne.
- The Incorporated Law Society; Mary Helly, University College Hospital, Galway; Clare Foley, Cavan College of Further Studies; and Mary Fields, Greendale Community College.
- The many students of the Athlone Institute of Technology and the Vocational School, now O'Fiaich College, Dundalk, with whom I had the pleasure of working over the years.

Part 1
Getting Started

▶▷▷▷▷▷▷▷▷▷▷▷▷▷

It has never been easier to save, retrieve and manipulate text. Before getting started, please check the names of the principal computer parts, as shown below.

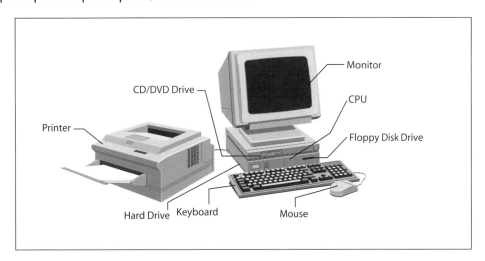

CPU The letters stand for Central Processing Unit. The CPU is the core of the computer and governs the operation of the computer and all connected input devices (e.g. keyboard), and all output devices (e.g. printer).

Disk Drive A device that reads information from disks and writes information onto disks.

A CD drive is a Compact Disc drive that is used to read CDs (also called CD-ROMs). A CD-RW drive can read and write to special CDs (either CD-Recordable or CD-ReWritable). A CD-Recordable disk can be written to only once, but can be read repeatedly. A CD-ReWritable can be written to repeatedly.

A DVD drive is a Digital Video Disc drive or Digital Versatile Disc drive that is used to read and/or write information using DVD discs. Digital Versatile Discs hold far more information than CDs. DVDs are used to store video and audio data, as well as traditional computer data.

Floppy Disk A removable disk; stores a smaller amount of information than a hard disk.

Hard Disk A sealed disk that can store a large amount of information electronically.

Keyboard An input device through which text or data is entered into a computer.

Monitor Also known as a visual display unit (VDU); displays the computer output onto a screen.

Mouse An input device, the movement of which controls the position of the I-beam or pointer on the monitor.

Printer An output device that produces printed text or other information.

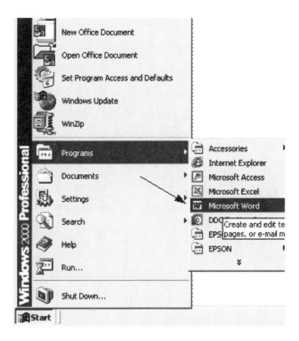

Activating Your Word Processing Program, Microsoft Word

Position the mouse pointer arrow on the **Start** icon at the bottom left of your screen, then push the pointer up to **Programs** and across to **Microsoft Word** – the Word 'window' then opens, as shown below.

The Word Document Window

Familiarise yourself with the parts of the Word window that are shown below.

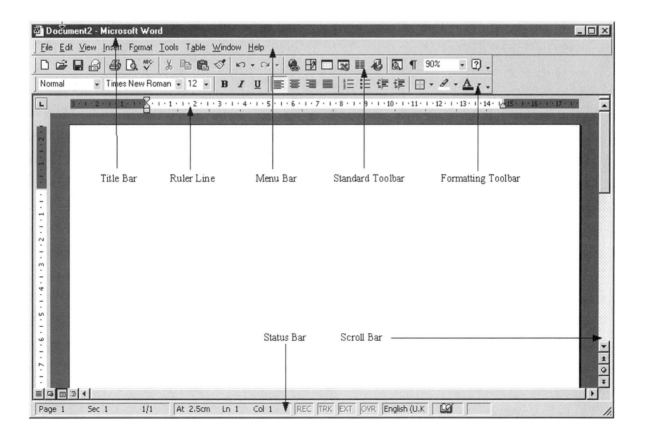

- The top, usually coloured, line is called the **Title Bar**. This shows the name of the software being used (i.e. Microsoft Word) and the name of the Word document being worked on. The names Document1, Document2, Document3, etc. will appear if a document has not been saved and given a name.

- The next screen element is usually the **Menu Bar**. Click one of the menus, such as **File**, **Edit** or **View**, to reveal a relevant drop-down menu. From the drop-down menu, click the option required.

- The next screen element is the **Standard toolbar**. Click the icons on this toolbar to perform general tasks such as opening, saving or closing files. If the Standard toolbar is not showing, click **View**, **Toolbars**, **Standard**.

- The next line is usually the **Formatting toolbar**. Icons on this toolbar allow one to embolden text, italicise and underline, etc. If the Formatting toolbar is not showing, click **View**, **Toolbars**, **Formatting**.

- The next line is usually the **Ruler Line**. This allows one to judge the position of text in a document window. If the ruler line is in inches, refer to 'Measurement units, centimetres versus inches' on page 11, as you may wish to change it to centimetres. If the ruler line is not showing, click **View**, **Ruler**.

- Note the **Scroll Bars** on the right and at the bottom of the Word window. By clicking the arrows in these Scroll Bars, the text on display may be moved up or down, or to the left or the right. If the Scroll Bars are not showing, click **Tools**, **Options**, **View**. Then, in the View dialog box, click the **Horizontal Scroll Bar** and **Vertical Scroll Bar** checkboxes.

- The **View Bar** is located at the bottom left side of the Word window. The buttons on this bar allow documents to be viewed in Normal View, Web Layout View, Print Layout View or Outline View.

- The **Status Bar**, near the bottom of the screen, shows information such as the page number and the line on which the cursor is positioned. If the Status Bar is not showing, click **Tools**, **Options** and **View**. In the Options dialog box click the **View** tab and then the **Status Bar** checkbox.

- The **Task Bar**, at the very bottom of the screen, shows the documents that are open and applications that are running.

 Tip 1 — Hold the mouse pointer over a toolbar icon for a second to activate a text box that gives the icon's name.

 Tip 2 — If one of the letters in a Menu Bar option is underlined (as <u>N</u>ew in the File menu), just key in this letter to activate the menu choice.

The left mouse button

The computer mouse has a left and right button. Click the left button unless instructed otherwise.

▶ Getting Started 1

Check that your Word window is showing all the screen elements mentioned on page 3 and key in the text My first document.

On the Standard toolbar click the **New** button 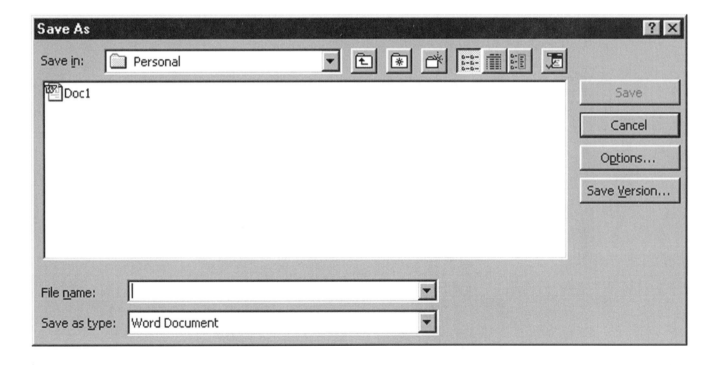 and key in My second document.

On the Standard toolbar Click the **New** button and key in My third document.

Now click **Window** on the Menu toolbar. The bottom part of the Window drop-down menu shows the three documents created, i.e. Document1, Document2 and Document3. Practise moving from one document to another by clicking the document names.

Saving work

Although three documents have been created, they have not yet been saved. Therefore, if there was a power failure or if the computer was turned off, these documents would be lost.

▶ Getting Started 2

Insert a floppy disk in the A: drive. Click the **Window** menu and click **Document1**, then click the **File** menu and select **Save As**. In the Save As dialog box, keep clicking the up arrow until it dims, then click the down arrow until 3½ **Floppy (A:)** appears. In the **File name** box, key in G2a. Then click **Save**.

Now click the **Window** menu again and select **Document2**. Repeat the above process. Rename Document2 G2b, and rename Document3 G2c.

Moving around text

As you move the mouse over text, an 'I-beam' appears. Click the mouse when the I-beam is in the required position. The I-beam changes to a (blinking) insertion point indicator called the 'cursor'.

Apart from using the mouse, the cursor position can also be moved by pressing the arrow keys.

Keyboard Commands (KBCs) may also be used to move the cursor, some of which are set out below.

Some keyboard commands (KBCs)

Make sure Num Lock is inactive when using the commands shown below (i.e. the Num Lock light must be off). These commands make use of the numeric keypad, which is located to the right of the keyboard.

- **Home** — moves the cursor to the start of a line.
- **Ctrl+Home** — moves the cursor to the start of a document.
- **End** — moves the cursor to the end of a line.
- **Ctrl+End** — moves the cursor to the end of a document.

Note — the plus symbol (+) means that the Ctrl key should be held down while the second key is pressed.

Num lock key

When the Num Lock key is active, a light shows above it. Press Num Lock again to deactivate it.

Correction of errors

Position the cursor immediately after the error and press the **Backspace Delete** key (i.e. the back-arrow above the return key), then key in the correct text.

Alternatively, position the cursor immediately before the error and press the **Delete** key.

▶ Getting Started 3

Key in the text below and save it as G3. Practise moving the cursor using (a) the mouse (b) the forward and back arrows and (c) the keyboard commands.

```
CREDIT CARD SECURITY HINDERS E-COMMERCE

Theft of credit card numbers over the Internet is the greatest
obstacle to e-commerce development. Until these security
issues are resolved, consumers remain hesitant about
purchasing goods and services.

Orbiscom is one of several Irish companies, including Trintech
and Baltimore, that are developing secure Internet credit card
payment services or products.

Source: The Irish Times, 30 June 2000
```

natural environment, the perfect location to produce the finest food	1722
products in Europe .	1742
Clean surroundings are important for pharmaceutical and chemical	1807
industries as well. It means that they often do not have to filter	1869
their air, and pay a great deal for water purification. Many	1925
industries absolutely need clean surroundings and when they do not	1993
get them, they have to spend huge sums of money cleaning them up.	2061
This can often be the reason why industries chose to locate in remote	2130
areas. Controlling and monitoring the activities of industries once	2194
they are in operation, and the decision as to whether they can or	2257
cannot locate in the first place are the issues, even if only to ensure	2323
that there are clean areas left in which to locate new industries. One	2390
of the central points raised by the study into Industry and the	2450
Environment, carried out by An Taisce and the Confederation of Irish	2517
Industry was the necessity of a toxic waste disposal facility in this	2581
country.	2589
Early this year, a report recommended that an €8 million incinerator	2656
with a capacity for handling up to 5,000 tonnes of waste a year be	2720
erected. The proposal was welcomed by interested bodies, some with	2788
varying degrees of caution, and the Department of the Environment	2854
is currently inviting tenders for it. However, both Earthwatch and	2918
An Taisce stress the importance of developing an overall waste	2979
management policy whereby we have to take responsibility for our	3044
own waste. They wonder if we would be actively encouraging	3103
companies with a high production of toxic waste to locate here if we	3168
accept a toxic waste facility without placing controls on waste	3227
production.	3238

Selecting text

Text must be selected before its format can be changed. This can be done in a number of different ways.

❶ Move the cursor to the beginning of the text, hold down the left mouse button and move (drag) the I-beam over the text.

❷ Move the cursor to the beginning of the text, then move the I-beam to the end of the text, hold down the Shift key and click.

❸ To select a word, position the I-beam over it and double click.

❹ To select a sentence, position the I-beam over it, hold down Ctrl and click.

❺ To select a paragraph, position the I-beam over it and treble click.

❻ To select all the text in a Word window, use the Ctrl+A keyboard command.

❼ To select a line of text, move the I-beam to the beginning of the line (until it changes to an inward-facing arrow), then click.

▶ *Getting Started 4*

Retrieve G3 and practise selecting the following:

(a) 'several Irish companies' — use method 1

(b) all the text except the first sentence — use method 2

(c) 'Internet' — use method 3

(d) the first sentence — use method 4

(e) the second paragraph — use method 5

(f) all the text — use method 6.

Inserting text

Position the cursor where the text is required and key it in.

The Insert key

The **Insert** key (the **Ins** key) on the numeric keyboard is sometimes pressed accidentally; this causes keyed-in text to replace existing text. Press this key a second time to deactivate it.

Deleting text

Select the text and press the **Delete** key, or the keyboard command **Ctrl+X**. Another convenient way of deleting a block of text is as follows:

❶ Select the text.

❷ Hold the mouse pointer over the selected text.

❸ Click the button on the right side of the mouse.

❹ Move the mouse pointer to **Cut** (on the menu that appears) and click again.

Copying a block of text

When text is copied it remains in its original position and a copy is made in a different location. To copy, select the text, click the **Edit** menu and click **Copy**. Note — the Edit menu shows the keyboard commands for the various edit options. For example, to the right of the Copy option is the keyboard command Ctrl+C.

Ireland's positive environmental image is central to the promotion of	69
food produce - our main export. Fishing, farming, and tourism jobs	136
are also dependent on natural resources. Yet, with environmental	201
interests often seen as conflicting with those of industry, are we	264
conscious enough of the commercial worth of conservation?	323
To many of us the notion of industrialisation and a healthy	382
environment are mutually exclusive. Images of damage, often	444
irretrievable, caused to the environment in heavily industrialised	509
areas like the Ruhr valley in Germany, are recalled, and at home the	577
dispute about setting up a pharmaceutical factory in the south, come	645
to mind. While the debate surrounding these incidents heightens	710
public awareness of the potential threat posed by industry to the	775
environment, they can also somehow create the impression that one	843
must be sacrificed for the other.	876
Environmental groups opposing new plants are frequently castigated	944
as being anti-industry and anti-employment. It is as if the choice is	1011
between industry, which generates jobs and revenue, and the	1073
environment. Nobody in Earthwatch would be ashamed to oppose	1139
toxic industries. They state that dirty industries do a lot more	1201
damage to an area in the long run, than creating a fuss at the time.	1267
After all, they say who is really doing the harm? Jobs in farming,	1331
fishing and tourism are jeopardised by pollution. The links between	1399
a healthy environment and the development of industries like	1461
tourism, agriculture and food are obvious, and are a significant	1523
selling point of those industries abroad. Coras Trachtala, for instance,	1592
promotes Ireland abroad as having 'lush pastures, clean waters,	1655

Moving text to a different position in a document, or to another document

Copy the text, move the insertion point to a different location, click the **Edit** menu and click **Paste**. Note — the keyboard command Ctrl+V is shown on the Edit menu to the right of Paste. Try to learn your keyboard commands!

Font and font size

A font is a style of typeface, such as Times New Roman. Each typeface is available in many different sizes. To change font, click the arrow in the **Font** button on the Formatting toolbar. To change font size, click the arrow in the **Font Size** button.

▶ Getting Started 5

Retrieve G3 and carry out the tasks below. Save it as G5.

(a) Select all the text and change the font to Arial.

(b) Select the heading and change it to 16 points.

(c) Select the remainder of the text and change it to 14 points.

The Undo Typing button

To undo changes made to text press the **Undo Typing** button on the Standard toolbar.

▶ Getting Started 5a

Retrieve G3 and carry out the tasks below. Save as G5a.

(a) Delete the second sentence using the Delete key.

(b) Press the Undo Typing button and delete the second sentence again using Ctrl+X.

(c) Press the Undo Typing button again and delete the second sentence again by clicking the right mouse button (i.e. the right side of the mouse).

(d) Key in a new paragraph, as follows:
```
Baltimore recently licenced its encryption technology to Visa
International to make secure Internet payments possible.
```

Underline (or underscore), bold and italics

Select the relevant text and click the **Underline**, **Bold** or **Italics** buttons on the Formatting toolbar.

▶ Getting Started 6

Retrieve G3 and underline the second sentence. Embolden the heading and format each of the company names in italics. Save as G6.

Centre, right align

Select the relevant text and click the **Centre** or **Right Align** button on the Formatting toolbar.

is now being achieved. The industrial authority has also courted	1634
component makers and subassembly specialists with some	1696
success. In short, it should be possible for Ireland to secure	1759
continued growth in the overall electronics and software	1818
industries, but the computer sector may account for a declining	1885
proportion of the jobs and the exports.	1926

The recent round of computer factory closures in this country	1991
and the fall in the value of system exports in 1990 show that all	2060
is not-well in the computer industry. Technology trends have	2126
combined with changes in the structure of the industry to create	2195
enormous challenges for all suppliers and chronic difficulties for	2263
some. The fortunes of the big computer vendors vary	2320
dramatically. Some companies have caught the mood of the new	2388
computing wave and are expanding fast and others misread the	2455
changes and are recording hefty losses. On a global level the	2519
majority of computer makers, including the mighty IBM, are	2583
struggling to match last year's sales and to achieve financial	2648
breakeven for 1991.	2668

To understand what is happening, it is only necessary to listen to	2738
the promotional cliches trotted out by the suppliers. Their claims	2808
that computers today are smaller, more powerful, less expensive	2877
and easier to network together than ever before are absolutely	2944
true.	2950

◗ *Getting Started 7*

Key in the text below and save as G7.

(a) Centre the first two lines.

(b) Right align the last two lines.

```
The Ground Beneath Her Feet
By U2
Featuring lyrics by Salman Rushdie
(Part of the soundtrack album for the movie Million Dollar Hotel.)
```

Justify
Select the relevant text and click the **Justify** button ▤ on the Formatting toolbar.
When text is justified it aligns both at the left and right margin.

◗ *Getting Started 8*

Retrieve G3 and (a) justify (b) centre and (c) right align it. Save as G8a, G8b and G8c, respectively.

Drag-and-drop text editing
Drag-and-drop editing allows the operator to move text around easily. To check that this facility is enabled, click the **Tools** menu, click **Options** and then click the **Edit** tab in the Options dialog box. Ensure that the **Drag-and-drop text editing** checkbox is ticked.

To drag and drop, select text, hold the I-beam (which changes to a pointer arrow) over it, hold down the mouse button and drag the text to a different position.

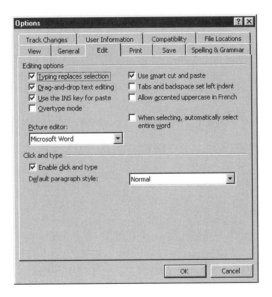

◗ *Getting Started 9*

Retrieve G7 and practise dragging and changing the position of the lines.

Drag and copy
Drag and copy is like drag and drop, except that the selected text stays in position and a copy is moved to a different position. To drag and copy, select the relevant text, hold the I-beam over it, hold down the Ctrl key, hold down the mouse button and drag the text to a different position.

Computers are a key part of the Irish electronics sector, but the	67
computer wave during which dozens of US vendors set up	128
manufacturing plants in Ireland is effectively over. There are	193
very few systems projects available for the IDA to chase these	258
days and most of the existing systems facilities are showing signs	327
of age.	335
The computer industry is feeling the heat. Established names are	404
disappearing, system manufacturers are diversifying into new	468
lines of business at a startling rate, and much of the clout of the	535
big computer companies has passed to microchip makers and	598
software firms.	614
These operations employ some 4,700 people, down from a peak	681
of 6,000 jobs four or five years ago. The best way to judge their	749
future viability is to look at the extent to which their owners are	818
investing in shopfloor data collection, automation equipment or	885
the flexible manufacturing systems that enable them to combine	953
volume production with a high degree of customisation. By these	1022
criteria no more than four or five plants in this country look	1086
secure for the long term.	1113
Most of the factories that have closed had not received sufficient	1182
investment for their processes to match the industry average.	1246
Looking beyond computer system manufacturing at associated	1310
production activities, the picture is much sunnier. In the mid-	1374
eighties the IDA began to grant-aid warehouses for software	1437
companies on a hunch that these firms would subsequently	1499
undertake serious development work in Ireland. This objective	1566

Retrieve G7, and without further keying in, format it to look as shown below. Save it as G10.

The Ground Beneath Her Feet

Featuring lyrics by Salman Rushdie

The Ground Beneath Her Feet

<u>By U2</u>

The Ground Beneath Her Feet

(Part of the soundtrack album for the movie *Million Dollar Hotel*.)

The Ground Beneath Her Feet

<u>By U2</u>

<u>By U2</u>

<u>By U2</u>

▶ *Getting Started 11*

Key in the sentence below once, return five times, and drag and copy the sentence five times. Apply the formatting shown for each line and save as G11. Note the fifth line is centred and the sixth line is right-aligned.

The Irish e-business market will be worth €6.4 billion by 2003.

The Irish e-business market will be worth €6.4 billion by 2003.

<u>The Irish e-business market will be worth €6.4 billion by 2003.</u>

The Irish e-business market will be worth €6.4 billion by 2003.

The Irish e-business market will be worth €6.4 billion by 2003.

The Irish e-business market will be worth €6.4 billion by 2003.

People skills are the key to successful quality effort. Formal   1530

Quality programmes have little chance of success unless effective   1596

interactive 'people skills' are in place at all levels. Managers and   1662

employees may understand and believe in the organization's   1724

quality concepts but if they have not developed the required   1786

skills to implement them, the process may not succeed.   1842

In this regard the role of education and training is crucial. Quality   1909

of service depends on the people who deliver that service and,   1973

without the support of training, staff cannot perform their job   2036

with confidence.   2054

Studies indicate that well over half of Irish employees do not   2116

receive any training. In fact, the percentage of payroll spent on   2180

training in Ireland is one of the lowest in Europe.   2229

Another crucial factor in the drive for improved customer care is   2295

setting goals and providing incentives for staff to reach these   2357

goals. Motivation research shows that people need to work for   2421

more than just money - they need to be convinced that what they   2488

are doing| is worthwhile.   2514

This is the benefit of incentive schemes such as the Quality Mark   2580

and Quality Awards. They set goals and standards to be achieved;   2648

provide recognition for employees; and raise morale throughout   2712

the organisation.   2730

Key in the text below in 12 points Times New Roman font. Save it as G12.

THE E-COMMERCE BILL

The E-commerce Bill became law in July 2000 when the President, Mrs McAleese, signed it with a digital signature. The President's signature was the first electronic signature to have the State's full legal recognition.

This Bill is seen as a cornerstone of e-commerce and is designed to enable businesses and citizens to do business over the Internet, ranging from registering property deeds to signing contracts, making tax returns, requesting medical information and corresponding with the government.

It sets out a formal legal framework for conducting business electronically, in nearly all cases giving equivalent recognition to electronic signatures. These signatures are not written names but an encoded sequence of characters that can be associated with an individual at a specific time.

The Bill also recognises electronic forms of writing and documents — until now, paper versions alone were guaranteed legal weight. It also clearly protects the right of businesses and individuals to use encryption — software programs that encode and decode electronic documents and e-mails.

One of the primary goals of the Bill is to guarantee the equivalency of electronic writing while ensuring technological neutrality. That is, that one form of technology, such as a smart card combined with a software program, is not the only allowed way of producing a signature.

The Bill is considered a good international model, according to privacy advocacy groups such as the Electronic Privacy Information Center in Washington, DC.

(The above text is based on an article that appeared in *The Irish Times* on 30 June 2000.)

Scrolling text up and down

To move text up or down, click the up or down arrow on the **vertical Scroll Bar**, or click and drag the button between the arrows.

Target speed — 50 wpm.

The 1990s are clearly becoming the Decade of the Customer. As	67
consumers become more sophisticated and competition for their	134
custom intensifies, quality of service is vital for business success.	202
This is being recognised not only by the services sector but also	268
by manufacturing industries, most of whom are now placing	328
greater emphasis on customer related activities.	378
Service quality means putting the customer first. It means	437
treating each customer as an individual, listening to them,	495
defining their needs, and not just meeting, but exceeding their	559
requirements each time. Customers are the mainstay of any	619
organisation. Dissatisfied customers mean loss of revenue,	677
reduced profits and redundancies.	712
Research has shown that while 30 per cent of customers will	773
complain about an unsatisfactory product, only 1 per cent will	836
complain about unsatisfactory service. They will simply not come	904
back to the supplier and what's more they will tell others. Sixty-	972
eight per cent of customers who leave service companies do so	1035
because of poor quality service. It costs five times as much to	1097
replace a customer as it does to keep an existing one.	1151
How can an organization become customer driven? This may	1215
necessitate a complete change in the management process. They	1282
must change from managing to leading. They must begin to see	1348
themselves as facilitators, ensuring that staff have all the means	1415
at their disposal to perform their tasks effectively.	1469

Retrieve G12 and make the following changes:

(a) Centre the heading and format it in bold.

(b) Format the name of the Bill in italics.

(c) Change the font to Arial and the font size to 8 points.

(d) Place the last paragraph after the first paragraph.

(e) Underline the words in the fourth paragraph as shown below.

THE E-COMMERCE BILL

The E-commerce Bill became law in July 2000 when the President, Mrs McAleese, signed it with a digital signature. The President's signature was the first electronic signature to have the State's full legal recognition.

The Bill is considered a good international model, according to privacy advocacy groups such as the Electronic Privacy Information Center in Washington, DC.

This Bill is seen as a cornerstone of e-commerce and is designed to enable businesses and citizens to do business over the Internet, ranging from registering property deeds to signing contracts, making tax returns, requesting medical information and corresponding with the government.

It sets out <u>a formal legal framework for conducting business electronically</u>, in nearly all cases giving equivalent recognition to electronic signatures. These signatures are not written names but an encoded sequence of characters that can be associated with an individual at a specific time.

The Bill also recognises electronic forms of writing and documents — until now, paper versions alone were guaranteed legal weight. It also clearly protects the right of businesses and individuals to use encryption — software programs that encode and decode electronic documents and e-mails.

One of the primary goals of the Bill is to guarantee the equivalency of electronic writing while ensuring technological neutrality. That is, that one form of technology, such as a smart card combined with a software program, is not the only allowed way of producing a signature.

Save the altered version as G13.

Measurement units, centimetres versus inches

We've got to get used to using metric measurements, so let's forget inches from now on. If inches are showing on your ruler line or in dialog boxes, change is called for! Click the **Tools** menu and select **Options**. In the Options dialog box, click the **General** label. At the bottom of the dialog box, click the arrow in the **Measurement units** box and select **Centimeters**.

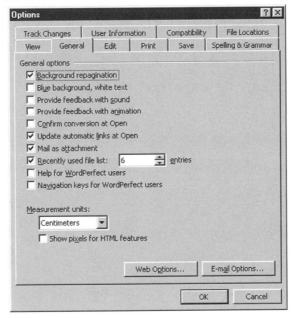

bays. This not only reduces manpower costs but also limits cage	1587
damage and the escape of stock in violent weather. This policy	1653
has elicited strong reactions from affected communities. If the	1719
call to remove all salmon cages from a radius of 12 miles from the	1787
mouths of wild fishery rivers is heeded, operating costs will	1847
increase. Reduced stocking densities will also increase costs.	1907
Most salmon rearing companies buy insurance to cover worker	1970
injury and the consequences of cage damage and the escape of	2033
stock. Opposing community organisations and affected wild	2093
fisheries have called for some form of local damage insurance that	2161
would compensate them for business losses or property	2218
devaluation attributable to salmon farming. This pushes further	2284
on costs.	2295
Farmed salmon are raised in high-density cages, giving rise to	2357
stress and the communication of diseases at rates unknown in the	2424
wild state. Disease, death rates and escape of salmon are high and	2492
show few signs of abating. The warmth of Irish marine waters	2555
may be contributing to the problem. Disease, death rates and	2617
escapes remain unresolved cost problems for the industry.	2677
Overall, operating costs can be expected to climb.	2727

Indenting text from the margins

To indent text from the left margin, highlight it and click the **Increase Indent** button on the Formatting toolbar, or drag the **Left Indent** control (i.e. the square under the two triangles at the left of the ruler line) to the right. To indent from the right margin, click on the **Right Indent** control (on the right of the ruler line) and drag it to the left.

▶ Getting Started 14

Retrieve G13 and change the font back to 12 points Times New Roman. Then indent the first paragraph by 1 cm from the left margin, and the second paragraph by 1 cm from the right margin. Save the document as G14.

Margins

Click the **File** menu and select **Page Setup**. In the Page Setup dialog box, click the **Margin** tab and set margins of 2.5 cm left, right, top and bottom.

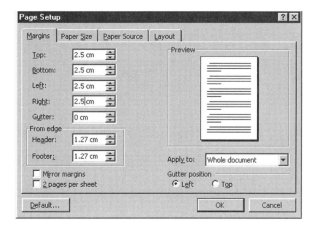

▶ Getting Started 15

Retrieve G11 and click **File**, **Page Setup** and the **Margin** tab, then check the margin setting. Click the **View** menu, click **Print Layout** and note the layout of the document. Change the margin setting to 4 cm left and 5 cm right — note again the layout of the document. Click the **View** menu and click **Normal** to change back to normal view. Save as G15.

Paper size

Click the **File** menu and select **Page Setup**. In the Page Setup dialog box, click the **Paper Size** tab. Now click the arrow in the **Paper size** box and select **A4 (210 x 297 mm)**. Other paper sizes may be selected as required.

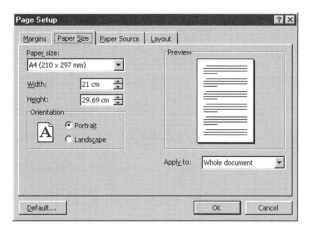

Irish fish farms are struggling in deep waters. Many companies	66
have collapsed, unable to withstand cut price selling from market	133
leaders, the Norwegians. There are also disease problems. Critics	200
argue that the industry, which has received €27m in State and	263
European Community grants over the last ten years, is capital	325
rather than labour intensive.	356
In the early and mid 1980s it looked as if the problems of	414
unemployment along the west and south-west coasts were about	480
to be solved as commercial fish farming began to take off.	538
Bord Iascaigh Mhara in a report upheld the industry as one with	603
great growth potential. It predicted that the output of fish farms	669
would increase from 13,000 tonnes valued at €8m in 1986 to	731
39,000 tonnes in 1991 at a value of €72m.	777
Salmon farming is a capital rather than labour-intensive business.	844
The salmon rearing business requires vast quantities of feed	905
stock, much of it consisting of pelletised sea fish and shellfish.	967
Here, too, the farms face the charge of disrupting the natural food	1033
chain of sea fish. The environmental issue aside, the feed sources	1099
are more difficult to tap, driving costs upward.	1147
To control costs the industry will try to automate feeding	1204
operations that can be triggered automatically or from land-based	1270
radio. Widespread use of such devices will reduce employment	1334
levels per tonne of harvested salmon. Efforts to control costs and	1399
minimise employment will cause operators to continue their	1459
policy of locating salmon cages near the shore or in sheltered	1520

Line spacing or leading

Line spacing is the space between lines of text. Most text is in single-line spacing; however, it is possible to use line-and-a-half spacing, double-line or treble-line spacing.

The quickest way to change line spacing is to use the Keyboard Commands:

- **Ctrl+1** — for single-line spacing.
- **Ctrl+2** — for double-line spacing.

Leading (pronounced 'ledding') is the term used in the printing industry for the spacing between lines. For example, 10 or 12 points of leading might be used. To specify the leading required, click the **Format** menu, select **Paragraph** and click the **Indents and Spacing** tab. In the **Line spacing** box, scroll down to **Exactly** and in the **At** box, key in the leading required, then click **OK**.

▶ Getting Started 16

Retrieve G11 and change the line spacing to double-line spacing. Save the document as G16.

Word wrap

When text is inputted, the cursor moves across the line until it reaches the right margin. It then automatically moves to the next line and takes with it any word, or part of a hyphenated word, which does not fit on the first line. This is called **word wrap**, and the automatic returns are called **soft returns**.

When a sentence takes up more than one line, resist the tendency to press the Return key at the end of the first line. Such returns are called **hard returns** and they make life difficult when editing text. For example, when text is added or deleted, hard returns may no longer come at the end of a line. In this case, each hard return would have to be deleted.

Note that the word 'accounting' didn't fit within the margins in the text below. So, guess what — it wrapped around to the second line!

```
Excel-based spreadsheets have been warmly greeted as
accounting and administration aids by many small firms in
Ireland.
```

In the case of the legal profession where a precise knowledge of national	1752
law is required, the rules for such tests will be somewhat stricter.	1820
This system is due to come into force two years after its formal adoption.	1995
Despite this wide-ranging application it is not, however, the final word	2067
on the subject. Engineers, for example, their professional bodies	2133
throughout the Community are seeking a separate regime that would apply	2203
special rules to govern its application to the profession.	2270
It is wonderful to have acquired this right. In the area of education	2339
many opportunities are now opening to study in European schools and	2405
universities and many exchange programmes are now being organised.	2469

▶ *Getting Started 17*

Retrieve G3 and enter a hard return after the first, second and third lines. Then change the font size to 16 points. Note — the hard returns are no longer at the end of a line and should be deleted. Save it as G17.

The above exercise aims to show that unnecessary hard returns at the end of a line can be a nuisance when text is reformatted.

Search and search and replace
To search for text in a file, click the **Edit** menu and click **Find**. Then key the text into the **Find what** box in the Find and Replace dialog box.

To replace text, click the **Edit** menu and click **Replace**. Then key the text into the **Find what** box, and key the alternative text into the **Replace with** box.

▶ *Getting Started 18*

Retrieve G9 and replace each occurrence of 'U2' with 'Bono and U2'. Save it as G18.

Printing a document
Click the **File** menu and click **Print**.

▶ *Getting Started 19*

Print one copy of G18.

Closing a file
Click the **File** menu and click **Close**.

▶ *Getting Started 20*

Close G18.

Target speed — 45 wpm.

The right to go and work in another Member State is probably the best	69
known of the rights we have acquired as a result of membership of the	138
European Community. This means that a person working in another	202
Member State may not be discriminated against on the grounds of	265
nationality. They should be treated equally and fairly, especially in	335
areas such as pay, living conditions, education and training.	396
A Community worker cannot be sacked from his job for reasons that differ	467
from those applicable to national workers. A Community worker who finds	538
a job in another Member State must, on applying, be issued with a	602
resident's permit. If a worker loses his job, it will not affect his	669
right of residence. At the same time, he will only be entitled to	733
unemployment benefit in his new country of residence if he has paid	798
sufficient contributions in his home country.	841
If you do not have a job, you have certain rights to stay in a Member	910
State for a limited period. You can stay for at least three months	977
while seeking employment. If a worker decides to become self-employed	1046
he is entitled to stay on in the Member State where he lives.	1106
The Community has been working for many years to win recognition for	1173
the professional qualifications held by people like architects, pharmacists	1245
and doctors. This has now been achieved and the Council of Ministers	1314
hopes to extend the principle of mutual recognition of qualifications to	1384
all other professions.	1406
The new rules take into account differences of education and training by	1476
providing compensating mechanisms. In some cases the authorities in the	1546
host countries can ask professionals to undergo either an aptitude test	1615
or training or adjustment period before being allowed tc practise.	1679

Part 2
The Keyboard

▷▶▷▷▷▷▷▷▷▷▷▷▷▷

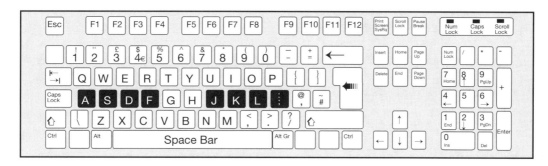

Now it is time to learn how to input text efficiently.

The Home Keys

There are eight 'home keys', one for each of the eight fingers. These keys can be thought of as 'springboards' from which the fingers spring and to which they return while covering the whole keyboard.

Place the fingertips on the home keys

Right hand: first finger on ⬚J⬚, second finger on ⬚K⬚, third finger on ⬚L⬚ and the fourth finger on ⬚;⬚.

Left hand: first finger on ⬚F⬚, second finger on ⬚D⬚, third finger on ⬚S⬚ and the fourth finger on ⬚A⬚.

Make sure your fingers are positioned correctly. Check that the G and H keys are uncovered and between your index fingers. Remember, G and H for Good Health!

How about a gentle workout?

Do the drill below a few times. Practise moving your fingers on and off the home keys as follows:

- fingers on lap
- fingers on home keys
- fingers on top of monitor (or VDU)
- fingers back on home keys.

Placement of your book

Text Production with Microsoft Word has a special spiral binding which allows it to stand upright. Place your book where you can see it comfortably, usually on the right-hand side of the computer with the right edge of the book angled towards you.

Do not look down at the keyboard

You will notice that there is a keyboard chart at the top of most pages in this section. Locate the position of the keys you require by looking at this chart. Do not look down at the actual keyboard.

Page setup

At this stage, you may wish to check how to set page margins, etc. To do this, refer to page 12.

for all children arose only in the nineteenth century.	1851
The emergence of public, tax-supported education was not solely a	1901
function of the stage of industrial development. It was also a	1966
function of the class structure in the society. In the United States,	2037
without a strong traditional class structure, universal education in	2107
publicly-supported free schools became widespread in the early	2168
nineteenth century; in England, the voluntary schools, run and	2232
organized by churches with some instances of state support, were not	2300
supplemented by a state-supported system until the Education Act of	2371
1870. Even more, the character of educational opportunity reflected	2441
the class structure.	2462

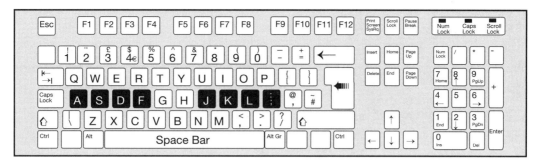

The space bar
Keep your fingers on the home keys and strike the Space Bar with the side of your right thumb.

Locate the position of each key from the keyboard chart and type the following exercise:

```
asdf jkl; asdf jkl; asdf jkl; asdf jkl;
```

Correction of errors
The correction of errors was explained on page 5. In order to develop smooth fingering, don't worry unduly about correcting errors at this stage. Try to work as accurately as possible.

Say the letters and spaces as you type
Get into the habit of naming the letters and spaces to yourself as you type. This promotes concentration, accuracy and the development of a smooth rhythm. For example, in the exercise above, say:

```
a    s    d    f  space    j    k    l    semicolon    space.
```

Starting a new line
When a line stops short of the right margin, as in the exercises below, one must press the Return key to get onto the next line. The Return key is the large key with the back arrow on the right of the keyboard.

The Return key
Keep your fingers on the home keys and strike the Return key with the little finger of your right hand.

Type the following exercise three times:

```
asdf jkl; asdf jkl; asdf jkl; (new line)
fdsa ;lkj fdsa ;lkj jkl; asdf (new line)
fdsa jkl; fdsa jkl; fdsa jkl; (new line)
```

The concept of equality of educational opportunity as held by members	70
of society has had a varied past. It has changed radically in recent	141
years, and is likely to undergo further change in the future.	202
In pre-industrial Europe, the child's horizons were largely limited by	279
his family. His station in life was likely to be the same as his	346
father's. If his father was a serf, he would likely live his own life	416
as a serf; if his father was a shoemaker, he would likely become a	483
shoemaker. But even this immobility was not the crux of the matter; he	555
was a part of the family production enterprise and would likely remain	628
within this enterprise throughout his life. The extended family, as	697
the basic unit of social organization, had complete responsibility for	766
him. This responsibility ordinarily did not end when the child became	837
an adult because he remained a part of the same economic unit and	903
carried on this tradition of responsibility into the next generation.	974
In this kind of society, the concept of equality of educational	1039
opportunity had no relevance at all.	1076
With the industrial revolution, changes occurred in both the family's	1151
function as a self-perpetuating economic unit and as a training ground.	1227
As economic organizations developed outside the household, children	1293
began to be occupationally mobile outside their families. It was in	1362
the early nineteenth century that public education began to appear in	1432
Europe and America. Before that time, private education had grown with	1504
the expansion of the mercantile class. This class had both the need	1573
and resources to have its children educated outside the home, either	1639
for professional occupations or for occupations in the developing	1706
world of commerce. But the idea of general educational opportunity	1774

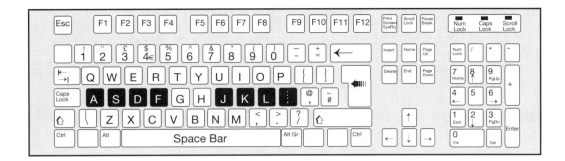

Posture

You will have to concentrate to become a competent keyboard operator. Adopting the correct posture will help you to develop the right mental attitude and spare that precious back of yours! Remember:

• Sit upright and back in your chair.

• Keep your shoulders back; try to avoid leaning forward too much.

• Keep both feet on the ground, not stretched out under your desk.

• Keep wrists low and relaxed, to avoid wrist strain.

• Curl fingers slightly.

• Keep elbows in.

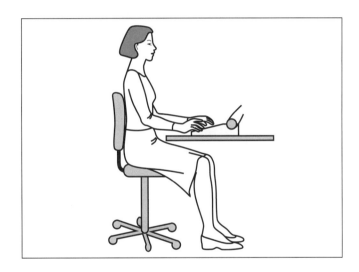

Type the following exercise three times:

```
fad lad jkl jlk dad ;lk jkl lkj asd fds jkl
```

Touch Typing

Remember, you are learning to touch type. This means being able to locate the keys without looking at them. Therefore, DO NOT look down at the keys. Look instead at the keyboard chart at the top of the page. Eventually, by looking at the chart you will remember where the keys are. However, if you look down at the keys, you won't remember where they are.

Keep your fingers on the home keys (remember those 'springboards' referred to on page 15) and your eyes on the book. You don't even have to look down to see if your fingers are on the home keys because most keyboards are built with a protruding dot on the F and J keys. You can therefore be sure you are on the home keys by touch alone.

programme by which the operator learns direct from the	1344
machine through a series of instructions on screen.	1396
The trainee can set his or her own pace but most training	1454
programmes take under 20 hours.	1475
The training programmes are deliberately restricted to	1530
the main functions and applications of the system's capability,	1595
although trainees will be able to progress to advanced	1649
exercises. However trainees at the basic stage will	1701
be fully capable and able to start up the system specifically	1764
for their own work station.	1791
On completion of training, competence is reinforced with	1846
an easy refresher course when a reference manual is used	1902
for each machine. Before terminating the Athcav Learn	1955
programme the trainee therefore has a satisfactory knowledge	2017
of several machines and packages and he or she has the	2069
flexibility to move from machine to machine or from application	2193
to application with the minimum of difficulty or delay.	2188

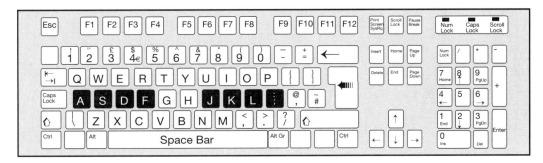

Producing neat sets of work

Type each line or sentence in an exercise three times. Try to produce a neat set of work by typing one line directly under the other. Leave a clear line between each set of three lines. You do not want to produce 'a dog's dinner' with work scattered all over the place!

Leaving a clear line

You leave a clear line by pressing the Return key twice.

Type each line three times; leave a clear line between each set of three lines.

```
fff jjj ddd kkk sss lll aaa ;;;
aaa ;;; sss lll ddd kkk fff jjj

fff jjj ddd kkk sss lll aaa ;;;
aaa ;;; sss lll ddd kkk fff jjj
```

Anchor your fingers on the home keys

Place your fingers on the home keys. Check that you can see the **G** and **H** keys.

Type each of the following lines three times, one line directly under the other. Leave a clear line between each set of three lines.

```
sss lll sss lll sss lll sss lll sss lll sss sls lsl
lsl lsl sls sls sls lsl lsl lsl sls sds lkl sds lkl
fad lad jal laj sad fas ;as as; kak jaj sas das lal
```

Your finished work should appear like this:

```
sss lll sss lll sss lll sss lll sss lll sss sls lsl
sss lll sss lll sss lll sss lll sss lll sss sls lsl
sss lll sss lll sss lll sss lll sss lll sss sls lsl

lsl lsl sls sls sls lsl lsl lsl sls sds lkl sds lkl
lsl lsl sls sls sls lsl lsl lsl sls sds lkl sds lkl
lsl lsl sls sls sls lsl lsl lsl sls sds lkl sds lkl

fad lad jal laj sad fas ;as as; kak jaj sas das lal
fad lad jal laj sad fas ;as as; kak jaj sas das lal
fad lad jal laj sad fas ;as as; kak jaj sas das lal
```

Target speed — 40 wpm.

This is the age of the computerised office and the number	58
of automated work stations per office employee has increased	120
in just four years from one in 400 to one in 40. This	174
change has come about very quickly in Ireland and there	229
are major implications in terms of the human factor.	281
There are many implications in terms of the number of	334
office employees which will be required in the future	387
and in terms of the sort of training needed.	437
To the Dublin branch manager of Athcav Temps this represents	449
both challenge and opportunity. This Manager has more	552
than 20 years' experience in supplying secretarial office	609
staff to many of Ireland's leading employers and he is	663
in a good position to comment on the shape of things to	718
come.	723
From the point of view of Irish employers, Athcav's capacity	785
to train operators in office automation skills gives	837
them a ready solution to training in large numbers, as	890
well as locating temporaries to cover gaps caused by	942
maternity leave, seasonal peaks or illness.	985
At the firm's training centre in Dublin, personal computers	1047
and word processors are maintained exclusively for training	1109
new operators, both Athcav's own temps and, by arrangement,	1175
the permanent employees of client companies. The training	1236
programme is called Athcav Learn and is a self-taught	1289

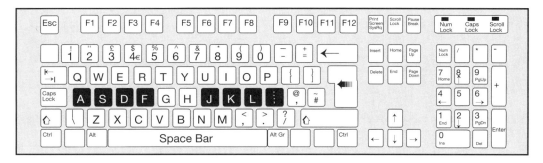

Type the following exercise three times:

```
a sad dad (new line)
a sad dad falls (new line)
all sad dads fall (new line)
ask all sad lads (new line)
```

 Tip — When using the fourth finger, resist the tendency to stick out the elbows and thus pull the other fingers off the home keys. Keep your elbows in and place your fingers on the home keys.

Type the following letters three times:

```
aaa ;;; aaa ;;; aaa ;;; aaa ;;; aaa ;;; a;a a;a ;a;
;a; ;;a ;;a aa; aa; ;a; a;a asa ;l; asa ;l; ada ;k;
```

Type the following words three times:

```
sad lad lass all adds salad falls salads lads sad fad
as jaffa fad lad dads fall add sad ask adds fads lads
```

Type the following phrases three times:

```
a sad dad falls; a sad lass falls; all sad dads;
a salad falls; dad adds a salad; a lass adds a salad;
a lad asks; as a lass falls; as all sad dads; ask all
```

Progress Report

Well done, you have learned how to use the home keys and already you can type various words and phrases. We shall now learn how to 'navigate' from the home keys. As we said at the beginning, there are eight home keys, one for each of the eight fingers. These keys can be thought of as springboards from which the fingers spring and to which they return while covering the whole keyboard. Remember — keep your fingers on the home keys!

 Errors — Try to avoid making errors. Saying the letters and spaces to yourself will help.

Target speed — 35 wpm.

Business is measured and reported on through numbers. Numbers provide	70
pictures of performance over a period, of conditions at a particular	134
point in time, or of future objectives and plans. These pictures	203
form the basis of virtually all major decisions within a business	268
and provide outsiders with the information they require in their	332
dealings with it.	349
It is important that those using them examine the communication and	416
use, or possible misuse, of financial numbers in business decision	482
making. This requires a look at the nature of these numbers, the	546
process by which complex business activities are measured, represented	615
in numerical terms, and presented in apparently factual and precise	682
form as management information. There are, I believe, misconceptions	750
concerning the nature of this information which have serious implications	823
for decision making. A greater awareness of what is involved will	889
lead to a more realistic and effective use of financial information,	957
and an ability to avoid some of the pitfalls. Business is complex.	1024
There are continual periods of change and reassessment, influenced	1090
by factors such as developments in technology, changes in customer	1156
preference and market demand, change in government policy, the national	1226
economy and international conditions. All of these factors mean	1289
that business is operating within a climate of uncertainty. Decisions	1360
are being taken in conditions of more and more doubt as to ultimate	1428
outcome.	1435
The availability of relevant and reliable information can reduce	1501
the uncertainty with which decision makers have to cope. Faced with	1570
ever-growing uncertainty, businessmen want facts in financial statements	1644
available to them. This desire for financial information arises at	1712
a time when developments in technology have enabled us to provide	1779
it in almost unlimited quantities.	1813

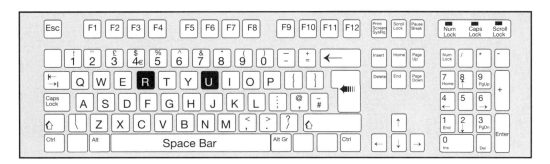

THE R AND U KEYS

The r key is typed by moving the first finger of the left hand from its home key f up to the r key.
The u key is typed by moving the first finger of the right hand from its home key j up to the u key.

 Remember — 'Spring back' to the relevant home key each time you strike a non-home key.

Letters — type three times:

```
frf juj frf juj frf juj frf juj frf juj frf juj rrr
jjj fff jjj frf juj rrr uuu frf juj fff jjj ral dud
dul dar uru rur sus srs ara ;u; srs lul uru rur ujr

fur ruf jur fuj ruj urj juf fur dur rud dud dur urd
lur kur ruk luk kul lar ral aru ura sar ras lur rul
ral lar dur rud jud duj raj jar rur uru ruj lud sur
```

Words — type three times:

```
suds far dark falls ark dull slur fur dual surf fluff
ajar afar fall fail lard dark lark dull full lull
dual sulk far fur furl jar; all salads dull sud rash
```

Phrases — type three times:

```
a full salad; a dull lad; a dull lass; a lark; a lull;
a rash; ask all dull lads; all full jars; all suds;
all surf; surf falls as suds; a dark lark falls
```

Just over 70% of sales personnel are men and 28% are women	1367
though women account for up to 43% in some industries like	1427
chemicals, pharmaceutical and distribution sectors. In Ireland	1490
professional women buyers lay more stress on representatives	1553
not being too pushy, having good manners and well groomed, being	1619
punctual as well as having a clear and concise sales presentation.	1686
On the other hand men put more stress on the need for good	1746
product knowledge, having a good personality as well as being	1809
direct and decisive.	1831
Irish people scored best for their willingness to satisfy	1887
customers needs and their pleasant manner. Unfortunately they	1950
were poorly ranked for probing to identify what the buyers needs	2014
are.	2019

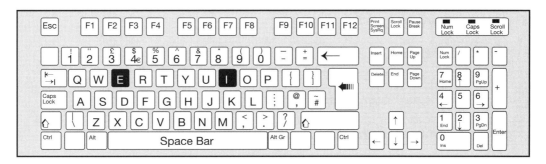

THE E AND I KEYS

The e key is typed by moving the second finger of the left hand from the home key d up to the e key. The i key is typed by moving the second finger of the right hand from the home key k up to the i key.

Letters — type three times:

```
ded kik ded kik ded kik eee iii eee iii ded kik fee
jii dee kii see lii lir ril lil rar jur ruj ije dei
```

Words — type three times:

```
sea flea lee lire ire fire sir life led dead lull
diddle fiddle led red lead are see fee dead lee see
sea die fill frill rill sill era rare ride side silk
fair fled flee rail sail duke rude fire lid fleas ire
```

Phrases — type three times:

```
ask if fred fell; did lee skid; a dull life; is life dull;
if asked; if fred asked; did fred fall; did sid slide;
is sid sad; is fred afraid; did a duke flee;
ask if fred is afraid; did i dare read; a rifle slid
```

Review work — type three times:

```
aaa sss ddd fff jjj kkk lll ;;; asd afd ;lk ;jk aru
aei ffd kfj kdk dkd sds sls jsd jkf ksl lsl sls a;a

rule jar lark lure lads adds lass dads jars full
salad falls lass ask lark dual duke fluke fuss flue
```

Target speed — 35 wpm.

Irish sales staff rate poorly when compared to their foreign	61
counterparts. Many of them are rough at the edges according to	125
purchasing managers who deal with sales representatives on a	188
daily basis.	201
A new survey of attitudes and reactions to salespeople indicates	266
that they often know little about the product; fail to listen to the	332
customers; turn up late or even without an appointment. In	392
addition there is a perception that Irish full-time selling staff	456
are less honest, reliable and sometimes over-pushy compared to	521
foreign sales teams.	542
With an open EC market, Irish manufacturers and wholesalers may	608
soon find that foreign competitors will beat them to closing a	671
sale ahead of their own salespeople. When asked to list the main	737
qualities they expect to find in a good salesperson, the great	798
majority mentioned a good knowledge of the product. Then they	862
listed honesty, integrity, reliability and follow-up, not being too	928
pushy, showing good manners and politeness, being well groomed	994
and neat, and they expected a person with good personality and	1058
character.	1069
About half Irish sales people measured up to these expectations	1134
compared to three-quarters of overseas sales people. No matter	1199
what the company size or its sector, its purchasing chief	1258
invariably had a better image of the foreigner.	1306

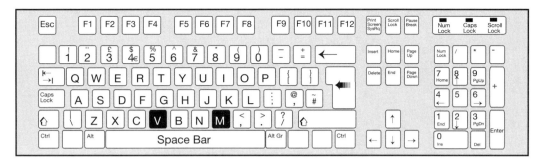

THE V AND M KEYS

The v key is typed by moving the first finger of the left hand from the home key f down to the v key. The m key is typed by moving the first finger of the right hand from the home key j down to the m key.

Type each line three times. Leave a clear line after every third line.

Letters

```
fvf jmj fvf jmj vvv mmm fvf jmj vvv mmm vmv mav vad
vmv mvm mvr vmv mvm vam mav vam mar vim mim rim vjm
jim sim fem mef rav var jum muj jum jum mud mak mjv
```

Words

```
ram rum mud mum slum sum valve rave slave seemed duke
dreamed mar fur valve rave jar jam jar jive film ram

mass vim mile file smile made servile slim middle
value vellum film lame flame dame leave fame maim
rave isle middle revile mile fume vile value mauve
```

Phrases

```
is vellum safe; is lee afraid; did i revile;
is lee servile; did fred drive far; did dad evade fire;
is silver safe; did red rum fall; a silver frame; a valve;
is rum safe
```

> **Remember** — Resist the tendency to look down when striking the Return key, as this will impede smooth skill development.

Target speed — 30 words per minute, i.e. 30 wpm.

The infant enters the world without knowledge of any sort. All that	69
each of us starts off with is his own potential talent, his individual	140
capacity for learning and remembering. The mind of the mature	203
individual represents all that he has learnt and remembered, and he	271
brings to bear the resources he has gathered both in order to meet	338
the demands of further new experiences and to support and encourage	406
the creation of new ideas. Thus given a certain inherited ability,	474
each of us is very much a product of his education.	526
The new-born child enters a going concern founded upon a social	600
tradition, and through his own learning he is able to take advantage	669
of the knowledge which his ancestors have already won by deep thought,	740
hard experience and bitter mistakes. Each generation makes its own	808
contribution to this tradition, and in turn hands on to its own	870
children a richer heritage; and in a sense each newcomer enters	936
through education into the collective mind of mankind.	991
This is what social scientists describe as the transmission of	1054
culture. The word 'culture' in this sense means all the ideas shared	1124
by a social group, whether it be a tribe, a complete nation or a	1189
whole civilization. These ideas are preserved, remembered, from	1254
generation to generation; and just as the proper functioning of our	1322
individual minds is dependent upon memory and the retention of	1385
knowledge from day to day, so the culture of a society depends upon	1453
its ability to keep alive its collective knowledge from age to age.	1521

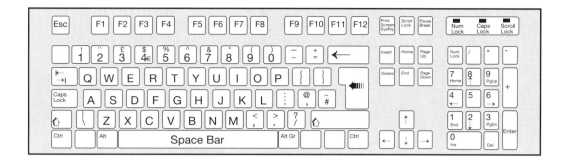

 Question — Are you saying the letters and spaces to yourself as you type? Saying the letters helps to promote concentration, accuracy and the development of a smooth rhythm.

Practise using the Return key

Type each line below three times. Leave a clear line after every third line.

```
a dull lad
sad lasses
did a kid lie
ask did a duke flee
```

Checking errors

When checking for errors, note the following:

• incorrect characters, spacing or punctuation marks

• omitted characters, spacing or punctuation marks

• incorrect margins.

 Remember — Do not look at the keyboard if you're unsure of the position of a letter. Look instead at the keyboard chart at the top of the page.

Part 16
Accuracy Tests

▷▷▷▷▷▷▷▷▷▷▷▷▷▷▶

A number of accuracy tests now follow, which should help students to prepare for examinations. A target speed has been set for each test and the point that should be reached has been marked. Note — the strokes are totalled at the end of each line.

Calculating keyboard speed
When calculating keyboard speed, each keyboard character and each space between words is deemed to represent a stroke. To calculate your speed, proceed as follows:

❶ Select the text keyed in.

❷ Click the **Tools** menu and select **Word Count**. In the Word Count dialog box, note the number of characters (with spaces).

❸ Click the **Start** button, click **Programmes**, **Accessories**, then click **Calculator**.

❹ Using the calculator, divide the number of characters (with spaces) by five. This will convert characters to 'standard words'.

❺ Divide the number of standard words by ten (as these tests are for ten minutes). The result is the number of standard words keyed in per minute, or the keyboard operator speed, e.g. 30 wpm or 40 wpm.

❻ Minimise the calculator and keep it handy on the Task Bar, ready for further calculations.

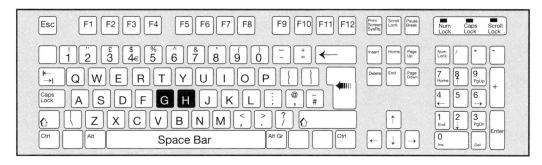

THE G AND H KEYS

The g key is typed by moving the first finger of the left hand from the home key f over to the g key. The h key is typed by moving the first finger of the right hand from the home key j over to the h key.

Type each line three times. Leave a clear line after every third line.

Letters

```
fgf fgf jhj jhj ggg jjj ggg jjj fgf jhj ggg hhh gah
hag gav hag gig hig dag hag lag hal gal sag hag lag
lav gaf hill dag kal lag gag rug mug hug lug gull
```

Words

```
he has heed gale hail hair fledge ledge edge hum hull
fledged ride hassle harass hear hare gale grime girl
grail hale hair vigil virile greed gravel ravel hedge
```

Phrases

```
he has fair hair; a gravel lodge; she hears a gale;
lee asked a frilled lass; ask if fred fired a rifle;
lee is afraid; is lisa fair; all fires add life; has a
lass fair hair; fred judged gale; had he a rifle safe

hire a gravel sieve; did gail evade; a hair hears her;
she has silver hair; did sid hire him; is silver hard;
has he heard; is gail fair; girl failed; did dave hug her;
is freda davis dull; his hair is dull; as safe as silver
```

Review the a key

```
ask ale aid ageless aura add address addle adder
arms alms aims assess amiss amid alive arrive arrival
```

Review the d key

```
did dive divide differ dash dual duel dire disease
dish disease differ drag drake dredge desire devil
```

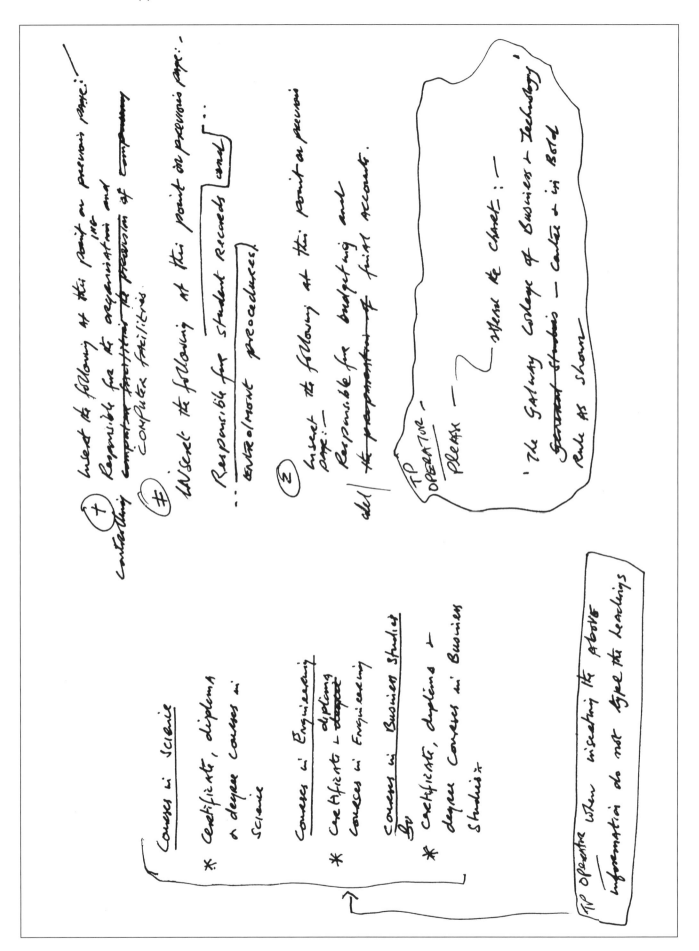

① Insert the following at this point on previous page :-
Responsible for the organisation and ~~computing~~ the provision of computing COMPUTER FACILITIES

Contrasting

Insert the following at this point on previous page :-
Responsible for student records and
... enrolment procedures.

② Insert the following at this point on previous page :-
Responsible for budgeting and
del | ~~the preparation~~ of final accounts.

TP OPERATOR -
PLEASE -
reset the chart :-

'The Galway College of Business + Technology'
Courses of studies — centre + in Bold
Rule as shown

Courses in Science
* Certificate, diploma + degree courses in Science

Courses in Engineering
* Certificate + diploma + ~~courses~~ courses in Engineering

Courses in Business Studies
* Certificate, diploma + degree courses in Business Studies+

TP Operator when inserting the above information do not type the headings

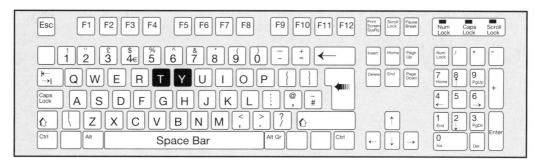

THE T AND Y KEYS

The $\boxed{t}$ key is typed by moving the first finger of the left hand from the home key $\boxed{f}$ up to the $\boxed{t}$ key.
The $\boxed{y}$ key is typed by moving the first finger of the right hand from the home key $\boxed{j}$ up to the $\boxed{y}$ key.

Type each line three times. Leave a clear line after every third line.

Letters

```
ftf jyj ftf jyj ttt yyy ftf jyj ttt yyy ftf jyj ftf
taf fat tay say lay day tat tit slit jilt yes ter yak
take tay tee yee yet tey yam tam mat fat yir yar ity
```

Words

```
tale stale yesterday dray slay slaked delayed slither
malady sit emit remit slit lit lady ladder shady
talked tease yacht utter stale slit
```

Phrases — type each paragraph three times:

```
a shady lady; he hit the staid maid; the mature man
had a rat; she muttered as she talked; he fumed as he
talked; he hit three trees first; has she a red tie

a style; sit here; light a fire; rake the yard; he
teased the staid lady; the tea lady; the shady lady;
a little red light; taste this dish; yes take a yam
```

Review the $\boxed{f}$ key — type each line three times:

```
fat frail flat fast fade fail fake fuel flue full
fugue fuse fused fuss fulfil frustrate frugal film
```

Review the $\boxed{g}$ key — type each line three times:

```
gate gale grail gift grit gritty get gather graft
garter grate guts gush gust grid griddle great gate
glitter glee ghastly gratify girl gravy gravitate
```

Key in the the chart below. Format it to print on A4 landscape paper. Save it as Test 6C.

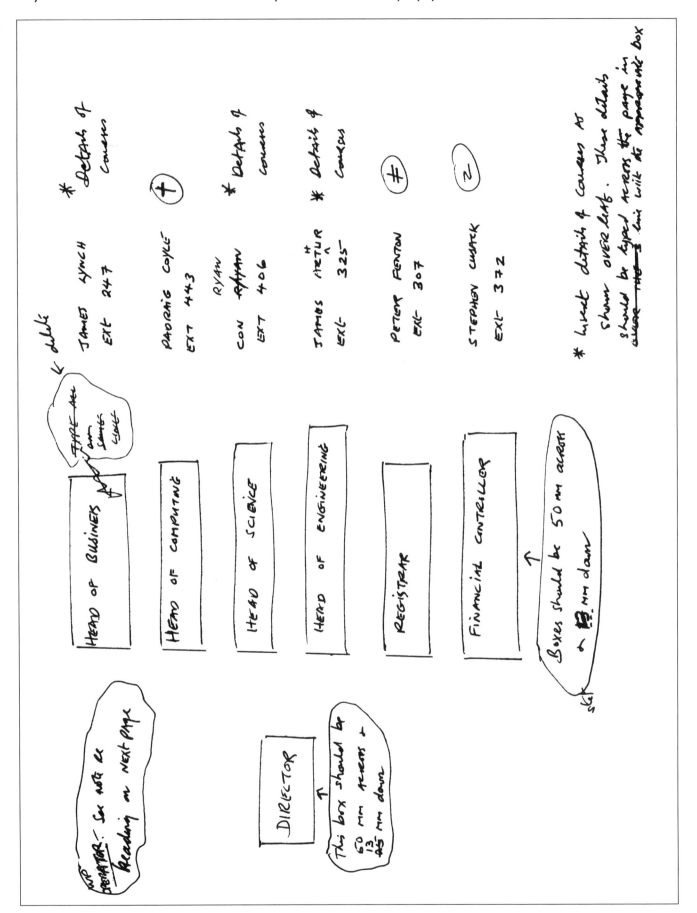

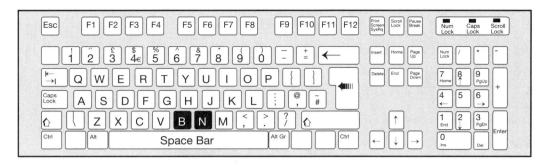

THE B AND N KEYS

The b key is typed by moving the first finger of the left hand from the home key f down to the b key. The n key is typed by moving the first finger of the right hand from the home key j down to the n key.

Points to remember

• Spring back to those home keys.
• Keep your eyes on the book.
• Do not look at the keyboard when pressing the Return key.
• Do not look at the keyboard when pressing the Delete key.

Type each line three times. Leave a clear line after every third line.

Letters

```
fbf fbf fbf jnj jnj jnj bbb nnn bbb nnn bbb nnn bbb
ban bin ben nib bib nin bat tab nab ban bab rab lan
gran nal bev bre baf jnj naj jun fbf fab frb ftb jun
```

Words

```
bad bash bay ten men hen nabbed tabbed babbled bend
bent blade ban man nab bay dumb thumb snail stumble
bumble fumble nib bib nibble nabbed ring making nibs

stumble snail darling starling alarming daring dab
staring sharing toiled thumb numb numbed badly begin
rugby bible ten names need bitter nimble stirring
```

Phrases — type each paragraph three times:

```
he hid the label under the table; the bent key; the
brandy is bad; he grabbed a rugby ball; she started;
bend it; did he bind the band and the finger; a band

is he at the table; give helen a hat; it is in the
big hall; she has a net; take this as a gesture;
drive the van as fast as he drives it; a stitch in it
```

Set out the information shown below in tabular form. The required column headings are underlined.
Save it as Test 6B.

WP OPERATOR
Under the heading insert the following sentence:
The following Irish companies are doing quite well and in some cases actually expanding during the current recession.

(1) COMPANY NAME - Dublin Crystal; Ayg Electric; D+S Packaging; Boxmore Plastics; Tellabs; Ros Air Condit;

(2) LOCATION - Blackrock; Skennen; Dublin; Spiddal; Scariff; Millstreet; Cork; Cavan;

(5) TELEPHONE - 288 7932; 70677; 392622; 26423; 471433; 8425522; 83464; 921355.

(6) FAX - 2633227; 70603; 393515; 26423; 471000; 8425979; 83464; 921477

(4) CONTACT - M. Taylor; J. O'Sullivan; M. Murphy; P. Shanahan; S. Ross; P. Cummins; J. Joyce;

(3) ACTIVITIES - Crystal; Graphite Parts; Polystyrene; Plastics; Telecom; Air Condit; TV/Film Prod.; Plastics;

WP OPERATOR - Retain 'Abbreviations'; use open punctuation

WP OPERATOR - TELEPHONE AND FAX
- AREA codes have been omitted please insert them. Note codes the following:
Clare & Clare - 061; Galway - 091; Dublin - 01; Cavan 049; Cork 021
Millstreet - 029. Show codes in brackets EX (061) 921355

Head the table 'Companies fighting the recession'; use Block capitals;
* KEY in columns to the order indicated as follows: (1), (2), etc
NOTE: SCARIFF & SHANNON ARE in Co. CLARE; BLACKROCK is in Co. DUBLIN;

WP OPERATOR - USE DOUBLE LINE SPACING in the body of the table

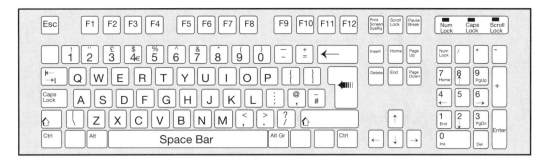

Type each line three times. Leave a clear line after every third line.

Review the **h** key

```
hair heart hassle had huddle hit heat heal halt hail
hard hardly heartless have half halve hairy hive hike
hide harry harries harness hell hatless hut hard halt
```

Review the **i** key

```
it item idle ivy idea idle if illegal illiterate
initial irrigate iris irate irregular irrigate isle
issue is irk islam irish issued idled imitate
```

Review the **j** key

```
jam jet jerk jar jittery jetty jade jaffa jasmine jab
jaguar jail jury jay jeer jelly jellyfish jerky jest
jet jig jiffy jiggle jilt jive jute justly jug jute
```

 Question — Have you seen anyone with the 'rocking head disease'? Unfortunate sufferers don't keep their eyes on the book; instead they move their eyes from the book to the keyboard and from the keyboard to the VDU.

TECHNOLOGY

u/c ✓ Information technology can ~~empower~~ allow people to achieve great things. ~~Having created common business goals, and t motivation that comes from IT, trust and Responsibility, I have t~~ people often exceed managements expectations. With the Right technology workers can be equipped to put their imaginations to work. In to-day's world this technology takes the form of "client-server computing." This enables the computer function that ~~typically~~ currently _ Reside on one computer to be split up and run on different-computer/ across a network.

stet

s/

The client is any ◯ system Requesting the services of another ◯ computer, the server is any system Responding to Requests. The benefit to customers is that it enables them to take full advantage of the new hugely powerful PCs and workstations. After more than a decade of talk and promises, business customers can now demand and obtain genuinely open systems without being locked into one supplier's offerings.

It seems that the legacy of the Recession will see the marrying of business, people and technology. This has brought about a new style of management, one very different from that used in the traditional hierarchical organisation. The "bridge to empire room" management Approach will not work for the empowered,* IT-oriented teams of to-day ~~and the next century~~. Instead the modern manager's role is closer to that of an ~~expert~~ experienced team coach, someone who demands a disciplined 100% team effort, yet who also knows how to talent-scout and motivate individual to initiative and imagination.

*OPERATOR - RETAIN ABBREVIATION

Once common business goals and shared systems of motivation are in place

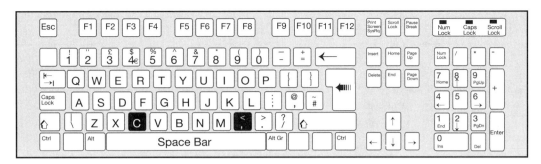

THE C AND , KEYS

The c key is typed by moving the second finger of the left hand from the home key d down to the c key. The , key is typed by moving the second finger of the right hand from the home key k down to the , key.

Letters — type each line three times. Leave a clear line after every third line.

```
dcd dcd dcd dcd k,k k,k k,k k,k ccc ,,, ccc ,,, dec
ac, bc, dc, ec, fc, gc, hc, ic, jc, kc, lc, mc, nc,
r,c s,c t,c u,c v,c y,c ,ca ,cb ,dc ,ec ,fc ,gc ,hc
```

Words — let's change activity. This time, type a line of each individual word. Leave a clear line and then type a line of the next word.

```
cake cash city cattle scene, screen, lace back track
yak flack black yacht care brace, face, disgraces
cat, curl, cecil track neck fleck viaduct vibrate

vibrant vice vicinity charming scheme schemes,
schemed, race, mace, brace, lace, calamity, cuisine
cart cabin city calf club cub clue clutch club

ace face mace lace dace brace embrace crush crime
back rack black flack attack lack hack crisis crib
cable charge large barge case ceiling crush slush
```

Phrases — keep typing each phrase until it wraps to the next line, then leave a clear line and type the next phrase.

```
the rabbit lunged at the cat; the cream cake; the
rabbit ate the meal; it is a cream bun; custard is
standard fare; the viaduct carries the rail track
```

Review the k key — type each line three times.

```
kaftan kebab keen knee keg kennel kerb kernel kestrel
khaki kilt kid kidney kill kiln kin kind kindred
kindly king kingfisher kink kinky kiss kitten kitty
```

millions of EUROS and are expected to yield even greater savings in the future.

The recession has certainly spurred on organisations to scrutinise their business overall. Integral to making things happen are two priorities — people and technology.

PEOPLE ← [WP OPERATOR — this heading and the next heading in BLOCK CAPS.]

The flatter structures of re-engineered org(s) almost invariably highlight the need for greater flexibility of people and their workplace. More than 60% of bus(s) already contract out certain activities, and three-quarters expect contracting out to grow over the next 4 years. For many org(s) this has led to contracting out to achieve greater flexibility

Run on [AND TO ALLOW ———— management to concentrate on / core business.]

Other flexible working practises such as home/tele-working, work-sharing and distance working have also come to the
u/l
l/c
#
fore. New practises such as these increasingly encompass the use of 'Intelligent Buildings'. An intelligent-building is located and designed to enable people to work at maximum efficiency by integrating all systems and
has ... building services including utilities and information technology.

This can mean a significant reduction in property-to-income ratios, energy savings, increased efficiency and greater speed and flexibility to react to market conditions.

WP OPERATOR

* please retain abbreviation here

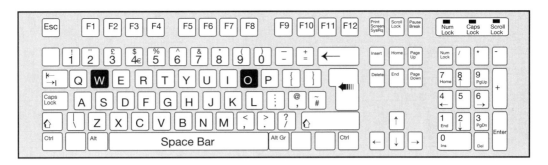

THE W AND O KEYS

The W key is typed by moving the third finger of the left hand from the home key S up to the W key. The O key is typed by moving the third finger of the right hand from the home key I up to the O key.

Letters — type each line three times. Leave a clear line after every third line.

```
sws lol sws lol sws lol www ooo www ooo sws lolo rolo
lolo solo wolo wer owo wow wwn bob dod wod awo owa
owo wao oaw oso sos wol loo koo roo rwo woe oew eow
```

Words — type a line of each word. Leave a clear line after every third line.

```
work wash worse yellow fellow wobble wool worsted
solo below water wash wealth wood would lobby sow row
mob mottled wood women wonder wolf won world worked

sloe woeful woebegone slog flog mouse louse hover won
omelette wrench you that voodoo trolley volute
resolute wobble wobbly noble hobble wholly woollen
worsted wood

lewd whistle frost cost lost loft bolt colt moult
watch orbit sloth float gloat remote devote revolt
wobbly trolley etiolate whistle worm worse worst
```

Phrases — keep typing each phrase until it wraps to the next line. Leave a clear line and type the next phrase.

```
he has the worst swivel; we will work with a wobbly
trolley; he wore a woolly coat; what has he done to
my woolly trousers; did he lie on the wooden floor

is there holly in the house; so near and yet so far;
a man among mice; it is worse today than yesterday;
take one day at a time; hard work brings rewards
```

Review the S key — type each line three times. Leave a clear line after every third line.

```
so sad sat same settle sow sew sign sent sense set
sentimental suggest submit sublime suitable sugar
sick sickly sit silt sidle scribble scratch subtle
```

Key in the manuscript below. Format it in double-line spacing. Correct spelling mistakes and other errors. Save it as Test 6A.

More than 90% of executives agree that service and customer focus are vital, but fewer than fifty percent believe their organisations are up to standard. For many organisations, the need for both cost-saving and greater customer focus is leading to radical new ways of doing things.

In the public sector, market testing, the citizen's charter initiatives and compulsory competitive tendering are having widespread impact.

Companies in the private sector are also having to look again at how they do things. Much leaner orgs are emerging with flatter, de-layered management structures. "Business process re-engineering" is the phrase used to describe this root and branch review and reconstruction of operating methods and organisation. Some well-known businesses, such as British Airways and ICI, have led the way.

Digital has also been through an intense period of bus. re-engineering. For example they have looked at their workstation business and found that they were manufacturing an astonishingly high number of parts which were clogging up their systems and overwhelming their salespeople. To date they have reduced the number of parts by a third. This has increased revenue, helped the salesforce and improved on-time delivery from 45% to more than 90%. Changes like this have saved the company

(side note)
NO OP
– please leave the phrase "The customer comes first"; see note at the end of the notes on next page

PARAGRAPH

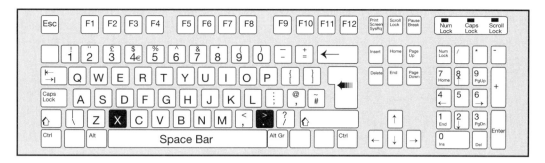

THE ⌷X⌷ AND ⌷.⌷ KEYS

The ⌷x⌷ key is typed by moving the third finger of the left hand from the home key ⌷s⌷ down to the ⌷x⌷ key. The ⌷.⌷ key is typed by moving the third finger of the right hand from the home key ⌷l⌷ down to the ⌷.⌷ key.

Letters — type each line three times. Leave a clear line after every third line.

```
sxs sxs sxs sxs l.l l.l l.l l.l sxs l.l sxs l.l xxx
... xxx ... xxx ... xen nex lex fax sax lax cax dax
gax hax jax kax max rax sex rex bex cex dex lex .x.
```

Words — type each line three times. Leave a clear line after every third line.

```
box fox rocks flex vex. relax. reflex. xenon flex vex
sex mix mixture texture vexation reflex relax xenon
texture. mixture. sex. annex maximum ox minimum
```

Phrases — type each phrase six times on six separate lines. Leave a clear line after every third line.

```
feel the texture of the woollen trousers; did the
viaduct vibrate; did the giant relax; with what
mixture did she dye the wool; rex wrote off his wagon

is silver better than gold; was the track too tough;
why was there silver in the box; he had to slog to
fix the trolley; he faxed an article about wrenches
```

Review the ⌷c⌷ key — type each line three times. Leave a clear line after every third line.

```
care cake care case calf cave class cave cuddle curt
cute cure cite cattle case cause cash carve
cackle cad caddie cadge cage cadet cadre cafe cake
```

Review the ⌷e⌷ key — type a line of each word. Leave a clear line after every third line.

```
emit error exam examination extra evoke elate
erstwhile elevate eradicate emulate evoke evade
evening even evensong enter entrance envy enemy
```

Dunne & Sons Ltd
44 High Street
Mullingar
Co Westmeath

.Name & Address of customer.

Liam Collins, Arden Vale, Tullamore, Co. Offaly.

Martin Moloney, Rahan Road, Clara, Co. Offaly

John Keane, Main Street, Birr Co. Offaly

g. Flannery, Castlepollard, Co. Westmeath.

X John Flanagan, Clara Road, Moate Co Westmeath. X

Kieran Kneafsey, Kilbeggan Road, Mullingar Co. Westmeath

Lounge	on inside wall	Bedroom 1	on inside wall
Dining Room	on inside wall	Bedroom 2	beneath window
Hall	on inside wall	Bedroom 3	beneath window
Landing	on bedroom 2 wall	Bathroom	on inside wall

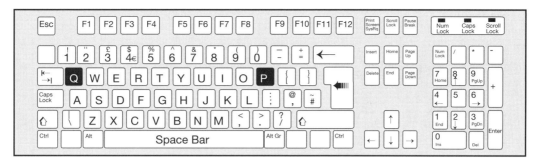

THE Q AND P KEYS

The q key is typed by moving the fourth finger of the left hand from the home key a up to the q key. The p key is typed by moving the fourth finger of the right hand from the home key ; up to the p key.

Letters — type each line three times. Leave a clear line after every third line.

```
aqa aqa ;p; ;p; ;p; qqq ppp qqq ppp aqa ;p; aqa ;p;
qat ;i; qit ;.; qiq pop pip pun qon noq nup qot pot
qit squ equ uip eqo qua qui que rep paq qap qiv viq
```

Words — type each line three times. Leave a clear line after every third line.

```
quibble rip pepper quick quirk spiral trollop flip
flipper slipper dapper voluptuous play ploy splay
trollop dollop possible prattle pair quire squire

perplex quick quire paid quip quipped prattle spoiled
lump bump plump plumb spiral duplex quarry query quip
presence patience pack quack parrot exquisite esquire
```

Phrases — type each phrase six times on six separate lines. Leave a clear line after every third line.

```
she needs a quorom; you need to queue to qualify;
pull and push; queen; it is quite possible;
he helped to fill the quota; did he grow parsnips
```

Review the b key — type each line three times. Leave a clear line after every third line.

```
bean bent bottle bulb bulbous burden bundle burnt
brittle broke brim bran bramble brat broad broker
brandish bit baby battle bounty bank banker banish
```

Review the t key — type a line of each word. Leave a clear line after every third line.

```
tape tame timid tired top tractor tame take tangerine
tangent truculent trundle take tacit table turtle
trundle tattered towel trowel train tram trot totter
```

Hot Water System

(a)   (b)   (c)   (d)

New copper indirect hot cylinder 36" X 18."

Existing cold feed tank

Hair felt / fibreglass insulation of tanks   and cold water feed pipes.

New ten-gallon fibreglass expansion tank, suitably lagged.

Note to W/P operator Please print off this letter in an appropriate manner on behalf of the Managing Director.

Design Temperature Standards.

The system is designed to provide the following indoor temperatures when the outside temperature is 30°F

Lounge and dining room. . . . . . .   70°F.
Bathroom, hall and landing .   .   .   .   .   65°F.
Bedrooms . . . .   ·55°F.

N.P. We enclose details of a Personal Loan Scheme and monthly Budget Scheme. [We hope to N·P hear favourably from you, in which case we should be pleased if you would complete and return the enclosed form of acceptance.

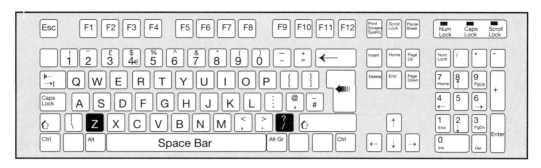

THE Z AND / KEYS

The z key is typed by moving the fourth finger of the left hand from the home key a down to the
 z key. The / key is typed by moving the fourth finger of the right hand from the home key ; down
to the / key.

Letters — type each line three times. Leave a clear line after every third line.

```
aza aza aza ;/; ;/; ;/; zzz zzz zzz /// /// zip piz
zot toz zon zot aza zan zit tiz zim miz liz piz ztz
zin niz zib biz zyz aza faz daz baz caz uza zul luz
```

Words — type each line three times. Leave a clear line after every third line.

```
zebra zephyr zeal zero zest zigzag zinc zone zombie
zither zoom zone zoo zone zip crazy lazy sleazy hazy
daze maze haze magazine mesmerize marzipan zinc zany
```

Phrases — type each phrase six times on six separate lines. Leave a clear line after every third line.

```
he read the magazine with zeal; the zebra has
a striped back; they found zinc in that zone; the
sleazy gypsy seemed half dazed; they tyrannised the zinc miners

she used marzipan and margarine; zeta read the crazy
magazine; the zombie took a zigzag route; there was a
haze over the maze; zany zealot; at zero hour; zenith
```

Review the l key — type each line three times. Leave a clear line after every third line.

```
lot liberal label level ladle lad lady lag lake label
lancer land lard large lament lanky languid lapel lap
lark largess larva lamb lash last lathe late latent
```

Review the m key — type a line of each word. Leave a clear line after every third line.

```
mat ham mantra middle muddle mutter muffle mark
marble mark marksman dame damsel drama arm anthem
main murmur mailing magnetic machine time memory
```

Note to WP Operator — Re typing of next 4 items.

1. Please number the items — leave ½" between No. & heading.
2. Type the headings using initial caps & underscore.
3. Please do not extend type under the Numbers.

Radiators

Supply and install Radiators in the position specified in prime coated finish, having a total surface area of 142 square feet, (see Note)

Note to WP OPERATOR

At this point please insert the tab (on page 289). Type the 1st and 3rd columns in Caps.

Boiler

Supply and install gas-fired boiler Rated at 50,000 b.t.u. per hour, complete with outer casing in blue/white finish; integral variable head circulating pump; electric four-stage clock programming; magnetic valve; electric thermostat. →

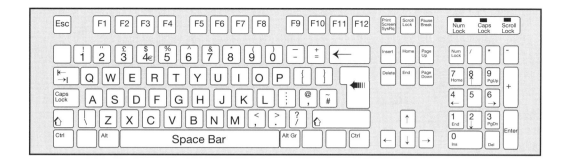

Well done, you have covered all the letters of the alphabet! It is time to learn how to type capital letters, i.e. to use the Shift key.

Capital letters

To key in capital letters, press and hold down either the left or right Shift key with the corresponding little finger, while keeping the other fingers in position on the home keys. The left Shift key is depressed when using the fingers of the left hand, and the right Shift key is depressed when using the fingers of the right hand.

 Note — Apart from capital letters, the Shift key is used to type other upper-case characters, i.e. the characters that appear on the top part of certain keys. For example, a colon : appears on the top part of the semicolon ; key.

Letters

```
Fr De Sw Aq Ju Ki Lo Fr De Sw Aq Ju Ki Lo :p
Rf Ed Ws Qa Uj Ik Ol Rf Ed Ws Qa Uj Ik Ol P;
```

Spacing after commas, semicolons, colons and full stops

Leave a **single** space between words and after commas, semicolons and colons. Leave **two** spaces after a full stop or a question mark at the end of a sentence. In the printing industry (as opposed to the world of word processing), it is usual to leave just one space after the full stop. Note the difference in the printed and typed text on this page.

Sentences

```
John Kelly came to Dublin.  Ask Ann Henry to come to
Cork.  Mr Smith and Mrs Murray will visit Galway.
Tell Joseph, Kate, Mary and Valerie to visit Susan.

Examination Requirements: Log Book, Calculator,
Ruler, Rubber, Geometry Set and Pens.  Present were:
Mr McNamara, Ms McGrath, Ms Walsh and Ms McKenna.
Flour, Tea, Currants, Sugar, Ginger and Margarine.

Ireland, Great Britain, The Netherlands, Germany,
France, Italy, Spain.  Dublin, London, Amsterdam,
Brussels, Paris, Rome, Madrid, Athens.  Belfast,
Cork, Limerick, Galway, Waterford, Dundalk, Drogheda.
```

Key in the letter below and save it as Test 5C.

Use margin of 25mm each side

Note to WP OPERATOR - you will find the name & address of the customer, (marked with "X") on the attached sheet, also the name & address of the Heating Contractor.

Use today's date: Ref: JF/DM

Insert a suitable Salutation

Thank you for your enquiry for gas-fired central heating, and I have pleasure in submitting the following Specification and quotation for your approval. [For carrying out installation N.P. in accordence with the provision of the Specification given hereafter, including testing and leaving installation in Satisfactory working order at a total cost of £1,000 subject to the quotation conditions specified

1 Tender and Specification for gas-fired central heating system (FIRED)

Note to WP OPERATOR Subject-heading in initial capitals

Optional Extras ←

WP OPERATOR - Leave 1½" blank   caps

General Description ←

Full central heating to designed temperatures, and domestic hot water; white Radiators with concealed Brackets. ⟶

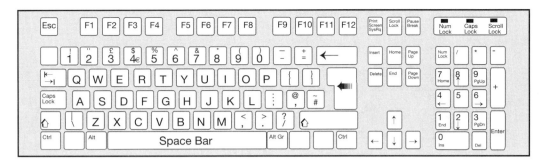

The position of certain characters

The position of certain characters, such as the question mark, hyphen, quotation marks, fractions and oblique / , varies from one keyboard to another. Computer keyboards generally do not show fractions; these are available through word-processing features such as 'Insert Symbol' (see page 75).

The question mark ?

Locate the question mark on your machine and practise reaching it from the appropriate home key (often the fourth finger of the right hand) while keeping the other fingers in place on the home keys.

Type each line three times and leave a clear line after every third line.

Words

    Who? What? When? Where? Why? How? Why? What? When?

Sentences

    Did he come? What is her name? Is she tall? Did
    the tall girl walk? How much is that? What is the
    difference? Is Thursday the day in question? Is it yellow?

    Is it a camera? Where is Fred? Is he far? Who is in charge? Did Ken
    do a careful job? When do the clocks go back an hour? Is there a
    time difference between Ireland and France?

Words

    dry, dried, numb, number, might, mighty, fry, fried,
    drug, drugged, guy tug they hug jug try fry but run
    nun gym mug fun rum gun buy ugh rub tub but try

    buy they jug run gun nun burn burnt, numb number,
    might mighty, cry cried, kit kite, fry fried, might
    mighty, their, therm, theta, thick, thieve, thigh

    fry, mug, nut, him, her, buy, hut, die, yet net
    certain, certify, dirt, dirty, dumb, dummy, dregs,
    dredge burn, burnt, they, their, there, cry, cried

Review the r key

    rash rasher rather rude rattle ram rabbit rabble rubbish rim
    rule rudder rabble remit remake reverse remember reset remake
    retake rupee rafter rankle

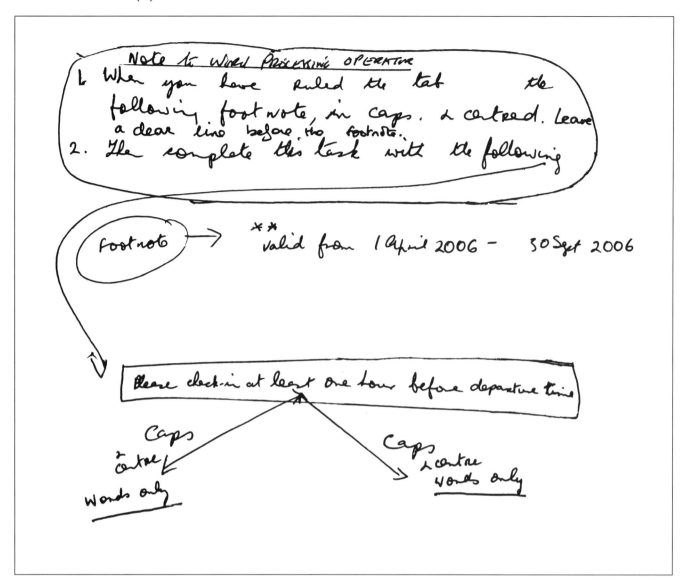

From this point on the keyboard chart no longer appears at the top of every page. You should photocopy a chart and look at it when necessary.

The colon

To type the colon, press the left Shift key and then the ⎡ : ⎤ key. There is only one space after a colon.

Letters, words and sentences — type each line three times. Leave a clear line after every third line.

```
::: ;;; ;:; :;: ;;; ::: :;: l;l l:l a;: a:; s:: :::
```
```
follows: following: details: dates: times: ideas:
suggestions: proposals: motions: recommendations:
```
```
In the following months: June, July and August.  The
following girls: Mary and Elizabeth and Margaret.
```

Review the ⎡ c ⎤ key

```
cake comfort creature calculate cancelled canter
capable cable cat cattle chattel civil cotton cut
club camp cave car carvery calculate campaign clamp
```

The hyphen/dash key

Locate the Hyphen/Dash key and practise reaching it from the appropriate home key. There is **no space before or after a hyphen.** Hyphens are used as follows:

❶ To separate the parts of a compound word, e.g. ultra-modern, post-date.

❷ To link words, e.g. the up-to-date situation, sister-in-law.

❸ Between the syllables of a word split over two consecutive lines.

```
the up-to-date situation; wide-eyed amazement; a grey-
green wash; mother-in-law; night-course students; half
of one-fifth is one-tenth; an on-off agreement
```

There is **one space before** and **after a dash** in word processing. Dashes are used as follows:

❶ Instead of a colon, e.g. Come home soon - we miss you.

❷ Instead of a set of commas, e.g. Seán - a strong lad - came first in the marathon.

```
Athenry - Town of the Kings - has impressive town walls.
New terms - like 'geek', 'nerd' and 'cyberspace' - are common
in computer magazines. Bill Gates - founder of Microsoft - is said
to have his sights set on the information superhighway.
```

Character drill — type each line three times.
```
colon: semicolon; question? colon: semicolon; question?
hyphen- hyphen- hyphen- dash - dash - dash -
colon: semicolon; question? hyphen- colon: semicolon; question?
```

 Note — In printing there is a special character for a dash, which is about twice as long as a hyphen. Can you spot the use of the printer's dash elsewhere in this text?

Note to Word PROCESSING OPERATOR

1. The following data is relevant to columns 3, 4, 5, and it is set out in that order.

2. Please use the 24-hour clock when typing "times".

3. Just type the first 3 letters when typing "days".

Wednesday —	10.00 am —	12.15.
Saturday —	9.00 p.m —	11.50 pm
Sunday —	11.00 am —	3.15 p.m.
Saturday —	6.30 pm —	10.20 p.m
Sunday —	8.00 am —	11.30 am.
Friday —	10.00 am —	2.10 p.m.
Tuesday —	1.00 p.m —	3.30 p.m.

FARO

Tenerife

Palma

Las Palmas

Malta

Malaga

Jersey.

cont. over ...

The apostrophe

Locate the apostrophe on your machine and practise reaching it from the appropriate home key. Remember — there is no space before or after an apostrophe in the middle of a word.

Type each line three times. Leave a clear line after every third line.

Words

```
mother's, boy's, child's, man's, people's, men's,
children's, women's, worker's; the boys' coats; one
week's holiday; the people's choice; a day's grace
```

Words again — remember to leave two spaces after a full stop.

```
flow.  glow.  low.  mow.  tow.  sow.  row.  cow.
row, sow, six, sixty, sixteen, sixteenth, exit,
exited; ignited; lost; sold; jinx; jinxed; who; west;

allow, allowed, professor, professional, quiz, zero,
zoology: zoological: promote: promotion: punctuate:
punctual.  quizzical.  zone.  zombie.  zoom.  zap.

apple.  appeal.  appear.  apply.  aqua.  aquarium.
applicator, professor, professional, quiz, zoology,
zealot; zoological; promotion; punctuate; punctilios;
```

Sentences

```
The girl's coat.  The girls' coats.  The child's hat.
The children's hats.  The man's jacket.  The men's jackets.
It's a large size.  Who's who?  Who's that?
```

Sentences again

```
When secretaries gain experience they may become "senior
secretaries".  Senior secretarial positions are given names
such as personal assistant, PA, executive secretary or even
executive assistant.  Secretaries are expected to handle
increasingly complex office systems.
```

Comma drill

```
a, d, e, f, i, j, k, l, r, s, u, a, d, e, f, i, j, k,
l, r, s, u, a, d, e, f, i, j, k, l, r, s, u, a, d,
```

Character drill

```
question?  question?  apostrophe' apostrophe' apostrophe'
colon: colon: colon: semicolon; semicolon; semicolon;
hyphen- hyphen- hyphen- apostrophe' apostrophe' apostrophe'
```

Key in the data below in tabular form. Save it as Test 5B.

Rule vertically, horizontally, & use double line spacing in the body of the tab.

(Heading:- Caps, u/s & centre) ⟶ ** Summer Schedule/2006 (refer to footnote below) ⟶ & desk

(Column headings):- ↓ Destination ①
Day ③
➤Airline ②

④ Dublin ² ⌐Depart⌐
⑤ Arrive Destination, also add a right-hand column for "Baggage Allowance".

Note to OPERATOR (WP)
Type the headings for the last 3 columns over 2 lines

(Destinations) ⟶ + Palma
+ Malaga
* Las Palmas
* Malta
* Tenerife
* Faro
* Jersey

Note to OPERATOR (WP)
1. Please type Destinations in alphabetical order.
2. * denotes 33 lbs. luggage allow,
+ denotes 44 lbs luggage allow.

Aer Lingus fly on all routes except Jersey – this is serviced by Ryanair

cont. over ... ⟶

Keying in a series of capital letters

To key in a series of capital letters, press the Caps Lock key. Press the Caps Lock key again to cancel the caps lock function to type in the normal way.

Sentences — key in each sentence three times.

```
To stay healthy YOU MUST EAT WISELY.  Many young people
eat TOO MUCH JUNK FOOD and not enough FRESH FRUIT AND
VEGETABLES.  EXERCISE is also important.
```

Using the Return key without looking down

Key in the following sentences:

```
It's a long way to Tipperary.
Only Alex played the game properly.
The girl smiled and made her departure.
They dismissed the people in this section.
Some people take annual leave in June, others prefer July.
Dublin, on the east coast, is the capital city of Ireland.
```

Well done! Now you are ready to move to an exciting stage in the development of your keyboarding skill, i.e. the calculation of your speed. This gives an idea of your progress to date and allows you to gauge future progress.

Calculating your speed

❶ A keyboard 'stroke' is any character or space. Every five strokes represents a 'standard word'. In the speed tests in this section, the number of standard words is shown at the end of the line.

❷ To calculate speed, select the text keyed in, click the **Tools** menu and click **Word Count**. Note the number of characters <u>with spaces</u> and divide by five. This gives the number of standard words.

❸ Divide the number of standard words by the number of minutes spent typing. This gives the number of words typed in one minute, i.e. speed in words per minute (wpm).

Use the calculator that comes with Windows — click **Start**, **Programs**, **Accessories** and **Calculator** — to calculate your speed.

One-minute speed test — target speed 16 wpm.

Note — You need to key in text as far as the point indicated to attain the target speed.

```
The play is showing at a larger theatre in the city        10
centre. We attended the Edu|cational Conferences in        20
Belfast last year. Your appointment has been fixed for     32
Tuesday afternoon.                                         35
```

 Remember — Leave **one** space after a comma, semicolon and colon, and **two** spaces after a full stop at the end of a sentence.

A patterned sisal carpet
which will give many years
of good service, even
when laid in hard wear
areas of hall and playroom.
Available in 6 colours.
Ref. No.   NC 16.
Price per sq. yd. €14.

re item 1.
Ref. No.   NC 4
price per sq. yd.
€11.00.

re item 2 —
Ref. No. WC 1
Price per sq. yd. €6.25.

Note to WP OPERATOR
① NO ruling required
② I omitted to include a paragraph 2:
please change paragraph numbers to
take account of this

Note to WP OPERATOR
As column 2 contains all the
information relevant to the
different types of floor
covering, make this the
widest column

Numbers

For general work it is better to enter figures from the normal keyboard, i.e. the fingers move to the numbers on the top row of the keyboard and spring back to the home keys.

Computers have special numeric keypads which are used when figures are typed repeatedly. Special numeric keyboard exercises are given at the end of this section.

Type the exercises below three times — spring back to the home keys shown.

```
a1a a1a s2s s2s d3d d3d aq1 aq1 sw2 sw2 de3 de3 a1q
```

```
1 from the a home key
2 from the s home key
3 from the d home key
```

```
s2w d3e a1q s2w d3e a1q s2w d3e a1q s2w d3e 123 123
```

```
Add 1 plus 2 to get 3. 1 plus 1 equals 2. Take 2
from 3 to get 1. Add 2 plus 1 to get 3. 11 plus 1
equals 12. 12 plus 1 equals 13. 13 less 1 equals 12.
```

Type the exercises below three times — spring back to the home keys shown.

```
fr4 fr4 fr5 fr5 fr4 fr5 fr4 fr5 f4r g5t h6y jy6 jy6
```

```
4 from the f home key
5 from the f home key
6 from the j home key
```

```
4rf 5rf 6yj j6j j6j j6j j6j j6j j6j j6j j6j j6j
```

```
4 plus 1 equals 5; 5 plus 1 equals 6; 44; 45; 46; 54;
55; 56; 64; 65; 66; 64 plus 1 equals 65; 64; 65; 66
```

Type the exercises below three times — spring back to the home keys shown.

```
j7j j7j ki8 ki8 l9l l9l l9l ;0; ;0; ;p0 77 78 79 80
```

```
7 from the j home key
8 from the k home key
9 from the l home key
0 from the ; home key
```

```
87 88 89 90 99 98 97 70 80 90 00 07 08 09 100 107 108
```

```
7 plus 8; 8 plus 9; 9 plus 1 equals 10; 10 minus 1
equals 9; 9 minus 1 equals 8; 8 minus 7 equals 1
```

all-nylon carpet. The special constructions of the fibres has made it possible for them to be fused together, thus eliminating the weaving process. Carpeting of this sort is suitable for use in any part of the house. Ref. No. for item 6 is NC 10, & it is €10.50 per sq. yd. Ref. No. for item 4 is NC 5, & it is €8.00 per sq. yd.

(3) A blend of Evlan and nylon is used in the manufacture of a plain, low-looped tufted tile carpet in two-tone colouring. It is suitable for light wear only in areas as bedrooms and bathrooms. A choice of 12 colours. (See end of question.)

(5) The deep texture of this nylon look tile carpet gives it an air of luxury. The surface pile which is in good quality nylon, makes it a suitable choice for any room in the house. Available in 6 colours.
Ref. No. NC 14
€9.50 per sq. yd.

(1) Newcomer to the field of carpet fibres is polypropylene, which is used in this cord type example. Although the carpet is very hard wearing, the surface is soft to the foot and resistant to water-borne stains. (see over)

Percentages

Locate the percentage sign on your machine and practise reaching it from the appropriate home key. Leave no space between a percentage sign and the number preceding it.

```
1%  2%  3%  4%  5%  6%  7%  8%  9%  10%  23%  45%  56%  78%  90%
```

Typing a solidus, or oblique [/]

Locate the solidus, or oblique, and practise reaching it from the appropriate home key. Leave no space before or after a solidus.

Type the exercises shown below.

July/August Wednesday/Thursday with/without and/or

Sentences

```
11 plus 12 make 23, 12 and 13 make 25, 13 and 14 make
27, 14 and 15 make 29, 15 and 16 make 31, 16 and 17
make 33.  Send sizes 10, 12 and 8 only.  The number
13 may be unlucky.  From a total of 70 Marion took
59 and Sean took 11.  Apply 4 drops 3 times a day.
Date of Birth: 26 October 1974.

In 1993 the Pretty Polly plant in Killarney produced
an average of 1.75 m pairs of stockings per week.
The plant is 140,000 sq feet and is one of the
largest production units in the EC, with 450 people
employed.  A stocking can be knit in sheer denier in
45 seconds - as quickly as it takes to pull them on.

205, 316, 427; 5389, 6721, 8273; 10902987
Account Number - 104367598
Telephone Number - 00-44-525-860-343
Invoice number 91826 relates to account no 45453.
All invoices from 125 to 300 were sent on 16/2/93.
```

Shift key drill

```
The They Their Our Hour Flour And Land Blank Ham Sham
Shame Ten Often Soften Par Park Spark Fit Flit Flight
Say Slays Slain
```

Words

```
quit quiz queen queer quench queue quid quip query
all; all; lad; lad; all; lad; all; lad; all; lad;
also load also load also load all load broad told

zeal; zealot; zealous; zebra; zap; zany; zone; zoo;
prig; prim; plus; pods; press; pray; prey; pup;
quit quiz queen queer quench queue quid quip zipper
```

Key in the text below and save it as Test 5A.

of 25 mm each side. Display the data following the opening paragraph in three columns, under the following headings :-

② Floor Covering   ③ Price per Sq. yd.   ① Ref. No.
Inexpensive

Inexpensive Floor Coverings

WP OPERATOR → Heading: in caps, u/s & centre →

Navan really believe in quality caps which is why they make carpets that can stand up to anything from years of hard wear to a close, close look. Now Navan have used all their caps craftsmanship to make the following range of carpets which sh. especially appeal to people with a limited l.c. Budget.

Note to WP OPERATOR: KEY in the items in Numerical order, but omit the Numbers

⑥ Attractive all-nylon carpet has the additional value of a built-in foam underlay. The lightly sculptured pile gives a pattern interest to the choice of 13 plain colours available in this range. See end of item 4

④ A completely new method has been applied to the manufacture of this

Note to WP OPERATOR: Re column headings : - all abbreviation in full, & Ref. No. & Price per Sq. yd. - type over 2 lines. "Inexpensive Floor Covering" - over 2 lines.

Backspace

The back arrow to the right at the bottom of the keyboard is used to move the cursor to the left.

Underline (or underscore)

To underline text, highlight the appropriate word(s) and click the **Underline** button on the Formatting Toolbar.

 Note — Punctuation marks should not be underlined, apart from those in the middle of a sentence, when a complete sentence is being underlined.

Type the exercise below three times:

<u>Urgent</u>, <u>Private</u>, <u>Confidential</u>, <u>By Hand</u>. Please send <u>ten</u> only. Give this matter your <u>immediate</u> attention. Don't forget <u>Mary</u>.

One-minute speed test — target speed 17 wpm.

Note — You must reach the point marked to attain the target speed.

Though the chairwoman's first duty is to be impartial, she	12
must also show considerable understanding|. There is no	23
point in appointing a woman who appears stubborn or	33
vindictive.	35

 Question 1 How did the above speed test go? Did you reach the target speed of 17 wpm?
Question 2 Did you make any errors? If so, how many?

Character drill — type each line three times.

percent % percent % percent % hyphen- hyphen- hyphen-
solidus/ solidus/ solidus/ question? question? question?
colon: colon: colon: solidus/ solidus/ solidus/

Page 3   Leah glasses   Ashford glasses

	Leah glasses	Ashford glasses
6 Sherry	36	36
6 White Wine	42	48
6 Red Wine/Claret	42	48
6 Water Goblets	48	54
6 Flute Champagne	60	66
6 Small Brandy	48	42
6 Brandy	60	72.

NB operator PLEASE insert euro symbol

Use the same format for the above as for Page 1

Additional keyboard drills

The drills set out below are useful for warm-up purposes and as aids to developing a smooth rhythm. You should aim to produce neat sets of work by typing the letters under each other as shown. If you make a mistake, ignore it and type the next letter in the appropriate place. Remember to leave a clear line after every third line.

The Rhythm Drill — type the set of three lines below three times.

```
fjdksla;sldkfjgh fjdksla;sla;sldkfjgh
fjdksla;sldkfjgh fjdksla;sla;sldkfjgh
fjdksla;sldkfjgh fjdksla;sla;sldkfjgh
```

The Alphabet Drill — type the set of three lines below three times.

```
abcdefghijklmnopqrstuvwxyz abcdefghijklmnopqrstuvwxyz
abcdefghijklmnopqrstuvwxyz abcdefghijklmnopqrstuvwxyz
abcdefghijklmnopqrstuvwxyz abcdefghijklmnopqrstuvwxyz
```

The € symbol

On some keyboards, it is necessary to hold down the 'Alt Gr' key while striking the '4' key to type the € symbol.

Type the exercise below three times:

```
€1, €2, €3, €4, €5, €6, €7, €8, €9, €10, €11, €12, €13, €14, €15.
```

Words — type each line below three times.

```
articulate belong before better cancel change clause course
early feel fact five full gone four cannot gave word ahead
charge custom give cast alive credit culprit cockpit concoct
```

The ampersand &

Locate the & and practise reaching it from the appropriate home key. Leave one space before and after the & .

Type the exercise below three times.

```
Burke, Farrell & Patterson; Mr & Mrs Farrell; 7 & 8 Sli an
Aifrinn; Jonny Carroll & The Sensations; Helen, Jane & Co.
```

Review the u key — type each line three times.

```
fur rum mum fun gun bun rut run hum hut guy buy hug
tug bug mug rug nut gut but hut fur rut run hum hug
tug rug nut hum munch bunch brunch lunch crunch hunch
```

Page 2

	Leah Collection	Ashford Collection
Flair Bowl 5"	75	75
Flair Bowl 9"	105	95
Salad Bowl 6"	72	80
Salad Bowl 8"	100	120
Rose Bowl 4"	60	60
Rose Bowl 6"	80	90
Footed Vase 6"	75	65
Footed Vase 10"	95	85.

€ PLEASE INSERT euro SYMBOL

WP OPERATOR

Show the above information in the manner shown below.

LEAH COLLECTION ←

Caps Bold block Underscored

2 clear lines →

€ clear line after € sign

Flair Bowl 5" 75

Flair Bowl 9" 105

Double line space.

Insert leader dots

2 clear lines

ASHFORD COLLECTION

Caps, Bold, Centred & Underscored.

€
Flair Bowl 5" 75

EXAMPLE

→ Please show the Leah Collection followed by the Ashford Collection on Page 2 as per example.

WP OPERATOR

One-minute speed test — target speed 18 wpm.

```
On first taking the chair, it is customary for the        10
chairwoman to thank members for placing| their confidence 22
in her. A few words are quite sufficient and will serve   32
to show that she is conscious of her duties and           43
appreciative of her position.                             49
```

> ❓ **Question 1** How did the above speed test go? Did you reach the target speed of 18 wpm?
> **Question 2** Did you make any errors? If so, how many?

Alphabetic sentences

The best-known alphabetic sentence tells of a quick brown fox and incorporates every letter of the alphabet! It's a great sentence for warming up before doing keyboard work. Key in the sentences below many times.

```
The quick brown fox jumps over the lazy dog.
The quick brown fox jumps over the lazy dog.
The quick brown fox jumps over the lazy dog.
```

Do not use the Caps Lock key when keying in the sentences below.

```
The QUICK brown FOX jumps OVER the LAZY dog.
The QUICK brown FOX jumps OVER the LAZY dog.
The QUICK brown FOX jumps OVER the LAZY dog.


THE quick BROWN fox JUMPS over THE lazy DOG.
THE quick BROWN fox JUMPS over THE lazy DOG.
THE quick BROWN fox JUMPS over THE lazy DOG.
```

I bet you have had enough of our nimble fox for now! Let's try some more sentences that stress keys such as x and z. Key in each sentence six times.

```
Zena zigzagged around the complex obstacle course.
The zany saxophone player joined the quartet in the plaza.
The zealous executive scrutinised the aquatic species in the
exotic aquarium.
```

Words — key in each line three times.

```
punctual puerile quote; quotation query; queries zircon;
zirconium; zone; zombie; zoom; zinc; zero; zing; zip, zany,
zeal, zealous zebra, zero, zinc, zipper, zip, zipper, zither
```

Word drill — key in each line three times.

```
apple appeal appear apply aqua aquarium applicator zeal;
zealot; zealous; zebra; zap; zany; zed; zoo; prig; prim; plus;
pods; press; pray; prey; pull; xenon xenophobia xenogamy
```

Key in the text below. Format it to print on landscape A4 paper which is folded vertically in the middle. Save it as Test 4C.

WORD PROCESSING OPERATOR — SET PLEASE — margins of 1.25 CM

Page I

Centre Bold & Caps → Ballinasloe Irish Crystal

WP OPERATOR → Giftware ← Centre Bold Caps.

Opening Hours

Monday — Friday
9AM — 5PM.

Leave 1 inch clear between each section →

Expand your collection with our exquisite crystal. Our collection

Or ~~comprehensively~~ ensures that ~~you can find~~

Or ~~a gift for~~

Or ~~every occasion~~ birthdays,

stet Weddings ~~or~~ AND anniversaries can be commemorated with just the right gift.

Double line spacing

For the purpose of the @ drill below, click the **Format** menu and click **AutoFormat**. Click **Options** and click the **AutoFormat as you type** tab, then deselect **Internet and network paths with hyperlinks**.

Key in the exercises below, which should help with those e-mail addresses! Note — the characters 4fr are used to reinforce the fact that @ is keyed in with the fourth finger of the right hand.

```
e-mail e-mail e-mail e-mail e-mail e-mail e-mail e-mail e-mail
4fr@ 4fr@ 4fr@ 4fr@ 4fr@ 4fr@ 4fr@ 4fr@ 4fr@ 4fr@ 4fr@ 4fr@
qw@eircom qw@eircom qw@eircom qw@eircom qw@eircom qw@eircom
```

Delete and Return key drills
Do not lapse into the habit of looking at the keyboard when pressing the Return or the Delete key. Try the drills below.

Drill one
❶ Key in John, delete John and key in Jack, press the Return key.

❷ Repeat the above six times.

❸ The result should be:

```
                        Jack

                        Jack

                        Jack

                        Jack

                        Jack

                        Jack
```

Drill two
Key in Kathleen, delete hleen, key in e, return and repeat six times.

Drill three
Key in Bernie, delete i.e., key in adette, return and repeat six times.

More alphabetic sentences

Key in each sentence three times.

```
Extra equipment such as microwaves and freezers make it quite easy
to provide wholesome food for the family.

The stalls in the zigzag streets of the quaint bazaar provide
yoghurt and yams for the anxious citizens.

The guest speaker dazzled her audience with a quick analysis of the
contentious issues of the epoque.
```

 Question — Did you see any 'Return Key Peepers' lately? RKPs, poor souls, look down at the keyboard when moving to a new line instead of keeping their eyes on their books!

Key in the table below and save it as Test 4B.

Centre vertically and horizontally and Rule. Use block style.

ITEM	COST	QUANTITY	RETAIL PRICE	VALUATION PRICE	PROFIT
	€		€	€	€
Cooker	300	6	450	1,800	150
Deep Fat Fryer	100	10	200	1,000	80
Dryer	200	5	300	1,000	100
Hoover	100	8	160	800	100
Iron	30	10	45	400	15
Microwave	280	10 8	350	2,240	70
Record Player	260 300	4	400	2,200	200
Toaster	50	20	75	1,000	25
Television	450 450	10	550	4,500	100
Video Recorder	290 290	5	350	1,450	60
Washing Machine	450	5	550	3,150	100
Refrigerator	300.	7	420	2,100	120
TOTAL	2,850	98	3,850	19,640	1,000

WORD PROCESSING OPERATOR — Insert the following heading in double line spacing above the tab.

Lynch's Electrical Superstore Valuation Report December 2006

Caps, Centre, bold & Underscore

Leave 3 clear lines after the heading

WP OPERATOR — Transpose last two columns

Check the profit and valuation figures that are circled.

Profit = Retail Price − Cost
Valuation = Cost × Quantity

Put all items in Col 1 in Caps

Open and close brackets

Locate the different types of open and close brackets on your machine and practise reaching them from the appropriate home key. Leave one space before and no space after an open bracket and no space before and one space after a closed bracket.

Key in the following exercises:

(a) (b) (c) (d) (e) (f) (g) (h) (i) (j) (k) (l) (m) (n) (o) (p)
(q) (r) (s) (t) (u) (v) (w) (x) (y) (z)

If I won €1,000,000 I would divide it up and put (1) €300,000 in government securities (2) €300,000 in a post office account (3) €100,000 in bank shares (4) €100,000 in ordinary shares in different Irish companies and (5) €200,000 in property.

Are you a Libra (22 September to 22 October) or a Scorpio (23 October to 21 November)?

Key in each line three times:

"Come in." "Do sit down." "It's great to see you." "How are your keyboard skills?" "Yes or no?"

(bracket) (bracket) (bracket) "quote" "quote" "quote"
'single quote' 'single quote' 'single quote'
he/she he/she he/she/ question? question? question?
hyphen- hyphen- hyphen- colon: colon: colon:
semicolon; semicolon; semicolon;

Underscore

never guess or alter figures
without referring to the originator.
of the draft. If you are at all.
in doubt on any point you must
refer. back. to the originator for.
confirmation /Clarification. OR

TYPOGRAPHICAL ERRORS ← Paragraph Heading

draft.

① In typing from typescript /
typographical errors of any kind ①
shd. be of course, likewise be del
corrected. Obvious inconsistencies in
presentation shd be corrected — for
example different styling for a
series of like – weighted headings.

CAUTIONARY NOTE ← Initial Caps & Underscore

In correcting errors
in drafts care is needed to be sure
that you correct only what is wrong.
Remember that in matters of punctuation,
spelling and English style generally
there can be equally acceptable
alternatives. In such cases, the pref. ie preference
of I author, & not of the typist must prevail.

Underlining again

Key in the following exercise three times. Do not underline the punctuation marks.

<u>Urgent</u>; <u>Private</u>; <u>Confidential</u>; <u>By Hand</u>; please send <u>ten</u> only; give this matter your <u>immediate</u> attention; <u>FOR THE ATTENTION OF MR SEAN WALSH</u>.

Further speed development

 Important — Don't push for a higher speed if you're making more than two errors in a one-minute test.

One-minute speed test — target speed 18 wpm. Try to reach the point marked.

Some senior secretaries oversee the work of junior staff	11
and are experts at delegating work.| Others assume a	22
personnel role or spend their time organising conferences	34
or travelling to meet foreign suppliers.	42

One-minute speed test — target speed 19 wpm. Try to reach the point marked.

Thanks to the American GIs, who wore them under their	11
uniforms for warmth, nylons found their| way to Europe	22
during the war years and became the coveted possessions	33
of many well-heeled ladies. They were incredibly	42
expensive, and many an Irish mammy will tell you	54
that you couldn't get a pair for love or money.	61

One-minute speed test — target speed 19 wpm. Try to reach the point marked.

This year the famous nylon stocking celebrates its	10
fiftieth anniversary and high kicks its leggy| way into	21
the twenty-first century. Founded back in the forties,	32
nylons caused a sensation when they were unfurled by the	44
Hollywood glamour girls and the smoothies in the movies.	55

Well done, you have established a typing speed! You now need to build speed and learn the conventions of document layout.

For further work on speed development, refer to the Speed Development section that follows and the Accuracy Tests at the end of the book.

two different figs may appear in the text though sense makes clear that the same one must be intended. Similar discrepancies can arise in names, places, dates, etc and much else.

WP OPERATOR
This stands for 'the'

2

Here yr. Role is Run on to be vigilant in scrutiny, but cautious about corrective action. For though it may be clear that something is wrong, it may not be at all obvious what is wrong & how the correction shd be made.

underscore

WP Where you can make a sure check for yourself — by referring to the file for instance example — you shd correct the error. Also if a fig. is not clear unclear it may be possible to confirm it by checking the total. You should

Numbers again

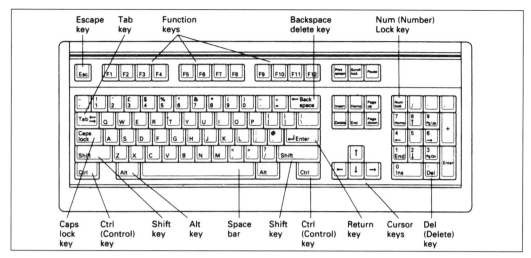

Computers have a numeric keypad which is generally located to the right of the alphabetic keyboard. It is more convenient to use the numeric keypad when keying in work that contains a lot of figures. Like the alphabetic keyboard, the numeric keypad is deemed to have 'home keys'; these are: 4, 5 and 6. The fingers should rest on the home keys as follows:

- the index finger or forefinger (i.e. the figure next to the thumb) on 4
- the middle finger on 5
- the ring finger on 6
- the little finger on $Enter$.

Getting ready

❶ Press the Num Lock key to activate the numeric keypad.

❷ Insert a table with two rows and six columns.

❸ Type the figures in columns and press **Enter** after each figure.

Numeric keyboard exercises

Home keys — 4, 5, 6		Bottom row keys — 1, 2, 3		Top row keys — 7, 8, 9	
555	456	111	312	777	987
666	546	222	213	888	779
555	654	333	131	999	879
444	456	111	213	888	799
666	554	222	313	777	989
444	664	333	322	879	898
666	546	111	211	789	789
555	654	222	133	987	887
444	465	333	122	889	888
456	546	123	221	988	889

 Remember — Your fingers must always return to the appropriate home keys.

incorrect use of capital letters and the like. With dictionary at hand, you shd watch spelling constantly. Thoughtful attention is all that is needed to spot √ a singular verb with a plural noun, or a vital comma omitted, confusing the meaning of a sentence. Sometimes | Reason for an error will be apparent, eg a hasty change in some respect, not √ carried Consequentially through. Thus the enumeration of sections & paras. can go wrong. Typists are expected to be on the lookout for all such obvious errors and to correct them without question

such things as

Insert ① here see two pages over

Paragraph Heading

DISCREPANCIES AND INCONSISTENCIES OF FACT Many other kinds of error can occur in drafts. For example, figs may be incorrectly totalled, or

Index finger keys — 4, 1, 7		Middle finger keys — 5, 2, 8		Ring finger keys — 6, 3, 9	
441	114	555	852	666	936
447	447	888	288	333	369
441	771	222	825	999	939
417	141	285	828	639	693
747	177	558	282	693	396
771	174	228	525	363	639
117	471	882	582	636	993
417	744	282	888	969	339
741	474	228	828	996	663
117	771	528	822	699	669

Now it is time to extend use of the numeric keypad. Note the additional key strokes below.

Character **Finger used**

Character	Finger used
0	thumb
+	little finger
-	little finger
/ (stands for divide)	middle finger
* (stands for multiply)	ring finger

Thumb key — 0		All the number keys		+ and -	/ and *
001	100	100	547	-120	/682
002	200	101	921	-250	*953
003	300	102	852	+621	/834
004	400	103	372	+720	*673
005	500	104	591	-937	/636
006	600	105	918	+450	*582
007	700	106	678	-168	*639
008	800	107	293	-247	/871
009	900	108	952	+853	*857
000	000	109	428	-628	/852

 Remember — With practice, an operator can become adept at using the numeric keyboard.

Key in and format the the manuscript below. Use double-line spacing and correct all errors. Save it as Test 4A.

WP OPERATOR

PLEASE REPLACE EACH OCCURRENCE OF "TYPIST" WITH "WORD PROCESSING OPERATOR"

THE ROLE OF THE TYPIST ← Centre, bold & Caps

One of the skills that mark an advanced typist is the ability to deal with accidental errors in drafts. The originators of drafts are very busy people. They often write or type with their mind very much on the business problem, & it can easily happen that mistakes creep into their draft unnoticed. Therefore, the typist can serve a most valuable function by applying a careful and intelligent cheque on such matters.

OBVIOUS ERRORS IN SPELLING AND GRAMMER ← Paragraph Heading

The simplest examples are mistakes in spelling, grammer, punctuation,

Part 3
Speed Development

▷▷▶▷▷▷▷▷▷▷▷▷▷▷

A top-class operator is expected to have a typing speed of 60 standard words per minute (wpm) with an accuracy level of 97% or greater, i.e. a maximum error level of 3%. Therefore, in a one-minute test with a target speed of 60 wpm, no more than 1.8 errors are allowed. So lots of practice is necessary!

Speed tests and errors
When developing speed, say the letters to yourself as you type. This will aid the development of a smooth rhythm. Do not correct errors when doing speed tests, but at the end of each test note the number of errors made. There is no point developing speed without striving for accuracy.

How to develop higher speed

❶ Ensure you can key in a speed test reasonably accurately, i.e. with no more than one error per minute's typing time. (Two errors per minute is the absolute maximum allowed.)

❷ Calculate your speed as explained on page 37.

❸ Now break out of your 'speed rut' by keying in the same test again three times at a faster rate — even if this causes you to make more than two errors.

❹ Re-establish control by keying in more carefully. Repeat the piece until you can again type it with no more than two errors per minute's typing.

❺ Key in a new speed test and repeat steps 1 to 4.

Half-a-minute speed tests
Work on half-a-minute tests until you can key in 60 characters in half a minute, i.e. 12 standard words. This is equivalent to a speed of 24 words in a full minute, or 24 wpm. Once you have reached a speed of 24 wpm, it is probably as well to concentrate on one-minute tests. In the tests below you need to reach the point marked to achieve the target speed.

HM/1 — Target 17 wpm, i.e. 8.5 words in half a minute.

```
Perhaps you could do an evening course afte|r work and learn      12
about the design side of the fashion business.                    21
```

HM/2 — Target 18 wpm, i.e. 9 words in half a minute.

```
She wore a peach-coloured embroidered cashmer|e sweater           11
combined with a delicious organza ballskirt.                      20
```

HM/3 — Target 19 wpm, i.e. 9.5 words in half a minute.

```
The model wore a painted and layered lace dress |and a            11
glorious ballgown in coffee-coloured satin.                       19
```

 Remember — Ensure you can type one speed test reasonably accurately, i.e. with no more than two errors per minute's typing, before proceeding to the next test. A maximum of two errors per minute is equivalent to one error per half a minute.

---

5. Probationary Period and Termination of Employment
The probationary period for all staff
should be not less than six (6) months.
After completion of six months, one
month's notice of termination of employment
is required on either side.

7. Office Hours:
Office hours shall be 35 hours per week.

8. Vacancies, Promotion:

8.1 All posts within the Agency (including
newly created ones) which become
vacant shall be filled by open
competition and shall be publicly
advertised.

8.2 Where possible, vacancies shall be
filled by closed internal competition.
On   If there are no applications for
such closed / internal competition, the
an   vacant post shall be advertised publicly.

8.3 Where a vacancy has been filled by
closed internal competition the point
on the scale used on appointment shall
be determined on the basis of the
/n   appointee's age.

9. Claims: (FINGAL)

9.1 Any Union organised within Fingal Agency
may   or the management / make claims on the
other.

stet 9.3. If such claims cannot be settled officially
by correspondence they shall be discussed at
a meeting at local level.

9.2. Such claims shall be made in WRITING.

Signed —————   Signed —————
(Block) Date   Date
for Fingal Agency   For General Workers Union

HM/4 — Target 20 wpm, i.e. 10 words in half a minute.

```
When the minutes of the previous meeting have been| read the      12
chairwoman asks if it is in order to sign them.                   21
```

HM/5 — Target 21 wpm, i.e. 10.5 words in half a minute.

```
Generally members are anxious to proceed with the bu|siness of    12
the day and they agree that the minutes should be signed.         24
```

HM/6 — Target 22 wpm, i.e. 11 words in half a minute.

```
The elegant office information processing student wore a| gold    12
cashmere sweater combined with a delicious organza ballskirt.     25
```

HM/7 — Target 23 wpm, i.e. 11.5 words in half a minute.

```
The girls who arrived late wore hand-painted and layered l|ong    12
lace dresses and glorious ballgowns in coffee-coloured            23
duchesse satin.                                                   27
```

HM/8 — Target 24 wpm, i.e. 12 words in half a minute.

```
Occasionally members question the accuracy of the minutes an|d    12
raise a query.  Finally the chairwoman signs the minutes and      24
adds the date.                                                    27
```

HM/9 — Target 25 wpm, i.e. 12.5 words in half a minute.

```
The quality mark signifies to the consumer that the              10
displaying |company has an approved system of quality            21
assurance.                                                       23
```

HM/10 — Target 26 wpm, i.e. 13 words in half a minute.

```
The quality mark is awarded only to companies who demonstrate    12
tha|t their standards of quality management are rigorous and     24
consistent.                                                      27
```

One-minute speed tests
There are 60 strokes (i.e. 60 characters or spaces) in each of the sentences below. As there are five strokes in a standard word, each sentence contains 12 standard words.

How many sentences can you type in one minute? Note — one sentence equates to 12 wpm, two sentences to 24 wpm.

```
People consider that the grass is greener on the other side.     12

Some people go abroad to get a few weeks sunshine each year.      12

Jack came to the aid of the frightened boys and the teacher.      12

Sportsmen say the harder they practise the luckier they get.      12
```

Key in the Agreement below. Use block style. Save it as Test 3C.

(Caps + u/score)

WP OPERATOR — PLEASE SHOW PARAGRAPHS in CORRECT order

Agreement between Fingal Personnel Agency and General Workers Union.

1. The Parties to the Agreement:
This agreement is between Fingal Personnel Agency and General Workers Union.

2. Negotiating Body:
The Agency recognises the GWU as the negotiating body for all employees who are members of that Union.

3. Information for New Employees:
The Agency shall inform all new employees, on appointment, of the existence of this and/or any other such agreements and apprise them of the contents.

4 Deduction of Union Contributions from Pay:
The Agency will deduct Union contributions from members' salaries, where authorised, and remit these contributions to the Union each month.

6 Pay and Conditions:
SHALL | Matters concerning pay and conditions, that is: pay; annual leave; sick leave; maternity leave; overtime; privilege days; incremental dates; tea breaks, be laid down in the relevant circulars which are issued from time to time.

Remember — Ensure you can key in one speed test reasonably accurately, i.e. with no more than two errors per minute's typing, before proceeding to the next one.

Can you reach the point marked and achieve the target speeds?

Test 1/1 — Target 20 wpm

Helen wore a satin blouse and a classic trousers while Mary	12
wore an elegant but a mannish trouser su|it.	21

Test 1/2 — Target 20 wpm

Please call to the boardroom after work on Friday next to	11
meet Mr Kelly who will be on hand to demon|strate the new	23
photocopying machine.	

Test 1/3 — Target 21 wpm

Yoga is a form of mental and physical exercise. It involves	12
a combination of exercising the body, concen|trating, and	23
breathing slowly and evenly.	27

Test 1/4 — Target 21 wpm

Paper recycling is an issue very close to home for	8
secretaries. It is estimated that every secretary ge|ts	21
through two trees worth of paper a year.	30

Test 1/5 — Target 22 wpm

Iced-pink, duchesse satin cocktail dresses trimmed with deep	12
black lace. Knickerbockers in rich brocades or d|eep black	24
velvet.	25

Test 1/6 — Target 22 wpm

There are two hundred standing and sitting poses in yoga.	12
Other poses are designed to refresh one after all |this work	24
and are called recuperative poses.	31

Test 1/7 — Target 23 wpm

Help to conserve the wildlife and landscape of Connemara.	12
Take litter away with you and dispose of it carefully. |Leave	24
wild flowers for others to enjoy, sketch/photograph them but	36
please do not pick them.	41

Key in the table below and save it as Test 3B.

BALLYMORE RFC

AIL FIXTURES 2005/2006

Date	Versus	Venue	Date	Versus	Venue	Date	Versus	Venue
4 Dec	Cork Con	HM	28 Dec	St Marys	A	22 Jan	Shannon	HB
29 Jan	Terenure	A	12 Feb	Clontarf	HM	26 Feb	DLSP	A
11 Mar	Garryowen	HB	25 Mar	Ballymena	A	8 April	Lansdowne	HM
22 April	Young Muster	A	29 April	Dungannon	HB			

HB= Home Ballymore   HM = Home Mullingar   A = Away

Test 1/8 — Target 23 wpm

```
Evening wear with beautifully beaded jackets and long evening      11
dresses in subtle, sophisticated colours.  Fine lace |layered      25
over satin and velvet columns.                                     31
```

Test 1/9 — Target 24 wpm

```
Key actions are needed. Commitment is required from all            11
sections of the economy, including the government, banks,          23
priva|te companies, and educational interests.                     32
```

Test 1/10 — Target 24 wpm

```
Due to the presence of computers and printers in most offices      12
the use of paper has skyrocketed.  When an error is spotte|d       24
in a document, rather than fumble with correction fluids or        36
pencil erasers, we simply print the page again and dispose of      49
the original.                                                      51
```

Test 1/11 — Target 25 wpm

```
The advent of the personal computer and its use for many day-      12
to-day tasks in the office has greatly improved efficiency.        24
Low|-cost computer equipment and those standard software           36
programs for word processing, spreadsheet, database                46
development and desktop publishing, make the breadth of            58
general-purpose possibilities almost limitless.                    67
```

Test 1/12 — Target 25 wpm

```
The business world of today is more dynamic and competitive        12
than ever before.  A new generation of bright, young               23
executives |have learned to thrive in this keen environment.       35
It is a world where the stakes and the rewards are high and        47
where margins for error just do not exist.                         55
```

Test 1/13 — Target 26 wpm

```
Training is separated into two general areas: job-specific         10
subjects and foundation subjects.  Foundation subjects are         20
very import|ant in the long term and are at the core of most       30
training programmes.  More specific job-related subjects are       54
provided depending on the particular training programme in         60
question.                                                          61
```

overtake Germany, whose Irish sales are plumeting.

This revolution redrawn the global wine map, it has has also created a different language because the starting point for the New World producers was different. Theirs was not the chateau re commune; it was the grape variety. They had to discover for themselves how best to turn it into wine, uninhibited by tradition. [I enclose a number of order forms on which I have marked the New World wines currently in stock. As I said, we hope to have the full selection within a fortnight. I also have pleasure in enclosing a leaflet giving details of a fascinating book about Robert Mondavi, one of the pioneers of viniculture in the New World.

notes:- the signatory is president of the club. The subject heading is New World Wines. Embolden the names of the grape varieties.

(margin notes: HAS not only / # / NP)

Test 1/14 — Target 26 wpm

```
Plastics, say environmentalists, may well be convenient but,      12
especially in the form of packaging, there is too much of it      24
around a|nd it is ruining the Irish countryside.  Thoughtless     37
disposal of rubbish on the sides of the roads and elsewhere       49
is common, with legislation having little or no effect on the     61
culprits.                                                         63
```

Test 1/15 — Target 27 wpm

```
Reusing paper is the first and best means of reducing our         12
consumption.  This is possible with a bit of imagination;         23
for example, draft| documents may be printed on the reverse       35
side of used paper and notepads may be simply made by using a     48
couple of staples.                                                51
```

Two-minute speed tests
Can you reach the target speeds which are marked?

 Note — Ensure you can key in each speed test reasonably accurately, i.e. with no more than two errors per minute's typing, before proceeding. A maximum of two errors in one minute is equivalent to four errors in two minutes.

Test 2/1 — Target 27 wpm, i.e. 54 words in two minutes.

```
It is not important that we speak or read a language fluently     12
in order to derive major benefits from it.  Basic knowledge       24
allows us to see the structure so that we can use similar         36
ways when explaining ideas, even in our own language, to          47
people from other cultures.  It i|s taken as a welcome            58
courtesy if one has a few words in a foreigner's language with    70
which to greet him.  After only a day or two of exposure to       82
the language sounds, it is much easier to catch the correct       94
sound of a 'local' name and repeat it correctly.  Many good       106
business relationships have started from the courtesy of a        118
few words and correct pronunciation of a person's name.           129
```

Test 2/2 — Target 27 wpm, i.e. 54 words in two minutes.

```
After many years of being bombarded with numerous messages        12
regarding CFCs, the greenhouse effect, recycling and the          23
demise of the rain forests, here in Ireland the message is,       35
generally, still going unheard.  Few people divide their          46
waste and dispose of it accordingly. | How many go out of         58
their way to use recycled products?  Our generation is            68
relatively lucky.  We enjoy the benefits of modern technology     81
to the full and as of now we have not had to pay the price        92
for it.  Future generations will be the ones who will have to     104
do that.                                                          106
```

use
l/c — 2

CHARDONNAY   CABERNET SAUVIGNON

varieties, chardonnay and cabernet sauvignon, have led the charge.

✓ It ~~used to be~~ ~~was~~ different in the 1980s. / wine we drank in Ireland then was overwhelmingly French, German and Italian; w Spain, Portugal, Yugoslavia (as was) and Bulgaria playing bit parts.

run on — Australian wines were a complete novelty — indeed to most people they were t joke. They did not even feature in official import figures. Today Australia is number four in / market and about to overtake Germany, whose Irish sales are plummeting.

M/

Tip — One way of developing speed is to key in the same sentence a number of times.

Test 2/3 — Target 28 wpm, i.e. 56 words in two minutes.

```
The strand of hair that we actually see, called the hair        11
shaft, is completely dead.  It is made of a form of protein      23
called keratin.  It forms scales which, if the hair is in        35
good condition, overlap each other to form a smooth layer.       46
The live part of the hair grows from a tiny p|ocket, called a    59
follicle, which is found just below the surface of the skin.     71
Hair grows fast - about one centimetre a month.                  80
```

Test 2/4 — Target 28 wpm, i.e. 56 words in two minutes.

```
The outer layer of the tooth is a hard, white substance         11
called enamel.  The next layer is called dentine and is like     23
bone.  The centre is soft tissue called pulp.  It contains       36
blood vessels and nerves.  The tooth is surrounded by gum and    46
anchored into the jaw bone by a root.  You|r teeth have          59
different shapes for cutting, chopping and chewing your food.     70
```

Test 2/5 — Target 29 wpm, i.e. 58 words in two minutes.

```
The investment level and creativity necessary to provide the     12
requisite level of technicians and engineers to service this     24
increasingly complex industry must be provided now. We must      36
also build up a strong research and development base to serve    49
both small and large industries.  Only then w|ill Ireland        60
continue to benefit substantially from the fascinating           71
electronics revolution.                                          76
```

Test 2/6 — Target 29 wpm, i.e. 58 words in two minutes.

```
The Irish plastics industry, quite apart from the convenience    12
value of its products, is quite a valuable one as far as         24
employment and balancing the nation's books are concerned;       36
but it is not an industry that escapes criticism from            46
conservationists who say that plastics have a serious            57
detr|imental effect on the environment in a way unmatched by     69
any of the traditional 'natural' materials such as paper and     81
timber.                                                          83
```

Key in the manuscript below. Use double-line spacing and correct all errors. Save it as Test 3A.

- Use 12-point Courier New font
- The letter must extend over two pages.
- The letter is from the club named below. The address is 46B O'Reilly Quay, Dublin 2. Telephone: (01) 7890123, E-mail: quaywine@eircom.net. Design a suitable letterhead.
- The letter will be signed by Carl Walsh
THE letter is being sent to Margaret Johnson, 52 Parnell Square, Cavan

Thank you f your enquiry and interest in the new world wines. A wide selection of these wines is already available from yr club, The Quay Wine Club. Relevant leaflet is w our printers and will be sent to all members WITHIN A FORTNIGHT, when our stock is complete. In past ten years, as you know, the whole business of making, naming and therefore understanding wine has taken an extraordinary leap forward.

Many new wines are fr vineyards that did not exist a generation ago: they come fr land where sheep once grazed or cherry orchards grew, and fr countries that had only ever made wine fr their own consumption.

What most of the new wines have in common, whether they come from South America, Australia or the rejuvenated south of France, is the emphasis they place on the grape — on the taste of fruit in glass and the name of grape on th label. Two

continued overleaf

Test 2/7 — Target 30 wpm, i.e. 60 words in two minutes.

Radioactive substances are used increasingly in medicine,	12
industry, research and for power and heat generation. At the	24
end of their useful life many of these have some residual	35
radioactivity and, in some cases, they are changed into	47
substances more radioactive than the original ones. These	58
wastes |have the potential to harm man as well as animals and	71
plants; it is important therefore that they be carefully	82
managed to prevent harm to ourselves and future generations.	94

Test 2/8 — Target 30 wpm, i.e. 60 words in two minutes.

Wastes have been classified in several different ways but no	12
one method is universally accepted. The simplest way is to	24
divide them into solid, liquid and gaseous wastes, that is,	36
describing them by their physical forms. Another method	47
classifies them by the degree of hazard they present, in	59
which| case they are labelled high, medium and low level	70
wastes: unfortunately no precise definition exists for each	82
level.	83

Test 2/9 — Target 31 wpm, i.e. 60 words in two minutes.

County Wicklow's natural boundaries best illustrate the	11
physical attributes of this beautiful county. Bounded on	23
the west, north and south by its hills and mountains and by	35
the sea on its eastern flank, the county is rich in scenic	47
beauty. The mountains for the most part are hills; gentle,	58
inviti|ng, well clad in fields and trees and accessible to	70
walkers. The higher hills lie to the west, dominated by	81
Lugnaquilla at 927 m.	85

Test 2/10 — Target 31 wpm, i.e. 62 words in two minutes.

There is still a peculiar attraction about the massive iron	12
knocker that could send thunder echoing to the remotest	24
slumbering person. Collectors can still find splendid	34
specimens, and demand is increasing. So, too, is the renewed	46
delight in that other, still weightier piece of door	57
'furniture', the door po|rter or door stop.	66
Both at their best are decorative, companionable curios.	77
There are changes in style and technique that make it	87
possible to determine a specimen's period, and a range of	99
metals from japanned iron to bronzed work and brass. Even	111
the more ornate may still be bought for a few pounds, but	122
they have to be sought.	127

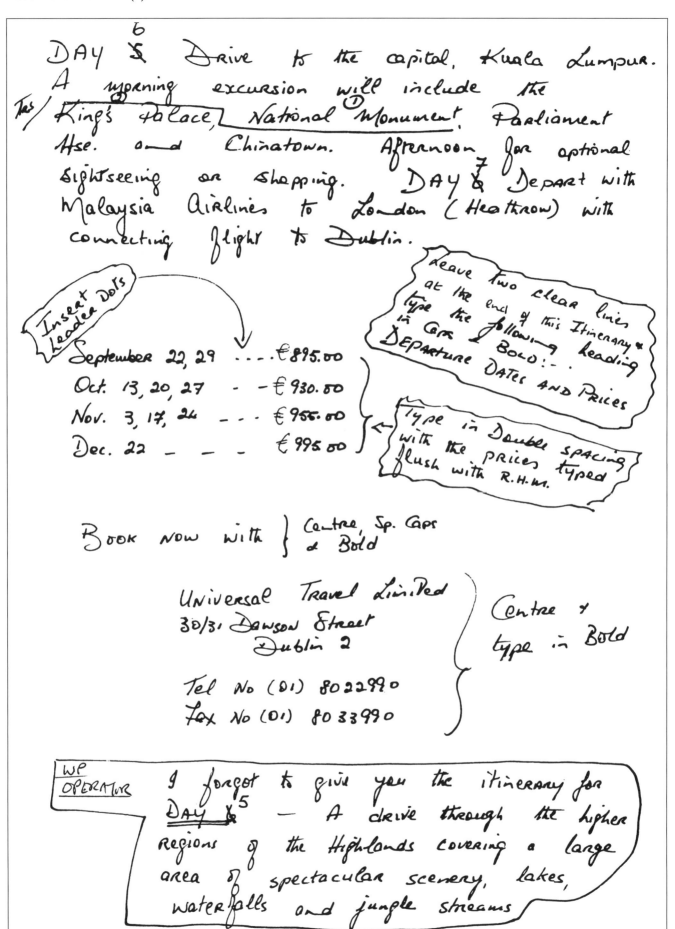

DAY 6 Drive to the capital, Kuala Lumpur. A morning excursion will include the King's Palace, National Monument, Parliament Hse. and Chinatown. Afternoon for optional sightseeing or shopping. DAY 7 Depart with Malaysia Airlines to London (Heathrow) with connecting flight to Dublin.

Insert Dots Leader Dots

September 22, 29 .... € 895.00
Oct. 13, 20, 27 - - € 930.50
Nov. 3, 17, 24 - - - € 955.00
Dec. 22 - - - - € 995.00

Leave two clear lines at the end of this Itinerary & type the following heading in Caps & Bold:- DEPARTURE DATES AND PRICES

Type in Double spacing with the prices typed flush with R.H.M.

BOOK NOW WITH { Centre, Sp. Caps & Bold

Universal Travel Limited
30/31 Dawson Street
Dublin 2

Tel No (01) 8022990
Fax No (01) 8033990

Centre & type in Bold

WP OPERATOR I forgot to give you the itinerary for DAY 5 — A drive through the higher regions of the Highlands covering a large area of spectacular scenery, lakes, waterfalls and jungle streams

Test 2/11 — Target 32 wpm, i.e. 64 words in two minutes.

He has achieved success who has lived well, laughed often,	12
and loved much; who has gained the respect of intelligent men	24
and the love of little children; who has filled his niche and	36
accomplished his task; who has left the world better than he	49
found it, whether by an improved poppy, a perfect poem, or a	61
rescued soul; w|ho has never lacked appreciation of earth's	73
beauty or failed to express it; who has looked for the best	85
in others and given the best he had; whose life was an	96
inspiration; whose memory is a benediction.	105

Test 2/12 — Target 32 wpm, i.e. 64 words in two minutes.

Any computer system is only as good as the operator.	11
Operator training which would maximise familiarity and	22
proficiency is the aspect frequently overlooked at the time	34
of purchase. It may also be underestimated at times of	45
internal employee change. The new operator is given unopened	57
operating manuals or, worse still|, shown the essentials by	69
another employee who is completely tied up with work of his	81
own.	82

Test 2/13 — Target 33 wpm, i.e. 66 words in two minutes.

Commercial constraints are a reality for most designers who	12
are subjected to the rules of productivity and efficiency	24
like anyone else in business. Occasionally really top	34
designers are free from such constraints and in a position to	47
explore their talent and hopefully redefine fashion's	58
boundaries. Also in some less developed |countries garments	69
are sometimes painstakingly made by hand, and they can take	81
months to perfect and complete.	88

Test 2/14 — Target 33 wpm, i.e. 66 words in two minutes.

The idea of using recycled paper may not be very popular.	12
Recycled paper has a bad image problem here in Ireland. It	23
is perceived as being more expensive and of poorer quality	35
than 'ordinary' paper. In fact the quality of recycled paper	47
is improving all the time. As more people use it the price	59
is also getting more competiti|ve.	66

Key in the itinerary below and save it as Test 2C.

DAY 1, 2 etc to be typed as side headings and in bold print. Leave a clear line between each day's itinerary.

A JOURNEY THROUGH MALAYSIA! / Sp. Caps & Bold

ITINERARY / Caps & Bold

DAY 1 Fly from ~~Dublin~~ via London to Kuala Lumpur (evening flight). DAY 2 Arrive Kuala Lumpur to connect with short flight to PENANG. Stay three nights at the

Close up / Shangri-La Hotel. Penang is situated

stet / just off the ~~east~~ west coast of Malaysia.

DAY 3 A morning tour of the island will include Georgetown and a drive past the

Run on / island's beaches and plantations. Afternoon at leisure to swim or for independent sightseeing or shopping. DAY 4 Morning departure by ROAD to Cameron Highlands. Stop at the Chinese Hindu limestone cave temples with their enormous statues of Buddha. Stay two nights in the Highlands.

Test 2/15 — Target 34 wpm, i.e. 68 words in two minutes.

Executive secretaries usually need excellent skills.	11
Typewriting must be effortless and a speed of 60 wpm is	22
commonly demanded. Nowadays a thorough knowledge of at least	33
one, if not two, word processing packages is essential.	43
Shorthand is still useful for many personal assistant	54
positions; this is particularly true in cities such as	66
L|ondon.	69

Test 2/16 — Target 34 wpm, i.e. 68 words in two minutes.

Thanks to the American GIs, who wore them under their	11
uniforms for warmth, nylons found their way to Europe during	23
the war years and became the coveted possessions of many	34
well-heeled ladies. They were incredibly expensive, and many	47
an Irish mammy will tell you that you couldn't get a pair for	59
love or money. There is no such shortage no|wadays.	69

Test 2/17 — Target 35 wpm, i.e. 70 words in two minutes.

This year the famous nylon stocking celebrates its fiftieth	12
anniversary and high kicks its leggy way into the twenty-	24
first century. Founded back in the forties, nylons caused a	35
sensation when they were unfurled by the Hollywood glamour	47
girls and the smoothies in the movies. Women simply adored	59
the silky feel of stockings and the contoured cling o|f these	71
subtle leg-enhancers.	76

Key in the tabulation below and save it as Test 2B.

TEST 2/B

Use single line spacing with a clear line between 'VEHICLE GROUPS'. Centre Vertically and Horizontally and Rule as indicated. Type in fully blocked style.

CAR HIRE IN LONDON / Caps & Bold

close up / Self-drive packages are arranged in ASSOCIATION with AVIS, who offer a wide range of vehicles at excellent rates. All prices are in euros per day.

Vehicle Group	Capacity	Vehicle Type	Consecutive Days		
			7-13	14-20	21+
A	5-Door (Seats 4)	Toyota Corolla	€32	€30	€28
C	4-Door (seats 4)	Toyota Camry	35	33	31
G	4-Door (seats 5)	Ford Mondeo	48	46	44
E	4-Door (seats 5)	Ford Falcon	39	38	35
F	5-Door (seats 5)	Nissan Primera Sunny	50	48	46
J	5-Door	Mazda	52	50	48

Type is in Bold →

Included in your hire:
* One transfer from airport or city to depot or vice versa
* Government Taxes and Stamp Duties

→ Not included in your hire:
* Vehicle insurance; Personal Accident Plan

Three-minute speed tests

 Remember — Make sure you can key in one speed test reasonably accurately, i.e. with no more than two errors per one minute, before proceeding. Try to reach the target speeds marked.

Test 3/1 — Target 35 wpm, i.e. 105 words in three minutes.

Irish fashion and design schools, both private and public,	12
are producing around 400 students each year. Students who	23
graduated 10 or 20 years ago have lasted the pace and have	35
now reached maturity. One of the best known of these is John	47
Rocha who was voted British Designer of the Year in 1993.	59
Graduates from Irish colleges acquire qualifications which	71
range from City and Guilds awards to degrees and most of them	83
find work in the industry. Some colleges have developed	94
reputations in particular sectors of the industry. | For	106
example, the Limerick College of Fashion and Design is well	117
known as a centre of excellence in the knitting sector.	128
Despite the efforts of the Craft Council and An Bord	139
Tráchtála to encourage young designers to establish	150
themselves at home most graduates in fact emigrate. They	161
head for the fashion centres of New York, London and Milan.	173

 Tip — If you finish a test within three minutes, start keying in the piece again and add the number of additional words keyed to the number of words in the piece. Divide by three to find your speed in words per minute.

Test 3/2 — Target 35 wpm, i.e. 105 words in three minutes.

For businesses in the current economic climate the management	12
of all types of expenditure is crucial as an aid to survival	25
and the generation of profit.	31
One area of expenditure, however, that is all too often	42
managed inefficiently is the maintenance of building and	53
plant. The absence of a planned maintenance policy is	64
generally due to the belief of building owners and users that	76
money not spent is money saved. The outcome is that most	88
property maintenance and repair work is carried out as a	99
result of defects and failur|es which have finally become too	111
serious to ignore.	114
As a consequence the cost of the work will be much higher	127
than it need have been. For example, it is likely that	138
additional work could have been avoided if a proper	148
preventative maintenance programme had been operating.	159

If you would like more specific details on what each city has to offer, please fill in the attached slip and return to us in the addressed envelope provided. We will be very happy to forward our Brochure to you.

If you cannot afford the luxury of getting away from your commitments for more than a few days at a time or do not wish to get 1st degree burns because of an errant ozone layer, then you shd. ~~definitely~~ ~~seriously~~ consider a European City Break.

word/

stet/

Yours sincerely

Finish the letter off appropriately and type the envelope mentioned in the last paragraph

- - - - - - - - - - - - - - - - -

European City Breaks / Caps & Bold

LONDON ☐   Amsterdam ☐   Paris ☐

city/lc (Please tick which you are interested in visiting)

Name _ _ _ _ _ _ _ _

→ Address _ _ _ _ _ _ _

(Leave two lines for the Address

Telephone No _ _ _ _ _

Test 3/3 — Target 36 wpm, i.e. 108 words in three minutes.

A company which has plant and machinery should have a	11
programme of preventative maintenance because such programmes	23
invariably save money and inconvenience in the long run. For	35
example, damage caused to the interior of a building due to a	48
defective roof would not have occurred if the roof had been	60
correctly maintained. Also, contractors usually charge a	71
premium for urgent work to compensate them for having to re-	83
allocate resources at short notice. Another factor which has	95
to be considered is the cost of disruption and loss of	106
produc|tion incurred in carrying out unplanned repairs. It	118
may prove necessary to shut down machinery and evacuate staff.	130
A factor less easy to quantify, but with equally serious	142
implications, is the potential loss of morale among staff who	154
work in buildings which show signs of lack of planned	165
maintenance.	168

Test 3/4 — Target 36 wpm, i.e. 108 words in three minutes.

Plant managers should stop reacting solely to crises and	11
instead introduce a planned maintenance programme. These can	24
be structured over periods from five years and are equally	35
applicable to new and existing buildings.	44
The first stage is a thorough building survey from which a	56
comprehensive schedule of defined work items can be	66
established. A detailed programme can then be drawn up	77
covering periodic maintenance as well as a schedule of major	89
repairs anticipated during the currency of the programme.	101
Financial resources can then be ef|fectively allocated with a	113
relatively minor contingency allowance for unavoidable	124
emergencies.	127
The property owner, or occupier, has therefore an effective	139
management tool for preventing deterioration and controlling	151
maintenance expenditure - and also planning ahead for	162
replacement once maintenance ceases to be cost-effective.	173

Indeed one of the biggest attractions of European City Breaks is their short duration. Business people and the self-employed in particular have always bn. attracted to the city break concept for the following Reasons :-

- ① Year-Round availability
- ⑤ Short durations
- ③ Relatively short flying time ④ High quality content.

/Close up

(margin annotation, left:) TP ORGANISE these points in Number order ② DO NOT type the Numbers i.e. USE BULLETS ⑦ HIGHLIGHT THESE POINTS

Although Numerous European destinations are featured within the programme of many Irish Agents, it is estimated that London, Paris and Amsterdam still A/c for more than 60% of all traffic, No doubt helped by the availability of very cheap Air fares. [These 3 destinations have retained their popularity over the years because of their proximity and perceived value for money. Whilst shopping and entertainment obviously feature highly on the itineraries of tourists visiting these cities, one cannot ignore the appeal of their architectural and cultural attractions, not to mention their gastronomic reputations.

(margin annotations, left:) 1. Travel Krs

(margin annotations, right:) / word

NP /

Test 3/5 — Target 37 wpm, i.e. 111 words in three minutes.

```
It is important to review the entire office environment when        12
a new computer system is installed.  Discussions with               22
suppliers will not provide all the answers for either               33
management or staff.                                                 37

For a start, things to do with the physical characteristics         50
of the user and the surroundings are more critical than they        62
were when typewriters were used.  Especially where visual           73
comfort is concerned, there are considerations that a typist,       85
as compared with a VDU user, would never need to bother with.       97
Working height, working distance, lighting - even colour           109
scheme|s have a part to play.  Much of this has to do with         121
ergonomics - the study of relationship between workers and         133
their environment, especially the equipment they use.             143

Since the VDU user is actually using a more sophisticated          155
work station than the typist - one that provides quite             166
different stress levels - it is important to consider how to        178
deal with these factors.                                           183
```

Test 3/6 — Target 37 wpm, i.e. 111 words in three minutes.

```
People often use the word 'eyestrain' to describe a variety         12
of symptoms, many of which have nothing to do with working          24
conditions.  All the same, there is a risk that users will          35
experience what might be termed visual fatigue if the right         47
things are not done by both users and employers.                    57

Focusing the eyes is a subconscious action.  They are               68
normally relaxed when focused in the distance, but increasing       80
effort is needed as the point of focus becomes nearer.              91
Looking at a VDU screen tends to concentrate the focus at one      104
or two specific near distances|; it calls for constant effort.     117
That is what creates fatigue.                                      122

So it is important to break this routine.  Every twenty            133
minutes or so change your angle of vision by looking away          145
from the VDU. Look at something outside the window or across       157
the room - that will focus your eyes in a way that causes them     169
to relax.  Five or ten minutes every hour doing something          181
other than operating the VDU can mean the difference between       193
accurate work resulting from comfortable vision and                203
carelessness brought about by fatigue.                             211
```

Key in the circular letter below and save it as Test 2A.

This letter is from Universal Travel Limited, 30/31 Dawson Street, Dublin 2. Tel No (01) 8022990 and the Fax No is (01) 8033990. Type the Tel No at the left-hand margin and the Fax No falling flush with the right-hand margin.

Alex Brown, Sales Executive, will sign the letter. The Ref. will have the letters CL followed by the writer's initials and then your own! Date as postmark.

Subject Heading: European City Breaks

Dear Traveller,

uc/ Being an island nation, we have always had a great sense of travel. Whilst the great irish diaspora in the past was due

oy/ to both economic & political factors, nowadays it has been replaced with the most benign [BENIGN] feature of the late 20th century lifestyle

Run on/ — international tourism.

NP/ Not only are more and more Irish people holidaying abroad, they are travelling further and more frequently. [Whilst growth in the long haul of cheap air fares, city breaks have experienced a renaissance in recent years because of a no. of disparate factors such as accessibility, frequency of services, choice of destination and, of course, price.

market has been due primarily to the greater availability

Test 3/7 — Target 38 wpm, i.e. 114 words in three minutes.

The normal eye does not need help in youth - it can focus	12
from very near through a normal VDU working distance of	23
approximately 14 inches or 35 centimetres to the stars	34
without a problem. If an individual's vision is normal,	45
operating a VDU will not make glasses necessary. If there is	57
a latent sight defect which does not show up in the usual	69
course of events, however, it is possible that repetitively	81
doing the things involved in VDU operation will make it	92
noticeable. That's when optical help may be needed,	102
specifically related to the work task.	110
Clues to be alert| for are eyes that feel tired or even sore,	123
headaches and fatigue in general. If they persist, an eye	134
examination will reveal whether the reason is a previously	146
unsuspected sight defect and, if so, what can be done to	157
correct it.	160

Test 3/8 — Target 38 wpm, i.e. 114 words in three minutes.

Whatever a VDU operator's age, if glasses are already worn it	12
will be worth making sure that they are right for the job.	24
The chance is that in some cases they won't be entirely	35
suitable for this particular purpose. If bifocal lenses are	47
used, for instance, it might be that, while being right for	59
normal everyday purposes, neither the distance portion of the	72
lens nor the reading segment seems right for working with a	84
VDU screen, or reading at arm's length. The answer may be in	96
lenses that correct vision for the particular focusing ranges	108
used at work and it may b|e that there are various	119
alternatives to be discussed with a registered optical	129
practitioner.	132
Other VDU operators have found that the screen's brightness	144
causes difficulties and, for some, this can be reduced by	156
tinted spectacle lenses or glare absorbent screen filters.	167
However, none of these represents a whole solution and should	180
be used only where nothing else - such as altering the	190
monitor's brightness setting, or improving the contrast of	202
text against background colour, or rearranging the lighting	214
of the workstation - seems to work.	222

are €500 for ~~the~~ ¹⁰ years.

⊗ The company will use the €50,000 to purchase a house qualifying for Section 23 relief.

○ ~~£15,000 of own capital and £85,000 of borrowed capital is put into a Rental Company to purchase property for £50,000.~~

NP   The company will let the property at a market rent of say €300 per month. The rent will not be liable to mainstream corporation tax for many years as a result of Section 23 Relief. It may be liable to corporation tax surcharge at an effective rate of 11%.

I trust the above example clarifies ~~will relate to y~~ the position with regard to Section 23 Relief. If you have ~~any~~ further queries or if you wish to speak to me in person, please do not hesitate to contact ^{THIS} ~~this~~ office ~~again~~. Stet

Five-minute speed tests

 Remember — Ensure you can key in each speed test reasonably accurately, i.e. with no more than two errors per minute, before proceeding.

Try to reach the target speeds which are marked.

Test 5/1 — Target 35 wpm, i.e. 175 words in five minutes.

Western blanket bog and heathland are the predominant	11
vegetation types to be found in the Connemara National Park.	23
The boglands, situated in the low-lying areas, are normally	35
very wet. Heathers clothe many of the mountain sides and	47
ling, cross-leaved heath heather and bell heather are all	58
very common. Probably the commonest plant in the park is purple	70
moorgrass. It grows in clumps particularly in the bogs and	81
is responsible for the colour of much of the landscape	92
throughout the year. Insectivorous plants form an integral	104
part of the bog community. Sundews and butterworts trap and	116
digest insects with their leaves to gain nutrients which are	129
in short supply in the bogs.	135
Much of the present park lands formed part of the Kylemore	146
Abbey estate and the Letterfrack Industrial School, the	158
remainder having been owned by private individuals. The	169
southern part of the Park| was at one time owned by Richard	182
(Humanity Dick) Martin who helped to form The Society for the	193
Prevention of Cruelty to Animals during the early nineteenth	205
century. The Park lands are now wholly owned by the State	217
and managed solely for National Park purposes. In the past	228
the lands were used for agriculture, mainly as grazing for	240
cattle and sheep. Vegetables were grown on some of the more	252
fertile lowlands. Today, these areas are easily recognised	264
by the old cultivation ridges and hollows. Several of the	276
bogs in the Park were used extensively as fuel sources, and	288
old turf banks, now disused, are commonly seen.	297

Test 5/2 — Target 35 wpm, i.e. 175 words in five minutes.

Many businesses fail because inadequate attention is paid to	12
stock control. Stock represents some of the capital of the	24
business. Holding excessive stock means that the business	36
may be short of cash. If too little is held, it may mean	47
disappointed customers and a consequent loss of sales.	58
Stock-taking involves the listing of every single item of	70
stock with the quantities held, after which the items have to	82
be individually priced and valued. There are three main	93
kinds of stock-taking - one of these is periodic stock-	104
taking. Periodic stock-taking, as practised in the chain	116
stores, is where the manager is usually required to take	127
stock every fortnight and return the figures to head office	139

Key in the letter below. Use block style and open punctuation. Save it as Test IC.

Letter from Barlow & Co, Chartered Accountants, The Mews, Chestnut Grove, Malahide, Co Dublin.

~~Dictated~~ Drafted by Ms Sally GUTKIN, Tax PARTNER — ref SG/55

Subject-heading — Section 23 Relief

Inside address: Mr Declan Byrne, 23 Watery Lane, Malahide.

Further to your letter of 10 May.

A special tax relief was introduced in 1981, to encourage the construction of moderate cost rented residential accommodation. The Relief became known as Section 23 relief after the relevant Section of the 1981 Finance Act.

Essentially the relief allows a person who purchases a Section 23 property to claim a deduction for a major part of the cost of that property against rents from that property and any other rental properties owned by him. The Relief is very attractive to persons with existing rental income in need of a tax shelter.

[The investment becomes even more BENEFICIAL where individuals form a rental company to purchase and let the property. Let us look at a specific example:—

* Individual subscribes €50,000 for ordinary shares in a newly incorporated private Rental Company.

* Assume €35,000 of the money is borrowed @ 11½% and the monthly repayments /....

Side notes:

OPERATOR PLEASE show all AMOUNTS in EUROS.

NB: Mr Byrne's reference was DB/MOM

NP

LEAVE CLEAR LINE BETWEEN EACH EXAMPLE

① USE BULLET POINTS, INDENT, + BLOCK TEXT INSIDE BRACKETS

Note — BRACKETS CONTINUED OVERLEAF

```
for valuation. With the large chain stores such as Dunne's       151
or Marks and Spencer's, total stocks at all branches will be     163
worth millions of pounds, and the business cannot wait |until    176
the end of the year to assess which goods are not selling, or    187
which goods have been stolen, so that a regular stock-taking     199
every week or fortnight is essential.                            206

In a manufacturing concern, stock control should be related     219
to production, so that only those goods which are low in         230
stock are manufactured and not the goods which are in            241
plentiful supply and which may not be selling.  Unless there     253
is good stock control, stocks may be lost through damage or      265
deterioration, or from pilfering.  Stock control is linked      276
with buying, and the purchasing department relies on accurate    289
information from the stores department.  Good stores staff       300
can ensure proper and prompt claims for damage, shortages or     313
defects in goods received.                                       318
```

Ten-minute accuracy tests

 Remember — Ensure you can key in each test reasonably accurately, i.e. with no more than two errors per minute, before proceeding. Two errors in one minute is equivalent to 20 errors in ten minutes.

Maximum errors permitted in an examination

As stated at the start of this section, an accuracy level of 97% or greater is usually required, i.e. a maximum error level of 3%. In a ten-minute test, with a target speed of 60 wpm, it is necessary to key in 600 words. As 3% of 600 words is 18 words, a maximum of 18 errors is allowed, i.e. 1.8 errors per minute. Try to reach the target speeds marked.

Test 10/1 — Target 35 wpm, i.e. 350 words in ten minutes.

```
Giving money to charity has never been easier.  Our consciences   12
pricked by emotive pictures in a newspaper or on the              23
television, we dip our hands into our purses on a seemingly       35
never-ending basis. No matter how much we give the charities      47
keep coming back for more.                                        52

In Dublin alone, there are four flag-day collections every        64
day of the year. Add the increasing number of sponsored           75
events, charity film premieres and banquets and the amount of     88
activity on the fund-raising front becomes clearer.               98

When we hand over our hard-earned cash, do we stop to think       110
where the money is going, or how much of it will reach the        122
cause we intended to benefit? Everyone knows that the             133
charitable organisations have overhead and administrative         144
costs, but how much do these add up to and can they be            155
justified?                                                        158
```

Key in the table below. Show the different employment sectors in alphabetical order. Save it as Test 1B.

SALARIES IN EUROS

Employment Sector	Function Head	Dept Head	Manager	Staff	Assistant
	€	€	€	€	€
Food Processing	32,824	27,321	22,307	18,833	15,152
High Tech	38,521	29,450	24,534	19,618	15,333
Manufacturing/ Construction	33,420	28,263	23,859	18,687	15,100
Engineering	30,666	26,574	22,228	18,106	14,800
Financial	36,951	28,120	23,605	18,944	15,750
Other	30,674	24,380	21,142	18,827	15,054

KEY IN "Set out above is a table showing the salaries paid to accountants in Ireland in 1988."

AT the foot of the table "

Rule THE TABLE AS SHOWN. ABOVE THE TABLE, CENTRE THE HEADING "High-tech Firms Pay Accountants Better", use block CAPS for heading. LEAVE A CLEAR LINE BETWEEN EACH EMPLOYMENT SECTOR.

BLOCK THE COLUMN HEADINGS BUT CENTRE THE TABLE (ie THE COMPLETE TABLE). CENTRE THE COMPLETE TASK VERTICALLY. DO NOT KEY IN INVERTED COMMAS IN THE HEADING OR THE NOTE AT THE FOOT OF THE TABLE

The recession is now biting deep - many companies have to cut   170
back on their advertising budgets. Charities are finding the   182
same to be true for them - there is a definite limit on the   194
amount of money they can hope to raise through purely   205
unselfish donations. They know that if the public do not   216
know you exist, they cannot give you money.   224

Many wealthy housewives organise gala dinner functions,   236
auctions and coffee mornings to help raise funds for a   247
certain charity. These functions are very successful and   258
raise large amounts of money for very deserving causes.   270
People who have money enjoy these functions and also happily   282
contribute to these charities. Film stars organise and   293
attend film premieres to help fund-raise for their favourite   305
charity. Bob Geldof wrote a song under the name Band Aid and   317
it reached top of the charts. All the proceeds of this   328
record went to aid the starving in Africa. He then went on   340
to organise Live Aid. It was the biggest fund-rais|ing event,   352
biggest TV event and biggest concert ever staged. The   362
proceeds went to relieve poverty in the third world   374
countries. Ireland contributed seven million pounds.   384
Poverty is still with us - we must give to charity.   394

Test 10/2 — Target 35 wpm, i.e. 350 words in ten minutes.

English Language summer schools are bracing themselves for a   12
drop in the numbers of teenage students coming to Ireland   24
this summer. The crippling effects of economic recession,   35
political uncertainty and currency devaluations in Spain and   46
Italy are being blamed for what may well signal the end of a   60
boom in educational tourism in Ireland.   67

Teaching English as a Foreign Language (TEFL) enjoyed a   79
dramatic spurt of growth in Ireland and elsewhere in recent   98
years. In 1988, about 47,000 foreign students came to   102
Ireland to study English and by 1991 the number had more than   114
doubled to 100,000. Bord Fáilte estimates that the revenue   126
generated by educational tourism was £81 million in 1991.   137

However, there will be a significant decrease in student   149
numbers coming to Ireland this summer. The French and German   161
markets have been in decline for many years; the numbers of   173
Spanish students dropped slightly in 1992 and is expected to   185
fall by about 15 per cent this year, and there may be a drop   197
of about 10 per cent in the numbers of Italian students this   210
summer.   211

Apart from the international recession, there are underlying   223
problems and trends which, if not addressed, will make it   235
difficult for the Irish educational tourism industry to   246
recover when Europe comes out of recession.   255

In many cases such projects are lodged now *tes*
in local libraries where they form part of
the archive collection on local history. This
is the objective of the *young historian awards,* *UC*
to encourage students to become detectives
researching the past of their local community
and thus adding one more piece to the broad
& patchwork of the history of their area. Any *NP*
aspect of local history can be chosen as a
COLON project study of a town, village, street or
building, a local family or person, a local
business, industry, organisation, institution or
publication; investigation of a particular
episode or period in local history, or of the
development of a national movement or organisation
at local level.   *— RECORDING —*

Or The idea of young people studying their *stet*
local areas and thus helping to build up
a *COMPREEHENSIVE* local history is central to
TYPE *in full* the Y.H. As.
RUN on The provincial newspapers around the country
WITH *UC* have joined the Irish Times in further emphasising
the local dimension of the competition. A *NP*
Young County Historian Award plus a € 50
prize will be presented for the best project in
each county; these awards are sponsored by the
provincial newspapers, who are helping to
promote and publicise the competition — and the
winners — at county level.'

Historians in their own right historical

The first problem is overcrowding in the Greater Dublin area.   267
More than 60 per cent of foreign students are concentrated in   280
the Dublin area in the peak month of July. Dublin is a small   292
city and the presence of even 40,000 foreign students each   304
July creates the impression of 'saturation'.   312

Students spend much of their time congregating in groups, and   325
it has been remarked that one can hear more Spanish in   336
Grafton Street any July afternoon than in a corresponding   348
street in Ma|drid.   351

This problem is finding its solution in a more even   362
distribution of students across the entire country. Over the   374
past five years the number of schools operating in cities and   386
towns all over Ireland has quadrupled. Almost every Irish   398
town with good sporting and recreational facilities now has   410
its quota of foreign students.   416

The second problem concerns standards. Bord Fáilte and the   428
Department of Education have stepped up control over   439
standards of teaching, accommodation and recreational   449
facilities. It is now much more difficult to gain official   461
recognition, and at least 15 schools were refused recognition   474
in 1992.   475

 Note — For further speed development work, refer to the Accuracy Tests on page 296.

Part 15
Production Tests

▷▷▷▷▷▷▷▷▷▷▷▷▷▷▶▶▷

A number of tests, containing three tasks, now follow. Try to complete each task within 40 minutes, and each test within two hours. Tests 1–4 are suitable for intermediate students and tests 5 and 6 are aimed at more advanced students.

▶ **Test 1A**

Key in the following manuscript in double-line spacing. Correct all spelling and other errors. Save it as Test 1A.

Part 4
Display Work, Stage One

▷▷▷ ► ▷▷▷▷▷▷▷▷▷▷▷

General style adopted in this book
Unless instructed otherwise, set up to work with:

❶ Margins of 2.5 cm.

❷ Single-line spacing.

❸ 12 points, Times New Roman font.

❹ A4 paper, portrait style.

Punctuation marks
As a general rule there is no space before, but one space after, a punctuation mark. However, the following important exceptions should be noted:

❶ There are two spaces after full stops, question marks and exclamation marks.

❷ There is one space before, but no space after, an open bracket or open quotation mark.

❸ There is no space before, but one space after, a close bracket or close quotation mark.

Standard and Formatting toolbars
Check again that the Standard and Formatting toolbars are showing. If not, click the **View** menu, select **Toolbars** and make sure the Standard and Formatting checkboxes are ticked.

Headings
The text-processing operator (the TP operator) must be familiar with different types of headings.

Main heading
Main headings come at the start of a piece of text and relate to an entire article or chapter. Such headings can be blocked at the left margin or centred; they are usually formatted in either closed or spaced capitals.

Subheading
A subheading relates to a subdivision or subsection of printed work. As such headings are less important than main headings, they are given less emphasis. For example, if the main heading is in spaced capitals, the subheading may be in closed capitals or initial capitals underlined. Like main headings, subheadings can be blocked or centred, but it is generally better if they follow the style of the main heading. As a general rule, leave one clear line between main headings and subheadings, and between subheadings and the text that follows.

Shoulder heading
Shoulder headings appear over individual sections of a document and are usually preceded and followed by a clear line. The term 'shoulder heading' is confusing, as one might reasonably expect such headings to be at the shoulder or side of text. However, this is not the case, so remember — shoulder headings are not at the shoulder! Shoulder headings should be given less emphasis than main headings or subheadings.

Key in the expressions below and save the document as Irish 2.

IRISH EXPRESSION	APPROXIMATE TRANSLATION
Ní hé lá na báistí lá na bpáistí.	A wet day is no day for children.
Is fearr na cáirde ná an t-ór.	Friends are better than gold.
Nuair a bhíonn an cat amuigh, bíonn an luch ag rince.	When the cat is away the mouse plays.
Is binn béal ina thost.	Silence is golden. (It's a sweet mouth that's silent.)
Is minic a bhris béal an duine a shrón.	A person's mouth often got him into trouble. (A person's mouth often broke his nose.)
An té is airde caint is é an té is ísle obair.	The one who talks most does the least work.
Is é triall na gcearc ag dul go hAlbain é.	All talk and no action. (This expression is about the hens who keep talking about going to Scotland but who never get there.)
Is fearr an tsláinte ná na táinte.	Health is better than wealth.
Bíonn blas ar an mbeagán.	A little (food) is very tasty.
Is maith an t-anlann é an t-ocras.	Hunger is a great sauce.
Marbh le tae agus marbh gan é.	Dead from drinking too much tea and dead from not having any (tea).
Ní líontar an bolg le caint.	Talk won't fill your belly.
Ní fhaigheann an duine an léann go saor.	Learning doesn't come cheap.
Is túisce deoch ná scéal.	A drink comes before a story.
Na trí amharc is géire amuigh: súil na circe i ndiaidh an ghráinne, súil an ghabhann i ndiaidh an táirne, agus súil an chailín óig i ndiaidh a grá.	The three sharpest eyes around: the eye of the hen after the grain, the eye of the blacksmith after the nail, and the eye of the young girl after her lover.
An áit a mbíonn iomad na lámh bíonn an obair luath.	Many hands make light work. (Literally, where there are many hands, the work is early.)
An áit a dtéann an chos téann an lámh.	Where the nose goes the rest must follow. (Where the foot goes, the hand goes.)

Key in the text below and save it as Display I.

F A T I G U E (Main Heading)

HOW TO OVERCOME THAT ALWAYS TIRED FEELING (Subheading)

<u>Too Much Sugar</u> (Shoulder Heading)

Sugar in sweet foods is rapidly absorbed into the blood, causing a swift rise in blood sugar. This triggers a surge of the hormone insulin, which knocks the sugar levels down and, after a few hours, leaves people feeling tired and hungry. This pattern is made worse by alcohol, excessive tea or coffee and smoking.

<u>Stress</u> (Shoulder Heading)

Stress is another common cause of fatigue. A brisk 20-minute walk after lunch reduces stress and boosts energy levels and combats the afternoon energy dip that many people experience.

<u>Not Enough Nutrients</u> (Shoulder Heading)

We're eating more processed food than ever before and we therefore risk becoming deficient in certain key nutrients. We should eat more fresh fruit and vegetables and remember 'if it grows eat it'.

▶ *Display 2*

Key in the text below and save it as Display 2. Format the main heading in bold and use 12 points Courier New font.

ONE WAY OF MAKING WORK EASIER

USE A COMFORTABLE CHAIR

If you intend to do a lot of text processing, you should consider buying a comfortable chair. Good chairs may be expensive, but they are a good investment as they permit one to sit in a variety of positions during the working day. Ideally you should be able to adjust the <u>height of the seat</u> so that your thighs are horizontal and your feet rest flat on the floor.

USE A FOOTREST

If your chair is too high for your feet to rest flat on the floor, you should consider buying a footrest. It is surprising how much relief such a simple device can provide.

Letters 'as Gaeilge'

The layout of letters in Irish is the same as that of English letters. Note — enclosures are indicated by the words 'faoi iamh' or 'istigh leis seo gheobhaidh tú'.

▶ *Irish 1*

Key in the letter below and save it as Irish 1.

```
25 Cnoc na Sí
Baile an Easpaig
Corcaigh

25 Samhain 2006

An t-Ardmháistir
Scoil Naomh Bríde
Sráid Dhíog Mhuire
Luimneach

A Ardmháistir, a chara

Míle buíochas as ucht do litreach. Cuireann an dea-obair atá
idir lámha agat meanma agus misneach orm.  Tagaim leat go huile
agus go hiomlán gur gá ár gcultúr féin a choimeád os comhair na
ndaltaí. Creid é nó ná creid é, téann rudaí mar sin i bhfeidhm!

Molaim duit, cuir i gcás, cuireadh a thabhairt do Chomhaltas
Ceoltóirí Éireann teacht chuig an scoil agus blas dár gcuid
traidisiún a thabhairt do na scoláirí.  D'fhéadfaí cuairt a
thabhairt ar na naíonraí agus ar na gaelscoileanna áitiúla
chomh maith.

Seift eile leis na daltaí a spreagadh i dtreo na Gaeilge, ná
comharthaí a chrochadh timpeall na scoile.  Dála an scéil, bhí
mé ag smaoineamh ar roinnt fhógraí feiliúnacha agus cuirimse
faoi iamh anseo iad maraon leis na haistriúcháin Bhéarla.

Guím gach rath ar do chuid oibre.

Is mise le meas



Seathrún Céitinn
```

 Some Irish expressions — *Is aoibhinn beatha an scoláire.* — Scholars have a happy life.
Nuair a chríonas an tslat, is deacair í a shníomh! — It's hard to teach an old dog new tricks! (Literally, when the stick gets old, it's hard to twist it!)

Paragraph headings

These headings are keyed in within paragraphs and formatted in upper case (capitals) or in initial capitals underlined.

Style 1

A horizontal space of about half a centimetre is left between the heading and related text, as shown below.

<u>Stress</u>   Stress is another common cause of fatigue. A brisk 20-minute walk after lunch reduces stress and boosts energy levels and combats the afternoon energy dip that many people experience.

Please note that a full stop or a colon is sometimes inserted after a Style 1 paragraph heading.

Style 2

Another style of paragraph heading runs on into the following text. In this case the heading is underlined or capitalised and only one character space is left after the heading, as in the example below.

<u>Stress</u> is another common cause of fatigue. A brisk 20-minute walk after lunch reduces stress and boosts energy levels and combats the afternoon energy dip that many people experience.

▶ *Display 3*

Key in the heading EXAMPLES OF PARAGRAPH HEADINGS followed by the two paragraphs above. Save the document as Display 3.

Side headings

Side headings appear at the side of the main body of a piece of text (see the examples on page 68). Such headings are usually in capitals or with initial capitals underlined. It is helpful to follow the procedure set out below when using side headings:

❶ Create a hanging indent so that the main body of the text is inset about half a centimetre from the longest line in the side heading.

❷ To set a hanging indent, select the text in question and then drag the **Hanging Indent**  control (i.e. the middle control at the left edge of the ruler line) to the required position.

❸ Press the Tab key after each side heading. (The Tab key is above the Caps Lock key.)

For more about tabs, see page 139.

See further reference to hanging indents on page 71.

Key in the letter below and save it as German 3.

Sender's Address ————————— HOTEL IN RUHE
POSTFACH 1261
2941 NORDSEEBAD LANGEOOG

Use to day's date ————————— – Unser Zeichen PG/GF
Reference —————

vom 18.04.2006

SUBJECT ————————— Ihre Schreiben

Inside Address ————— MR MARK Doyle
College of Hotel & Catering
Dublin Road
Drogheda
Ireland

TEXT —

Sehr geehrter Herr Doyle,

herzlichen Dank für Ihr freundliches Schreiben.

Wir bestätigen hiermit, dass wir gerne 4 Studenten
nach Möglichkeit für 6 Monate beschäftigen.

Die Arbeitszeit beträgt an 6 Tagen je 8
Stunden. Die Entlohnung beträgt netto €1,500 bei
freier Kost und Wohnung.

Für Fragen stehe ich Ihnen gerne noch bis zum
6. November und dann wieder ab 10. Dezember
zur Verfügung.

Mit freundlichen Grüßen
HOTEL IN RUHE

Petra Grohe

▶ Display 4

Key in the text below, which illustrates the use of side headings, and save it as Display 4.

```
EXAMPLE OF SIDE HEADINGS

IRELAND     After centuries of growing British influence, Ireland
            joined with Britain in 1801. In 1921 the 26
            southern counties gained independence and became the
            Republic of Ireland in 1948.

SPAIN       Spain regained its monarchy in 1975 after an
            interruption of 44 years. King Juan Carlos is
            currently leading the nation.
```

▶ Display 5

Key in the text below, which also illustrates the use of side headings, and save it as Display 5.

```
EXTRACT FROM A SPECIFICATION

External Walls    The external walls are of concrete block to be
                  built in two 100 mm thicknesses with a 100 mm
                  cavity between.

Lintels           All lintels shall be of concrete 75 mm
                  high.

Chimney           The chimney breasts shall be constructed
                  in concrete block. The flues shall be 200
                  mm in diameter and lined with flue liners.
```

Headings with closed and spaced capitals

When formatting text in spaced capitals, expand the default character spacing.

```
THIS TEXT IS IN CLOSED CAPITALS

T H I S   T E X T   I S   I N   S P A C E D   C A P I T A L S
```

To expand character spacing, click the **Format** menu and select **Font**. In the **Font dialog box** click the **Character Spacing** tab. In the **Spacing** box click down to **Expanded**. Then in the **By** box enter the number of points by which you wish to expand the character spacing. (In the example above the character spacing has been expanded by 5 points, which is rather a lot.)

 Remember — Unless instructed otherwise, set left and right margins of 2.5 cm.

Key in the letter below. Check your work with the letter on the previous page. Save it as German 2.

References: Their Ref = EL/UM   OUR REF = EK/GF

Letter to: Mahlzeit, Internationaler Küchendienst   V.
            Engerser Straße 75, D-56564 Neuwied 1

DATE: 29/9/200 6 SUBJECT HEADING: Praktikantenstellen
für irische StudentInnen der Fachrichtung Hotel
Management im Sommer 2007.

Complimentary Close: Mit freundlichen Grüßen
Name of Signatory: Eimear Kelly
Letter from: College of Catering, Moate, Co Westmeath
Body of Letter:
den Namen Ihrer Organisation habe ich von Herrn Joe
Gallagher, einem Angestellten des Blackrock Hotel in
Dublin, Irland, erhalten. Ich bin Dozentin für Deutsch
am College of Catering in Moate, Irland, wo ungefähr 80
StudentInnen Hotel Management studieren. Einen
Prospekt lege ich diesem Schreiben bei.

NP [Als Teil der Anforderungen für das Diplom müssen die
StudentInnen zwei Praktika ableisten. Das erste
Praktikum wird Ende des zweiten, das zweite Ende
des vierten Semesters gemacht. Diese dauern ungefähr
acht bis neun Wochen.

NP [Zwar lernen einige StudentInnen erst an der Fachhochschule
Deutsch, andere aber haben schon fünf Jahre Deutschunterricht
hinter sich; sie verfügen also über gute Deutschkenntnisse,
und möchten eventuell eines der zwei Praktika in Deutschland
ableisten. Somit würden sie sowohl einem anderen Weltblick
als auch anderen Methoden ausgesetzt, was ihnen bestimmt
bei der künftigen Arbeit von großem Vorteil wäre. Die
StudentINNEN würden ihrerseits engagiert ihren Beitrag

NP leisten. [Wären Sie in der Lage, einer/einem irischen
Studenten/Studentin eine Praktikantenstelle bei Ihrer Organisation
anzubieten?

▶ Display 6

Key in the exercise below and save it as Display 6. Underline the heading and expand the character spacing by 4 points.

<u>W H A T   S K I L L S   D O   S E C R E T A R I E S   R E Q U I R E ?</u>

Aspiring secretaries need complete mastery of two word-processing packages, for example Microsoft Word and Word Perfect. They also need a speed of 60 wpm in typewriting. Indeed, some of the top positions require a typing speed of 70 wpm.

At a guess, only one in five positions now require shorthand. However, in cities such as London there is a niche in the job market for secretaries with shorthand speeds of 90 or 100 wpm. Such jobs tend to be better paid and offer better long-term prospects. This is particularly true of personal assistant positions, which take the secretary out of the 'typing pool' and into contact with top executives. Clear articulation, good presentation and grooming are other requirements for positions such as these.

Horizontal centring

Centring across the line is a useful display feature. To do this, select the text and click the **Centre** button on the **Formatting toolbar**, or use the keyboard command **Ctrl+E**.

▶ Display 7

Copy the piece below, in which all the lines have been centred, and save it as Display 7.

SOME THINGS TO DO IN ENNISKILLEN

BOATING

FISHING

GOLF

HORSE RIDING

SHOPPING

SIGHTSEEING

Key in the letter below and save it as German I.

College of Catering
Moate
Co Westmeath

Mahlzeit   Moate, den 29.09.2006
Internationaler Küchendienst e.V.
Engerser Straße 75

D-56564 Neuwied 1

Unser Zeichen   Ihr Zeichen
EK/GF   EL/UM

**Praktikantenstellen für irische StudentInnen der Fachrichtung
Hotel Management im Sommer 2007**

Sehr geehrte Damen und Herren,

den Namen Ihrer Organisation habe ich von Herrn Joe
Gallagher, einem Angestellten des Blackrock Hotel in Dublin,
Irland, erhalten. Ich bin Dozentin für Deutsch am College of
Catering in Moate, Irland, wo ungefähr 80 StudentInnen Hotel
Management studieren. Einen Prospekt lege ich diesem
Schreiben bei.

Als Teil der Anforderungen für das Diplom müssen die
StudentInnen zwei Praktika ableisten. Das erste Praktikum
wird Ende des zweiten, das zweite Ende des vierten Semesters
gemacht. Diese dauern ungefähr acht bis neun Wochen.

Zwar lernen einige StudentInnen erst an der Fachhochschule
Deutsch, andere aber haben schon fünf Jahre Deutschunterricht
hinter sich; sie verfügen also über gute Deutschkenntnisse,
und möchten eventuell eines der zwei Praktika in Deutschland
ableisten. Somit würden sie sowohl einem anderen Weltblick
als auch anderen Methoden ausgesetzt, was ihnen bestimmt bei
der künftigen Arbeit von großem Vorteil wäre. Die
StudentInnen würden ihrerseits engagiert ihren Beitrag
leisten.

Wären Sie in der Lage, einer/einem irischen
Studenten/Studentin eine Praktikantenstelle bei Ihrer
Organisation anzubieten?

Mit freundlichen Grüßen

Eimear Kelly

Anlage
Prospekt

Vertical centring (or alignment)

Vertical alignment refers to centring information down, as opposed to across, the page.

Click the **File** menu, select **Page Setup**, and click the **Layout** tab in the Page Setup dialog box. Then click the arrow in the **Vertical Alignment** box and select **Center**.

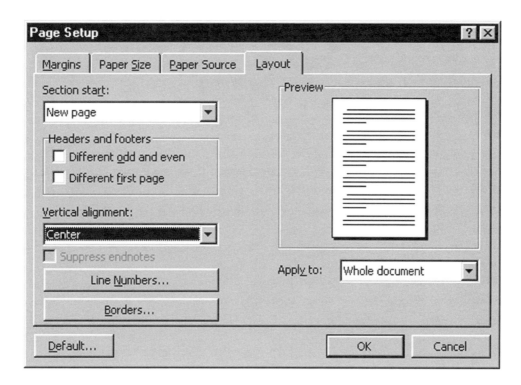

Checking vertical centring

To check that text has been centred vertically, click **File**, **Print Preview**. (Click **View**, **Normal** to return to Normal View.)

▶ Display 8

Centre the text below, both vertically and horizontally, and save it as Display 8.

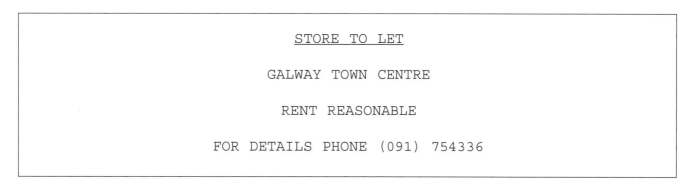

STORE TO LET

GALWAY TOWN CENTRE

RENT REASONABLE

FOR DETAILS PHONE (091) 754336

 Note — When centring vertically, use the Show/Hide button on the Standard toolbar to check that no non-printing characters, such as returns, have been keyed in before or after the lines to be centred. Otherwise, such characters will be treated as additional lines to be centred.

German business letters

Study the steps below in conjunction with the sample letter overleaf.

❶ Leave two clear lines after the printed letterhead.

❷ Key in the inside address in open punctuation at the left margin. Leave a clear line before the name of the town.

❸ Key in the date and the town from which the letter is sent opposite the first line of the inside address so that it ends flush with the right margin.

❹ Leave two clear lines and key in the reference at the left margin.

❺ Leave two clear lines and key in the subject heading.

❻ Leave two clear lines and key in the salutation.

❼ Leave one clear line and key in the body of the letter. If the salutation is followed by an exclamation mark, commence the letter with a capital letter. If the salutation is followed by a comma, begin the letter with a lower-case letter.

❽ Leave one clear line and key in the complimentary close using an expression such as 'mit freundlichen Grüßen'.

❾ Leave four clear lines for the signature.

❿ Key in the name of the signatory.

⓫ On the next line, key in the signatory's designation, if given.

⓬ If there are enclosures, leave four clear lines and key in 'Anlage(n)' at the left-hand margin.

⓭ On the following line(s) at the left margin, indicate the nature of the enclosure(s).

The mixed plural

The use of the upper case 'I' in the word 'StudentInnen', in the letters that follow may appear a little odd. This usage is intended to convey the '**mixed plural**'. In this instance it refers to a group of male and female students. If the mixed plural was not used, the masculine plural 'Studenten' would be used — even if there was only one male student among a group of 100. The feminine plural, 'Studentinnen', would only be used if the group was comprised exclusively of females. (The use of the mixed plural is a relatively recent trend, and by no means widespread — yet!)

 Accents — For notes on keying in accents, refer to page 244 at the start of this section.

Centre the text below both vertically and horizontally and save it as Display 9.

A COMPUTER PROGRAM FOR LEARNING IRISH

EasyReader is an Irish language learning program that provides a framework for learning, teaching, and using the Irish language.

With just a click, the program gives the definition of any word in any text and, with a second click, it explores relevant points of grammar.

For further information on EasyReader go to http://www.irishforlife.com.

Paragraphing

Paragraphs separate text into different topics or sections. We have already discussed paragraph headings; now we shall consider different paragraph styles. Block paragraphing is the standard style advocated in this book, i.e. all lines start at the same point, usually the left margin. When using single-line spacing, leave one clear line between paragraphs, i.e. two returns. When using double-line spacing, leave three clear lines between paragraphs, i.e. two double-line returns.

To set a particular paragraph option, select the paragraph(s) you wish to work on. If working on a complete document click the **Edit** menu and choose **Select All**, or use the keyboard command **Ctrl+A**.

Example of Blocked Paragraph
Intel supplies the computing industry with chips, boards, systems and software. Intel's products are used by industry members as 'building blocks' to create advanced computing systems for PC users.

Example of Indented Paragraph
    Intel supplies the computing industry with chips, boards, systems and software. Intel's products are used by industry members as 'building blocks' to create advanced computing systems for PC users.

Example of Hanging Paragraph
Intel supplies the computing industry with chips, boards, systems and software. Intel's products are used by industry members as 'building blocks' to create advanced computing systems for PC users.

(a) To create an indented paragraph, click on the **First Line Indent** control (i.e. the top control at the left end of the ruler). Hold down the mouse button and drag the marker to the right, then release the mouse button.

(b) To create a hanging paragraph, click the **Hanging Indent** control (i.e. the middle control at the left end of the ruler). Hold down the mouse button and drag the control to the right, then release the mouse button. Note — although the bottom control also moves, a hanging indent is created.

Key in the letter below and save it as French 3.

DATE - *Today's date*

LETTER FROM BRigitte Delamere
Oakdale,
Athlone

Please note Typist

⟨ *no reference necessary* ⟩

OBJET: demande d'emploi

P.J. : CuRRiculum Vitae

Monsieur,

Ayant lu votre annonce dans "Le Monde"
du 3 janvier, je me permets de poser ma
candidature au poste de secrétaire actuellement

NP vacant dans votre entreprise. [J'ai fait un
programme de secrétariat (l'équivalent du BTS)
AU ATHLONE INSTITUTE OF TECHNOLOGY.

couramment, ⟶ Ma langue maternelle est l'anglais mais je parle
et j'écris sans faute, le français.

⟨*EFFECTUÉ*⟩ J'ai déjà ~~complété~~ un stage professionnel dans
une entreprise à Dublin. Les qualités que
vous recherchez pour le poste semblent
correspondre à celles que j'ai développées

NP pendant ma formation. [Veuillez trouver
ci-joint mon curriculum vitae et je me
tiens à votre disposition pour vous fournir
tout renseignement complémentaire.

NP [En espérant que ma candidature retiendra
votre attention, je vous prie d'agréer,
Monsieur, l'expression de mes sentiments
distingués.

Key in the piece below; use indented paragraphs. Save it as Display 10. Note — the symbol in the left margin means marked text should be deleted.

MISSION STATEMENTS AND ALL THAT! ← (Bold + CAPS)

Many companies now insist on formulating a mission statement. For example Kentucky Fried Chicken, KFC, were once happy to call their food "finger-licking good"; now they also have a mission statement which states that the organisation's aims "to provide families with affordable, delicious chicken-dominated meals."

Other mission statements come from Lada the car manufacturers and Pepsi. Lada aim "to provide the lowest price and best value for money." Pepsi meanwhile state, "we will be an outstanding company by exceeding customer expectations through empowering people guided by shared value".

Indeed, much of management theory these days is about, not only formulating mission statements, but also about "empowering people" and "exceeding customer expectations."

Can you think of a mission statement for your friendly Saturday night discotheque?

Key in the letter below. Use the style suggested on page 245. Check your work with the typed version on page 246. Save it as French 2.

REFERENCES : THEIRS - JM/1194, OURS - PMcN/SC

Letter to 'Le Directeur d'Établissement, Kaoline de France, 129, Cours de Chazelles, BP 1229, 35014 Rennes, France'

Date - the second of November 2002

Subject heading - 'Visite des professeurs et des étudiants du PTC Tullamore, Irlande.'

Enclosures - '1 prospectus' and '5 photos'.

AIMABLE

Complimentary close - 'Je vous remercie, Monsieur, de votre aimable co-opération et vous prie d'agréer, Monsieur, l'expression de mes sentiments distingués.'

Designation of signatory - 'Maître de Conférences'

Name of signatory - Patrick McNamara

Letter from - Polemore Training College, Clara Road, Tullamore, Co Offaly, Ireland, Tel (0506) 72649, Fax (0506) 72641

MONSIEUR

Body of letter - JE TIENS, AU NOM DE MES COLLÈGUES ET MES ÉTUDIANTS, À VOUS REMERCIER POUR L'ACCUEIL QUE VOTRE COMPAGNIE NOUS A RÉSERVÉ PENDANT LA VISITE À VOTRE MINE. GRÂCE À DES EXPLICATIONS DONNÉES PAR M CHOUX, NOTRE VISITE ÉTAIT AUTANT INTÉRESSANTE QU'INSTRUCTIVE.

NOTRE SÉJOUR EN FRANCE ÉTAIT FORT INTÉRESSANT PARCE QU'IL NOUS A PERMIS DE VISITER DES DIVERSES MINES EN BRETAGNE ET EN NORMANDIE (MINES DE KAOLINE, ANDALUSITE, URANIUM, ARDOISE ET FER).

LES ÉTUDIANTS ONT NON SEULEMENT DÉCOUVERT L'INDUSTRIE MINIÈRE FRANÇAISE, MAIS ILS ONT ÉGALEMENT EU UN PETIT APERÇU DE LA CULTURE FRANÇAISE. CE VOYAGE CONSTITUE DONC UNE NOUVELLE ÉTAPE DANS LE DÉVELOPPEMENT DES RELATIONS ENTRE LA SECTION MINIÈRE DE NOTRE IUT ET LE MONDE PROFESSIONEL.

COMME PROMIS, JE JOINS À CETTE LETTRE UNE COPIE DE NOTRE PROSPECTUS ET QUELQUES PHOTOS QUE NOUS AVONS PRISES DANS LES ALENTOURS DE VOTRE MINE.

▶ Display 11

Retrieve Display 10 and reformat it with hanging paragraphs. Save it as Display 11.

Paper orientation

Paper is **portrait style** when the narrow side is on top and **landscape style** when the widest side is on the top. Unless instructed otherwise, use portrait style.

To change paper orientation, for example from portrait to landscape, click the **File** menu, click **Page Setup**, then click the **Portrait** button under **Orientation** in the Page Setup dialog box.

More about paper size

Paper	Millimetres	Inches
A4 portrait	210 x 297	8¼ x 11¾
A4 landscape	297 x 210	11¾ x 8¼
A5 portrait	148 x 210	5⅞ x 8¼
A5 landscape	210 x 148	8¼ x 5⅞

Other paper sizes include the following: A3 (double A4), A2 (double A3) and A6 (half A5).

Enumerated text and bullet points

It is often necessary to format text using numbers or bullet points. This is easily done in Word, as follows:

❶ Key in the relevant text without numbers or bullets.

❷ Select the lines to be numbered or shown as bullet points.

❸ Click the **Format** menu and click **Bullets and Numbering**. Click the **Numbered** tab in the **Bullets and Numbering** dialog box when enumeration is required; click the **Bulleted** tab when bullet points are required.

❹ If open punctuation is being used, one can opt for numbered items without full stops by clicking the **Numbered** tab in the **Bullets and Numbering** dialog box and then clicking the **Customize** button. In the **Customize Numbered List** dialog box, delete the full stop after the number in the **Number font** box.

❺ If an enumeration style is not available, for example (a) (b) (c), click the **Customize** button. In the **Customize Numbered List** dialog box, key (a) into the **Number format** box, then click the down arrow in the **Number style** box and select a, b, c.

▶ Display 12

Key in the text below. Press the Return key after 'investment' and 'speculators', then drag and copy it four times and apply:

❶ Standard enumeration, i.e. 1. 2. 3.

❷ Open punctuation enumeration, i.e. without full stops after the numbers.

❸ Alphabetic enumeration, i.e. (a) (b) (c).

❹ Bullet points.

❺ Save it as Display 12.

```
Dealing in stocks and shares online has revolutionised investment.
More than a million Americans have left their jobs to become full-time
share speculators.
Over 20 million individuals manage their portfolios online.
```

Key in the letter below and save it as French I.

POLEMERE TRAINING COLLEGE
CLARA ROAD
TULLAMORE
CO OFFALY
IRELAND
TEL (0506) 72649
FAX (0506) 72641

Le Directeur d'Etablissement
Kaoline de France
129, Cours de Chazelles
BP 56103
50400 RENNES
France

V/réf: JM/1194
N/réf: PMcN/SC   Tullamore, le 2 novembre 2006

Objet: Visite des professeurs et des étudiants du PTC Tullamore, Irlande

Monsieur,

Je tiens, au nom de mes collègues et de mes étudiants, à vous remercier de l'accueil que votre compagnic nous a réservé pendant la visite à votre mine. Grâce à des explications données par Monsieur Choux, notre visite était autant intéressante qu'instructive.

Notre séjour en France était fort intéressant parce qu'il nous a permis de visiter de diverses mines en Bretagne et en Normandie (mine de kaoline, andalusite, uranium, ardoise et fer).

Les étudiants ont non seulement découvert l'industrie minière française, mais ils ont également eu un petit aperçu de la culture française. Ce voyage constitue donc une nouvelle étape dans le développement des relations entre la section minière de notre IUT et le monde professionel.

Comme promis, je joins à cette lettre une copie de notre prospectus et quelques photos que nos avons prises dans les alentours de votre mine.

Je vous remercie, Monsieur, de votre aimable co-opération et vous prie d'agréer, Monsieur, l'expression de mes sentiments distingués.

Patrick McNamara
Maître de Conférences

P.J: 1 prospectus
            5 photos

Key in the enumeration exercise below. Use the appropriate automated numbering style. Save it as Display 13.

YOUTH AND COMMUNITY SPORT

General Rules for County Competitions

(i)   These general rules shall apply to all county competitions at both the area rounds and the county finals.

(ii)   It is the responsibility of the leader who completed the entry form to ensure that all the members are familiar with the rules.

(iii)   All competitors must be bona fide current members of the organisation or club they represent.

(iv)   All competitors should be at least 14 years of age, but not over 21 years of age, on the date of the county final. Where a competition has a junior and a senior section, the ages shall be 14 but not more than 16 for juniors and over 16 but not more than 21 for seniors. In all cases, age refers to a competitor's age on the date of the county final.

(v)   Only <u>one</u> complete team may enter each competition from each youth group.

(vi)   Appropriate dress must be worn – this must be provided by the competitors or their organisation.

(vii)   Personal playing equipment, e.g. rackets, bats, shuttles, etc., must be provided by the players or their organisation.

(viii)   The County Board must sanction requests for postponement of any competition at least one week before the scheduled date. However, in the case of bereavement, the captain of the team should notify the county board as soon as possible.

(ix)   The decision of umpires, referees and adjudicators is final and binding.

Decimalised enumeration

When a subdivided numbering system, such as decimalised enumeration, is required, click the **Format** menu and then click **Bullets and Numbering**. In the **Bullets and Numbering** dialog box, click the **Outline Numbered** tab and select the type of enumeration required. Note the example below.

1   _____

           _____

    1.1   _____

           _____

    1.2   _____

2   _____

Layout

A number of different styles are used in countries such as France and Germany. However, in the interest of simplicity, just one style is suggested in this text.

French business letters

Study the steps set out below in conjunction with the sample letter overleaf.

❶ Leave one clear line after the letterhead.

❷ Key in the longest line of the inside address/town line. Select it and click the **Align Right** button on the Formatting toolbar.

❸ Tab in the remaining lines of the inside address/town lines. Note the use of a comma after the street number in '129, Cours de Chazelles'.

❹ Leave a clear line.

❺ If there are references, these should be keyed in at the left margin so that the last reference is on the same line as the town line. The recipient's reference should have the style 'V/réf:', standing for 'vos références', and the sender's 'N/réf:', standing for 'nos références'.

❻ Tab in and then key in the sender's town and date.

❼ Leave one clear line.

❽ If there is a subject heading, it should be keyed in at the left margin and commence with the word 'Objet', followed by a colon and the subject details in lower case.

❾ Leave a clear line.

❿ Key in the salutation, which usually consists of a word such as 'Monsieur'.

⓫ Leave a clear line and key in the body of the letter.

⓬ There is no complimentary close (as we know it) in a French business letter. The French equivalent is contained in the final courtesy paragraph, which includes words such as 'mes sentiments distingués'.

⓭ Leave two clear lines and key in the name and designation of the sender at the left margin.

⓮ Leave a clear line.

⓯ If there are enclosures, these should be keyed in as P.J.: (standing for 'pièces jointes') followed by details of the enclosures, as shown in the sample letter overleaf. Note we cannot use our usual open punctuation style here, as full stops are required after 'P' and 'J'.

Sorting text

When asked to sort text alphabetically, select the text in question, click the **Table** menu, click **Sort** and in the **Sort Text** dialog box select the type of sort required.

▶ *Display 14*

Key in the text below and sort it in ascending alphabetical order. Save it as Display 14.

```
Helen
Breda
Adam
Michael
Brendan
Seán
```

Accents

Click the **Insert** menu and select **Symbol**. In the Symbol dialog box, click the **Symbols** tab. Click the arrow in the **Font** box and select (normal text) in the **Subset** box. Click the down arrow and select **Latin-1**. Now click the accented letter required and click **Insert**.

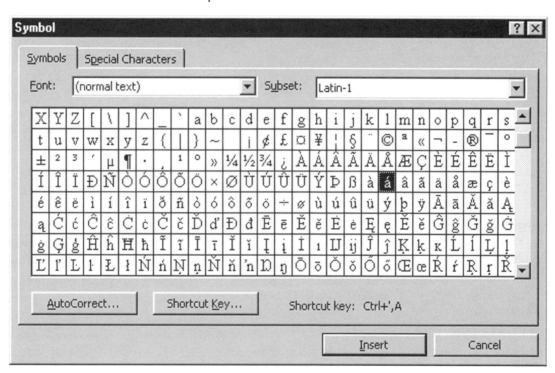

Keyboard Commands

You know your ABCs, but do you know your KBCs – your Keyboard Commands?

When certain characters are selected, relevant keyboard commands are shown at the bottom of the **Symbol** dialog box. For example, when á is selected, the bottom of the **Symbol** dialog box shows, 'Shortcut key: Ctrl+', A'. This tells us to hold down the Control key and the apostrophe key together and to then press the letter a.

```
To key in á — Ctrl +', a
To key in Á — Ctrl +', A
```

For more details on accents, refer to page 244.

Part 14
Work in French, German and Irish

▷▷▷▷▷▷▷▷▷▷▷▷▶▷▷

It has been said that one may use English when buying abroad, but when selling (or indeed when looking for a job!) it is better to use the appropriate foreign language.

Accents

The quickest way to key in an acute accent, or the Irish 'síneadh' fada, is to hold down the Alt Gr key and the relevant letter.

 Note — In the commands below, the plus symbol (+) means that Ctrl should be **held** down while the second key is pressed.

Press **Ctrl+'** (apostrophe), then press the relevant lower-case letter for the following:
á, é, í, ó, ú. Use upper-case letters for Á, É, Í, Ó, Ú.

Press **Ctrl+`** (accent grave), then press the relevant lower-case letter for the following:
à, è, ì, ò, ù. Use upper-case letters for À, È, Ì, Ò, Ù.

Press **Ctrl+,** (comma) then the letter for ç, Ç.

Press **Ctrl+Shift+:** (colon) then the letter for ä, ë, ï, ö, ü. Use upper-case letters for: Ä, Ë, Ï, Ö, Ü.

Press Ctrl+Shift+&, 's', for the German letter 'scharfess', i.e. ß. Alternatively, press Alt+225 using the numeric keypad.

Other accents

For information on other accents, use the Word Help feature. Information on accents is somewhat hidden, but you can find it as follows: press the **Help** button on the Standard toolbar. In the **What would you like to do** box, key in 'international characters', press **Search**, select **Insert symbols or special characters**, then select '**Type international characters**'.

Accents using the Insert menu

Position the insertion point where an accented letter is required. Go to the **Insert** menu, select **Symbol** and click the **Symbols** tab in the Symbol dialog box. In the **Font** box scroll down until (**normal text**) is showing. Click the required accented letter, then click the **Insert** button.

Assigning alternative keyboard commands to accents

Anther way to key in accents is to assign additional easy-to-remember key combinations to letters that take accents. For example, 'é' may be assigned Ctrl+e. To do this, go to the **Insert** menu and select **Symbol**. In the dialog box click 'é', then click **Shortcut** key. In the dialog box, enter the key combination Ctrl+e. A further example — Ctrl+Shift+e might be selected as the key combination for 'É'.

 Note — As most of the easy-to-remember key combinations have already been assigned, e.g. Ctrl+E centres a paragraph, assigning such combinations to accented letters is only advisable when menus or toolbars are used instead of function keys.

The Undo button

You can undo changes to a document by simply by clicking the Undo button on the Standard toolbar. Click the arrow to the right of the button to undo multiple actions.

The Redo button

Click the Redo button to redo actions that have been undone.

Practise using the Undo and Redo buttons

❶ Key in the following: One, Two, Three, Four, Five, Six, Seven, Eight, Nine, Ten

❷ Delete each word, one at a time.

❸ Undo the ten deletions.

❹ Redo the ten deletions.

❺ Undo the ten deletions.

Using Word's Clipboard

The Clipboard is an underused but very handy tool for carrying out certain editing tasks, like putting together parts of an existing document.

Practise using the Clipboard

Assume you have six items in one file and, for some reason, you need a separate file for each of them. The exercise below demonstrates how the Clipboard can be used for this task.

Key in the text below using drag-and-copy. Remember – hold down the Ctrl key while dragging.

Item 1
This item is about . . .
Item 2
This item is about . . .
Item 3
This item is about . . .
Item 4
This item is about . . .
Item 5
This item is about . . .
Item 6
This item is about . . .

Click **View** menu, **Toolbars**, **Clipboard**. On the Clipboard, click the Clear Clipboard button.

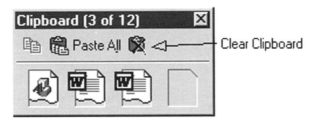

Now copy the different items, **one at a time**. Click the New Blank Document button on the Standard toolbar. Click the first clip on the Clipboard to paste it, and save the document as Item 1 File. Proceed in the same way for clips 2 to 6.

▶ Construction 3

Key in the following extract from a Bill of Quantities. Use bar tabs (see page 240). Save it as Construction 3.

INDEX	DESCRIPTION	QUANTITY	UNIT OF MEASURE	UNIT RATE	TOTAL
	Mount Temple Sports Centre				
	DRAINAGE				
	Surface Water Drainage				
	Excavating trenches to receive pipes 225 nominal size; grading bottoms; earthwork support; disposal of surplus excavated material by removing from site				
	Excavations starting from reduced level; filling in above 450 thick beds or coverings with 10-20 nominal size granular material				
a	not exceeding 2m deep, average 1m deep	21	M		
b	Extra over trenches of any depth for breaking up rock met with in excavations	5	M3		
	Plain insitu concrete; BS 5328, ordinary prescribed mix C15P 20 aggregate				
c	Beds 525 x 100 to 225 internal diameter pipes	21	M		
d	Coverings 525 x 350 to 225 internal diameter pipes	21	M		
	Drains; uPVC pipes and fittings, BS 4660; ring seal joints 225 pipework in trenches				
e	laid in position, in runs not exceeding 3m; 10 nr	21	M		
f	long radius bends	9	NR		
			to collection		

Key in the text below without the numbers, then use Word's enumeration feature to enumerate the text as shown. Save as Display 14a.

The Fourth-Generation iPod

1 Offers up to 12 hours of battery life.
2 Weighs in at just 5.6 ounces.
3 Slips into your pocket with ease.
4 Lets you carry your entire music library with you wherever you go.
5 Available in 20GB and 40GB models.
6 A musical dream come true, letting you easily slip up to 10,000 songs into your pocket.
7 Lets you enjoy your music wherever you go.
8 Incorporates the same touch-sensitive Apple Click Wheel that started life on iPod mini.
9 Without lifting your thumb from the wheel, you can select play lists, scroll through thousands of songs and start the music playing.
10 Want that song to play from the beginning again? A single click will do the trick.
11 You can put the Apple Click Wheel to use the next time you want to set your music to shuffle. Right there on the main menu — where it's very easy to find — you'll spot a new option: Shuffle Songs. Everyone's favourite option for mixing things up, Shuffle Songs randomly plays the songs in your music library. You'll never guess what's coming up next, so you're always surprised by startling juxtapositions — like a U2 number right after an aria from one of the great operas.
12 Play your music for hours and hours.

◗ *Display 14b*

Retrieve exercise 14a and use the Clipboard toolbar to arrange the text so that point 6 comes first, point 3 second, point 5 third, point 2 fourth, point 7 fifth and point 11 sixth. Change the enumeration to the 'a, b, c' format and save as Display 14b.

◗ *Display 14c*

Retrieve exercise 14a and see if you can complete exercise 14b more quickly by using drag-and-drop text editing rather than the Clipboard. Change the enumeration to the '(i), (ii), (iii)' format and save as Display 14c.

Construction 2

Key in the following extract from a Specification. Use the correct format. Save it as Construction 2.

ROOFING

TILES

1. The tiles and fittings for the main roof slopes are to be plain red sand-faced concrete tiles to comply with BS 473.

GROUNDWORK

2. Cover the rafters with reinforced roofing felt lapped 100 mm at joints and carried over hips and ridge and down into gutters.

Provide and fix 20 x 35 mm sawn and impregnated battens to the requisite gauge with similar tilting fillet ex 75 x 50 mm at eaves.

TILING

3. The tiles are to be laid to 100 mm gauge and each tile in every fifth course is to be secured with 40 mm aluminium nails. The alternative courses at verges and abutments are to have tiles of width and a half to ensure bond. Verges are to have undercloak of plain tiles bedded and pointed in cement mortar and into every course of all abutments lay one G173 lead soaker. Lay a double course of eaves.

Cover the ridges with hog back pattern ridge tiles bedded, jointed and pointed in cement mortar with four ends filled solid and with slips.

TP OPERATOR PLEASE Block text under reference numbers

Columns

With Microsoft Word, work can be easily set out in columns.

▶ Display 15

❶ Key in the text below in the normal way, without using columns.

❷ Select all the text except the first two lines.

❸ Click the **columns** icon on the standard toolbar, then draw the mouse pointer across the first two columns in the pop-up icon, and click again. The selected text is now formatted in two columns but appears in the first column, as it is not long enough to run over to the second column.

❹ To balance the text between the two columns, click at the end of the text that needs to be balanced, click the **Insert** menu, click **Break** and then **Continuous**.

❺ Save as Display 15.

Note

1   At any point in columns, text after the insertion point can be 'forced' to move to the next column by clicking the **Insert** menu, **Break** and then **Column**.

2   To delete column breaks, click **View** menu, **Normal**, then select and delete the breaks.

CULTURAL ACTIVITY COURSES IN DONEGAL

http://www.oideas-gael.com

HILL WALKING

The Sliabh Liag peninsula offers some of the most breathtaking settings in Ireland for walking.

CELTIC POTTERY

The native skills of pottery making are taught by a professional art teacher and potter.

ENVIRONMENT & CULTURE

This course offers an exploration of both the natural and man-made heritage of the region, with morning presentations and afternoon field trips.

MARINE PAINTING

This course is under the direction of professional Irish painter **Kenneth King** of Straid Studio, Gleann Cholm Cille.

FLUTE & WHISTLE PLAYING

An 'Exploration of Irish Music' through the flute and whistle, presented by a leading traditional musician, offers tuition to both the learner and the improver.

ARCHAEOLOGY

'5,000 Years in Stone' is the theme of this programme.

CELTIC ART

Interpret and create Celtic art with **Patrick Gallagher**, internationally renowned artist and designer. Lectures, workshops and visits to local Celtic sites.

DONEGAL DANCES

Tuition is by a leading instructor in traditional two-hand dances such as the Mazurka, the Highland, Shoe the Donkey and the Peeler & the Goat.

▶ Display 15a

Retrieve Display 15 and insert a column break at the end of the paragraph about Marine Painting. This will force the following text to move to the second paragraph.

▶ Construction 1

Key in the following extract from a sample Specification. Save it as Construction 1.

A sample extract from a Specification is shown below. You should copy this and then type the manuscript Specification on the following page using the same layout.

SPECIFICATION OF WORKS

required to be done and materials to be used in the erection and completion of a house at the entrance to Slí an Aifrinn, Tralee, Co Kerry, for Michael O'Sullivan, Esq, under the superintendence and to the satisfaction of

John B Liston Esq FRIAI
Chartered Architect
7 Denny Street
Tralee, Co Kerry

2 April 2006

PRELIMINARIES

WORKS GENERALLY

1 The whole of the works are to be executed under the supervision and to the satisfaction of the Architect.

SCOPE OF THE WORKS

2 The works comprise the erection and completion of a brick built house two storeys high on the south-western side of the road at the entrance to the estate, as shown on the block plan. The main roof is pitched and tiled, the wall brick faced, the ground floors of solid construction and the first floor is of timber construction.

ACCESS TO THE SITE

3 As the private road shown on the site plan is in continuous use, the access for these works is to be by means of a new opening to be made in the fence on the north side of the new house.

FORM OF CONTRACT

4 The Contractor will be required to sign the current Form of Contract (Blue Form) Private Edition 1996 (without Quantities) issued under the sanction of the Royal Institute of the Architects of Ireland, a copy of which may be viewed at the Architect's office by appointment. The Conditions of Contract therein contained are to be read in conjunction with and as a part of this Specification.

Columns versus tables

When dividing text into columns, it is often more convenient to use the Table function (without gridlines). Tables are covered on page 148.

▶ Display 16

Key in the text below. Put the place names in bold and the Irish words in italics (refer to page 7 if necessary). Centre vertically and horizontally. Save it as Display 16.

THE POSSIBLE DERIVATION OF SOME ← (*TITLE — CAPITALS AND BOLD*)

DONEGAL PLACE-NAMES

(*italics please*)

Donegal from DUN NA NGALL, fort of the foreigners. The foreigners were the Vikings who took possession of a fort here in the 10th century.

Letter kenny from Leitir Ceanainn, wet hillside of the O'Cannons.

TORY ISLAND FROM TORAIGH, place of towers. The towers are the high cliffs and isolated tors in many parts of the island.

Source: A Dictionary of Irish Place-Names by Adrian Room; published by Appletree Press

---

Tailpiece

Some display pieces, such as menus or advertising material, incorporate what is known as a tailpiece. Characters such as 0, hyphen, full stop and colon are used to create the desired effect. An example of a tailpiece is set out below.

```
0 – 0 – 0 – 0 – 0
  – 0 – 0 – 0 –
    0 – 0 – 0
      – 0 –
```

 Tip — When using tailpieces, or indeed any other forms of display, avoid overelaboration.

Layout of construction documents

The layout of construction documents varies. However, **Specifications** and **Bills of Quantities** have certain characteristic features, e.g. each clause has a reference number or letter. Bills of Quantities usually have seven columns for the following:

- reference letter
- further reference
- description
- number of units
- unit of measurement
- price per unit
- the extended price in euros and cents.

To key in the specification overleaf, proceed as follows:

❶ Set up to print on A4 portrait paper with margins of 2.5 cm top, bottom and right. However, set a left margin of 7.5 cm.

❷ Set a left indent at the 8 cm mark and key in the heading SPECIFICATION OF WORKS and format it in block capitals. Key in the details that follow, including the name and address of the architects or engineers, as shown overleaf.

❸ Clear the left indent and key in the date. Set a tab and complete the body of the Specification, as shown overleaf.

Bar tabs

Bar tabs are required for the exercise on page 243. To set bar tabs, select the lines where bar tab lines should appear. Click the **Format** menu, **Tabs**. In the Tabs dialog box, click the **Bar** button and set bar tabs at 1.5 cm, 2.5 cm, 7 cm, 9 cm, 10 cm, 12 cm and 14 cm. Click **Set** each time a tab is entered, then click **OK**. The result will be as shown below:

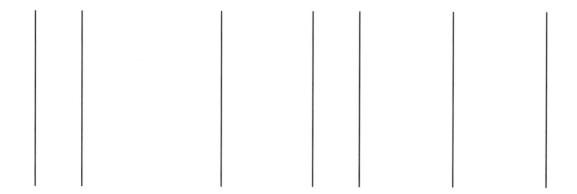

> ▷ **Note** — It is probably easier to use tables than bar tabs. Only the vertical lines required are retained.

Key in the exercise below and save it as Display 17. Please note that it requires a suitable tailpiece.

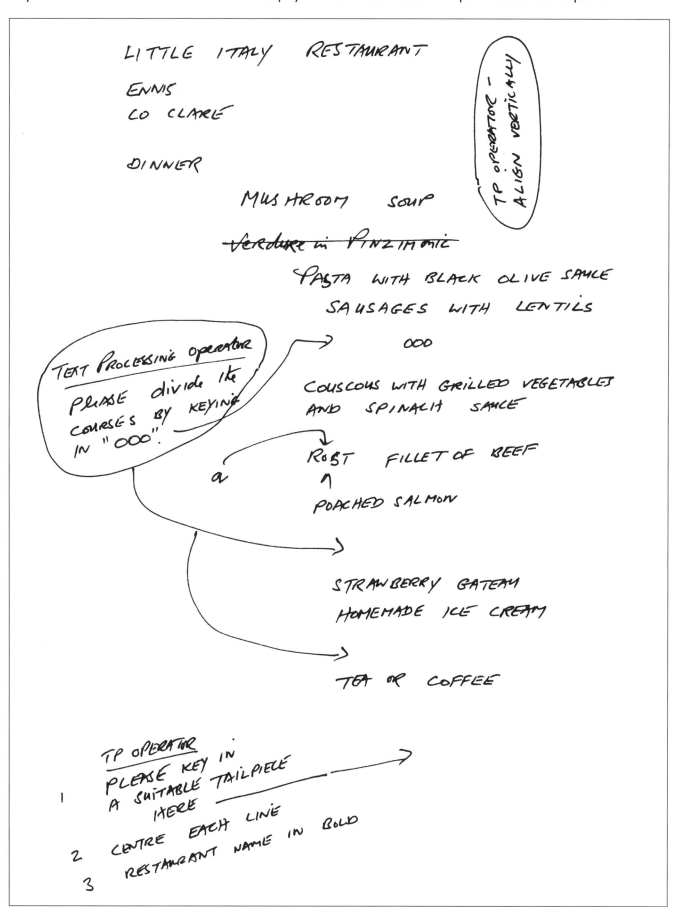

LITTLE ITALY RESTAURANT

ENNIS

CO CLARE

DINNER

MUSHROOM SOUP

~~Verdure in Pinzimonio~~

PASTA WITH BLACK OLIVE SAUCE

SAUSAGES WITH LENTILS

ooo

COUSCOUS WITH GRILLED VEGETABLES AND SPINACH SAUCE

ROAST FILLET OF BEEF

POACHED SALMON

STRAWBERRY GATEAU

HOMEMADE ICE CREAM

TEA OR COFFEE

TP OPERATOR – ALIGN VERTICALLY

TEXT PROCESSING OPERATOR
PLEASE divide the courses by keying in "ooo".

TP OPERATOR
PLEASE KEY IN A SUITABLE TAILPIECE HERE

1
2 CENTRE EACH LINE
3 RESTAURANT NAME IN BOLD

Construction Work

Some of the documentation used in the construction industry is referred to below.

Tender

A Tender is a formal offer to do a job at a stated price.

Estimate

Before a job gets under way, a firm of chartered quantity surveyors may be asked by a client to prepare an Estimate or Cost Plan. Estimates are used, among other things, as a basis for arranging finance.

Specification

A Specification sets out, or specifies, details of the workmanship and the nature of materials to be used in a particular job. It does not, however, state the **quantity** of materials to be used. Specifications are usually prepared for a client by a firm of consulting engineers or chartered architects and are sent with drawings to building contractors who wish to tender. Consulting Engineers' Specifications deal with such matters as the structure of a building, soil tests, the make-up of the materials to be used, 'live and dead weight' and the amount of reinforcement required. Chartered Architects' Specifications, on the other hand, deal with interior finishes and such matters as doors, lighting, ventilation and plastering.

Without details of quantities, contractors have to tender at a fixed or 'lump sum' price.

Bill of quantities

For bigger jobs costing in excess of about €300,000, a Bill of Quantities is prepared along with the Consulting Engineers' Specification. A Bill of Quantities itemises, where possible, the **quantities** of materials and the detailed work required to complete a particular job. It usually contains separate Bills relating to different parts of the job, such as Preliminaries, Substructure and Superstructure. Details similar to those contained in a specification are set out in a section of a Bill of Quantities known as 'Preambles'. Like Specifications, Bills of Quantities are sent out with drawings to contractors who wish to tender. Contractors arrive at their tender price by filling in prices opposite each item on the Bill of Quantities.

Acceptance of a tender

When Tenders are received, they are studied and factors such as price, the track record of a contractor and any qualifications which may have been made are taken into account. Finally, a Tender is accepted, i.e. awarded to a particular contractor.

▶ Display 18

Key in the poem below and save it as Display 18.

I

ST RIOCH'S MONASTERY, INISBOFIN, LOUGH REE

A SUMMER SUN IS SETTING AS I DRIFT NEAR
                                    CLUSTERED TREES
AND A LAZY MIND IS LISTENING TO THE MURMER
                              OF SOME BEES
AND EVERYWHERE A SAINTLY HUSH
THE ISLAND DRAWS ME NEAR

II

AND NOW UPON THE ROCKY SHORE, A PILGRIM, RAPT,
                                    UNSEEN
A SOUL IS CAPTIVATED WHERE SAINTLY MEN HAVE
                                    BEEN
AND THEN A WAVE, A MUFFLED SOUND FROM OVER BY
                              THE SHORE
OR WAS THIS VOICE OF RIOCH ON HIS ISLAND HOME
                              ONCE MORE?

III

AND STILL THE SCENE IS CHANGING AS I CLIMB TO
                              THE ANCIENT PLACE
THE CHURCH NO LONGER FALLEN DOWN; FULL OF
                              BENEDICTION'S GRACE
I STAND AND GAZE A MOMENT, UNSEEN BY THE SAINTLY
                              THRONG
AS INCENSE LIFTS TO HEAVEN ON CLOUDS OF PIOUS
                                    SONG

IV

AND NOW THE BEES FROM DROONING, TO SOME MONKS
                              IN GENTLE CHANT
TO THE LORD ABOVE THEIR MAKER, THEY PRAISE HIS
                              LOVING HAND
AND NATURE TOO IS TALKING TO THE LORD OF ALL THE
                              LAKE
AS LITTLE CREATURES ALL AROUND THEIR EVENING
                              HOMAGE MAKE

V

BUT SOON THE HYMN IS DYING AND THE SAINTLY MEN DEPART
TO DO THE LITTLE THINGS THAT KEEP THEN ON THIS EARTH
THEIR FIRE IS OUT, THEIR SMOKE STILL RISES THROUGH THE
                                    TREES
THESE MEN WERE NOT GOD'S SOWERS BUT HIS FULLY RIPENED
                                    SEEDS

▶ Display 19

Retrieve the above exercise and use colons to add a tailpiece, as shown below. Save it as Display 19.

::::::
:::
:

Key in the exercise below and save it as Medical 3.

COURSE FOR MEDICAL SECRETARIES

Aims and objectives

To introduce students to the work of the medical secretary, to the medical departments of a hospital and to the use of medical terminology.

Syllabus

Cardiology (heart)

Dermatology (skin)

Endocrinology (glands)

ENT (ear, nose and throat)

Gastroenterology (digestive system)

Gynaecology and Obstetrics (female reproductive tract and childbirth)

Mental Health

Neurology and Neurosurgery (nervous system and surgical treatment of disorders of brain, spinal cord or other parts of the nervous system)

Ophthalmology (eye)

Orthopaedics (bones, joints, muscles, tendons and ligaments)

Plastic Surgery (operations to repair or reconstruct skin and underlying tissue)

Haematology (blood)

Oncology (tumours, particularly cancer)

Vascular Surgery (blood vessels)

Paediatrics (growth and development of children)

Checking spelling and grammar

The relevant Word dialog box must be set so that the software works in a way that suits the user. Some users forget this and as a result lose the benefit of Word's powerful spelling and grammar checker.

To set the spell checker, click the **Tools** menu, select **Options**, click the **Spelling & Grammar** tab, then click the relevant checkboxes.

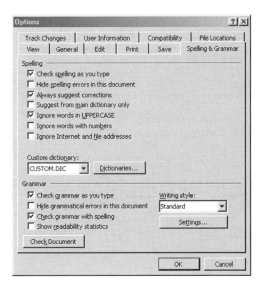

It is suggested that the following checkboxes should be ticked:

❶ Check Spelling as you type.

❷ Always suggest corrections.

❸ Check grammar as you type.

On the other hand, it is recommended that the following options should not be ticked:

❶ Hide spelling errors in this document.

❷ Ignore words in UPPERCASE.

Checking up on the spell checker!

To check the Spelling and Grammar settings, key in a sentence which incorporates both a spelling and a grammatical error. For example, 'He done it yesterdayy.' A red line should appear under 'yesterdayy' when the Space Bar is pressed. Also, at the start of the next sentence, a green line should appear to indicate that there is a grammatical error.

 Remember — The spell checker is not foolproof, so treat it as an aid rather than a magic cure for all spelling errors.

For example, the following sentences were not challenged by Word's spell checker:

❶ Mr Walsh, the college principle, was first to address the meeting.

❷ A new subject, The History of Art, was added last year to compliment the children's education.

❸ The council for the defence asked for added time to consider their position.

We should of course have used the words 'principal', 'complement' and 'counsel'.

 Tip — Right click on a word which has been underlined in red. If possible, Word will suggest the correct spelling.

Key in the table below and save it as Medical 2.

AREAS OF MEDICAL WORK			
Term	**Relates to:**	**Term**	**Relates to:**
cardiology	heart	dermatology	skin
ophthalmology	eye	endocrinology	glands
plastic surgery	operations to repair or reconstruct skin and underlying tissue	orthopaedics	bones, joints, muscles, tendons and ligaments
haematology	blood	gastroenterology	digestive system
gynaecology	female reproductive tract	obstetrics	childbirth
psychiatry	mental health	bacteriology	study of disease-causing microbes, including bacteria, viruses, and fungi
immunology	study of immune system	histopathology	biopsy and postmortem examination of tissues
blood transfusion	blood typing and matching	clinical biochemistry or chemical pathology	analysis of chemical indicators of disease
oncology	tumours, particularly cancer	vascular surgery	blood vessels
paediatrics	growth and development of children	neurology	nervous system
neurosurgery	surgical treatment of disorders of the brain, spinal cord and other parts of the nervous system	pathology	study of disease process

Time

Time is stated using the 12-hour clock system. The 24-hour clock is usually reserved for itineraries, time-tables, military operations and the like. The following points should be noted:

❶ A full stop is required when using the 12-hour clock format — even when using open punctuation. A space should be inserted between the figures and am or pm.

❷ A full stop should not be used in the 24-hour clock format — even when using full punctuation. A space should be inserted between the figures and 'hours'.

Example 6.15 am = 0615 hours and 9.45 pm = 2145 hours

Itineraries

When a person has a number of appointments, it is often helpful to set out the details in the form of an itinerary. There are no rigid layout rules, but it is common to leave about half a centimetre between columns. Itineraries that relate to more than one day are sometimes printed on better-quality paper.

▶ Display 20

Key in the itinerary below and save it as Display 20.

ITINERARY

Mr J O'Hara's visit to Tullamore

11 and 12 December 2006

Tuesday 11 December 2006

Time		
1230		Taxi from Dublin office to Heuston Station.
1310	**Depart**	Heuston Station.
1430	**Arrive**	Tullamore. Accommodation booked at the Bridge House Hotel. Taxi from station to hotel.
1500		Taxi from hotel to Tullamore Software plc.
2000		Dinner at the Nook and Cranny restaurant, Tullamore.

Wednesday 12 December 2006

Time		
0930		Room reserved at Bridge House hotel for interviews for new positions with Tullamore Software. Refer to File TS 1892.
1115		Coffee break ✗
1300		Lunch at Tullamore Court Hotel ✗
1400		Meeting with interview panel and company executives at Tullamore Court Hotel ✗
1600		Taxi from hotel to Tullamore Station ✗
1615	**Depart**	Tullamore ✗
1735	**Ariive**	Dublin ✗

(handwritten note: TO ENSURE CONSISTENT USE OF THE FULL STOP, INSERT FULL STOPS AT THE POINTS MARKED 'X'.)

Medical Work

The role of medical secretary is performed in a number of different professional settings. Anyone planning a career in this field would do well to have an appreciation of the work of the key medical environments and administrative areas.

Key medical environments

• Hospitals

• Clinics

• Medical and dental surgeries

• Health Boards

Key administrative areas

• Patient admission

• Patient assessment

• Patient release

• Patient billing

▶ Medical 1

The secretary should also understand the medico-legal implications of the professional relationships between medical personnel, administrative personnel and patients.

Key in the text below and save it as Medical 1.

General medical terms			
acute	antral	aneurysm	abdominal
bacteria	bilious	bruits	central nervous system
crepitus	cyanosed	cardiovascular	carotid
dysphonia	duodenum	dysphagia	degenerative
expiratory	inspiratory	bronchi	effusion
emphysema	exacerbation	fatigue	haemoptysis
cirrhosis	hiatus hernia	cortex	sputum
mass	pleural effusion	pylorus	common bile duct
oesophagus	costalgia	abrasion	vital signs stable
neurological	epilepsy	sinusitis	rhinitis

Notes

❶ The Dublin Institute of Technology, Kevin Street runs a Medical Records and Patients Service Management Course.

❷ The Cavan College of Further Studies runs a Certificate in Business Studies — Medical Secretarial Course.

 Tip — When preparing for an interview with one of the Health Boards, candidates should find out as much as possible about the activities of the Board in question. It is also worth learning some basic medical terminology, particularly the names of the main hospital departments.

Meetings

Informal meetings are held to work out a common course of action. For example, a group of friends might meet to work out the details of a proposed holiday. However, the directors of a company or the members of a society usually hold **formal** meetings to decide on matters of importance. Such formal meetings are governed by generally accepted procedures.

Notice of meeting and agenda

The notice calling a meeting and the relevant agenda are usually combined. The notice must include the name of the organisation, the type of meeting involved and the date, time and venue.

Agenda

An agenda is a list of the items to be discussed at a meeting. The items are usually numbered and listed in order of importance.

Minutes of a meeting

Details of the business discussed at a meeting and any decisions or resolutions passed are recorded and preserved in the form of minutes. Minutes are recorded in the order in which they appear on the agenda; they must be accurate. Before a meeting may commence, the minutes of the last meeting must be read and agreed. They are then proposed, seconded and finally signed by the chairman.

IRISH WILDLIFE ASSOCIATION
6 Tudor Grove
Tullamore
Co Offaly

A meeting of the committee of the Irish Wildlife Organisation will be held in the Shannon River Hotel, Limerick on Sunday, 18 July 2002 at 3.00 pm.

AGENDA

1 Apologies
2 Secretary
3 Matters arising from the minutes
4 Correspondence
5 Review of Limerick conference
6 Venue for next conference
7 Youth development programme
8 Any other business
9 Date and time of next meeting

FRANK HUGHES
Secretary

---

after the payment thereout of all my just debts & testamentary and funeral exps for such of my sisters Annette and Christina Carroll 42 Old Meadow Estate Attenry 6 Galway as shall be living at my death and if more than one in equal shares absolutely

In Witness whereof I have hereto set my hand on this ─ ─ ─ ─ ─ day of ─ ─ ─ ─.

Signed published and declared by the ABOVE named ─────── as and for her last Will in the joint presence of herself and us who at her request and in such joint presence have hereunto subscribed our names as WITNESSes. This Will having been printed on the front side only, of the foregoing ( ) pages of SIZE A4 paper.

PLEASE ENDORSE this Will. The Solicitors are AS FOLLOWS:

FLYNN & Co
The Mall
Ballinasloe
Co GALWAY

TP OPERATOR
① Key in the TOTAL NUMBER OF PAGES
② Key in the PAGE NUMBERS (AS SHOWN IN THE EXERCISE "Legal 1") AT THE FOOT OF EACH PAGE

Reports

In business or the academic world, it is often necessary to gather information on a particular topic. Such information is often presented in the form of a report.

Formal reports often include the following parts:

❶ Title — usually on a cover page.

❷ Procedure — sets out the method used to collect the information.

❸ Findings — details the information collected.

❹ Conclusion — a summary and conclusion drawn from the findings.

❺ Recommendations — what action(s) should be taken.

In long reports, particular attention should be paid to ensuring that headings, subheadings and the enumeration style are consistent. See pages 73 and 74 for information on enumeration.

▶ *Display 21*

Key in the piece below and save it as Display 21.

INFORMAL REPORT ON CARAVAN THEFT

Because of their high value and mobility, caravans represent prime targets for thieves. Each year the number of thefts increases alarmingly and this report was prepared to indicate some of key theft prevention measures which can be taken to deter a thief.

delete

1   LEAVE YOUR MARK
    Mark your caravan and etch the windows with your house number.

2   USE A HITCHLOCK
    The tow bar is the first thing a thief will examine. If it is not locked into a cover, he can hitch your caravan to his vehicle and tow it away.

3   FIT AN ALARM
    Alarms are becoming smaller and cheaper and are an excellent way of scaring away intruders and alerting neighbours.

4   INSTALL A NIGHT LIGHT
    At night a light, either battery or electronically operated by a time switch, can suggest you caravan is occupied.

It is recommended that all of the above measures should be put into effect on your next caravan holiday.

John Heaton
Security Advisor to the Caravan Club

31 January 2002

(d) To Franciscan Abbey Athenry the sum of €5,000

(e) To ISPCA the sum of €500.

③ To my sister Jacinta Carroll of 48 Old Meadow Estate Athenry Co Galway I give devise or bequeath the contents of my holiday home situated in Lisdoonvarna Co Clare

④ My jewellery and Waterford crystal I bequeath to my ~~Nephew~~ Niece Mary Carroll of 49 Parkgrove Ave Ballinasloe.

⑤ I give devise and bequeath all my estate both real and personal whatsoever and wheresoever situated not hereby or by any codicil hereto otherwise specifically disposed of unto my trustees UPON TRUST

Key in the report below. Refer to shoulder headings on page 65. Save it as Display 22.

REPORT ON OUTGOING CORRESPONDENCE ← *Heading in block caps and boldface*

Managers spend a considerable amount of time composing and dictating letters. Many of these are similar and contain relatively routine information. It has therefore been decided to introduce the use of standard paragraphs and letters.

HOUSE STYLE ← *SHOULDER HEADING*

A study of sample correspondence in our five departments has revealed a lack of uniformity. Some of the styles used, for example the semi-blocked style, are rather dated and do nothing for the image of the company. It has therefore been decided to introduce a "house style".

HOUSESTYLE FEATURES ←

Our house style will come into effect on the first day of the new year, and will include the following features:

    blocked style layout
    open punctuation
    minimum underlining
    no signature line at the end of letters
    minimum division of words at line ends
    use of open window envelopes

COMPANY MANUAL ←

A manual containing standard letters in our new house style will be available shortly

Key in the Will below. Use the correct legal format. Save it as Legal 6.

I Martina Josephine Carroll of 42 Old Meadow Estate Athenry Co. Galway hereby revoke all former wills & testamentary dispositions heretofore made by me and declare this to be my last will. ① I appoint Rose Roche of Main Road Athenry to be executrix and trustee of this my will ② I bequeath the following pecuniary legacies: (a) To my brother John Carroll now residing in 49 Parkgrove Ave Ballinasloe the sum of €1000 (b) To my sister-in-law Catherine Carroll-Cook now residing in Maynooth Co. Kildare the sum of three thousand pounds. (c) To my friend Clare Mannion living in Trim Co. Meath the sum of one thousand euros.

Clearing the Word window

Let's do a little exercise to reinforce our knowledge of the parts of the Word window — refer back to page 3 if necessary. Let's clear the Word window.

Click the **Tools** menu, click **Options** and click the **View** tab in the Options dialog box. Deactivate the **Status Bar, Horizontal Scroll Bar** and **Vertical Scroll Bar** checkboxes by clicking them.

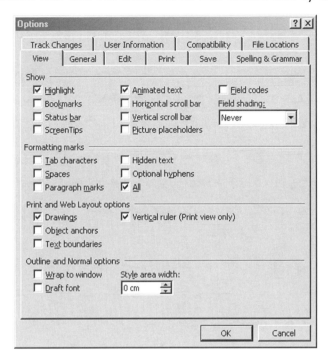

Now click the **View** menu, click **Toolbars** and deactivate any checkboxes that are ticked.

Click the **View** menu and deactivate the **Ruler** checkbox if it is ticked.

Click the **Start** button at the bottom left-hand side of the screen, click **Setting**, click **Taskbar** and **Start Menu**. In the Taskbar Properties dialog box, click the **Taskbar Options** tab and deactivate the **Always on top** checkbox.

Now that you've done the damage, doesn't your screen look rather emasculated!

Key in the Will below. Check your work with the previous exercise. Save it as Legal 5.

This is the last will & testament of me SEATHRÚN O'BOYLE of Harbour Village, Dunmore East, in the County of Waterford and I hereby revoke all wills and other testamentary dispositions at any time theretofore made by ME.

I appoint my sons Michael O'Boyle and Stephen O'Boyle to be my executors of this my will and I direct them to pay all my lawful debts, funeral and testamentary expenses.

I give devise and bequeath all my property of whatsoever nature and kind, both real and personal, that I may die seized, possessed of or entitled to unto my wife Helen O'Boyle for her own benefit and use absolutely.

In the event of my said wife pre deceasing me or in the event of the concurrent deaths of my wife and myself (concurrent deaths in this context to mean deaths following a common tragedy and within thirty days of each other) I give devise and bequeath all my property of whatsoever nature and kind, both real and personal, that I may die seized, possessed of or entitled to unto my four children Michael, Stephen, Lorraine and John in equal shares.

In witness whereof I have hereunto set my hand this —— day of — One thousand Nine Hundred and ——

Signed & acknowledged by the above named testator as and for his last will and testament in the presence of us, both present and at the same time who in his presence and in the presence of each other, at his request, have hereunto subscribed our names as witnesses.

—————————   —————————

—————————   —————————

Rebuilding the Word window

Now let's get our Word window back together again, as follows:

❶ Reintroduce the Task Bar by pressing the **Ctrl+Esc** keys together. Click **Settings**, click **Taskbar**, then click the **Always on top** checkbox. (The Esc key is on the top left of the keyboard.)

❷ Click the **View** menu and select **Ruler**.

❸ Click the **View** menu, click **Toolbar** and click the checkboxes for the toolbars required (usually the Standard and Formatting toolbars suffice).

❹ Click the **Tools** menu, click **Options** and click the **View** tab. In the Options dialog box click the **Status Bar**, the **Horizontal Scroll Bar** and the **Vertical Scroll Bar** checkboxes, i.e. make sure a tick appears before them.

Key in the Will below and save it as Legal 4.

THIS IS THE LAST WILL AND TESTAMENT of me SEATHRÚN O'BOYLE of Harbour Village, Dunmore East, in the County of Waterford and I hereby revoke all Wills and other Testamentary Dispositions at any time theretofore made by me.

I APPOINT my Sons MICHAEL O'BOYLE and STEPHEN O'BOYLE to be my executors of this my Will and I DIRECT them to pay all my lawful debts, funeral and testamentary expenses.

I GIVE DEVISE AND BEQUEATH all my property of whatsoever nature and kind, both real and personal, that I may die seized, possessed of or entitled to unto my Wife HELEN O'BOYLE for her own benefit and use absolutely.

In the event of my said Wife pre-deceasing me or in the event of the concurrent deaths of my Wife and Myself (concurrent deaths in this context to mean deaths following a common tragedy and within thirty days of each other) I GIVE DEVISE AND BEQUEATH all my property of whatsoever nature and kind, both real and personal, that I may die seized, possessed of or entitled to unto my four Children Michael, Stephen, Lorraine and Colin in equal shares.

IN WITNESS WHEREOF I have hereunto set my hand this   day of   Two Thousand and Six.

SIGNED AND ACKNOWLEDGED by the above named Testator as and for his last Will and Testament in the presence of us, both present and at the same time who in his presence and in the presence of each other, at his request, have hereunto subscribed our names as Witnesses.

_____   _____

_____   _____

_____   _____

Page 1 of 1

Part 5
Letters

▷▷▷▷▶▷▷▷▷▷▷▷▷▷

Letters

There are a number of recognised letter styles, but this text favours the use of the **fully blocked with open punctuation** style, as it is both up-to-date and straightforward.

For reference purposes only, examples of two other letter styles are given on pages 107 and 108.

 Note — Once a particular letter style has been selected, the rules governing its layout and punctuation must be strictly adhered to. Above all, elements of different styles should never appear in the same letter.

Blocked sytle

Blocked style means that each line starts at the left margin, as shown below:

A blocked style address	A non-blocked style address
Ms Maureen Moore	Ms Maureen Moore
Irishtown	Irishtown
Wexford	Wexford

Open punctuation

The following guidelines should be followed when using open punctuation:

❶ Standard grammatical punctuation must be used in the usual way, e.g. full stops at the end of sentences.

❷ When an abbreviation is followed by a full stop, as is the case when using the full punctuation, the full stop is omitted and a single character space is inserted instead, e.g. Mr. V. P. O'Neill becomes Mr V P O'Neill.

❸ In letters, no punctuation is used in the reference, date, inside address, salutation, complimentary close, name of the firm, name of the signatory or title of the signatory. Envelopes should be typed in exactly the same way as the inside address.

❹ When separate details appear on the same line, as in the subject heading of letters or memos, the rules of open punctuation are not infringed by the insertion of commas between the different details. Alternatively, an extra space may be inserted. Consider the examples below:

```
RE 105 CHURCH STREET, ATHY, CO KILDARE

RE   105   CHURCH STREET   ATHY   CO KILDARE
```

House style

House style is the style favoured by a particular organisation. For example, it may be that a particular organisation does not favour the use of open punctuation. In this case the typist must conform to the style in use in her or his organisation.

▶ Legal 3

Key in the Agreement below. Check your work with the previous exercise. Save it as Legal 3.

Agreement made 2/5/2006 between Seamus O'Brien of 46 Munster Street, Mallow in the county of Cork of the one part and Joan West of The Walk, Dunmore East, Co Waterford of the other part.

WHEREAS:

1 Seamus O'Brien holds the premises set out in the schedule hereto under lease from Joan West for a term of 21 years from 1 January 1990.

2 Seamus O'Brien has complained that works carried out by the said Joan West at 45 Munster Street, Mallow adjoining the shop of Seamus O'Brien have caused disturbance and financial loss to him.

3 The said Seamus O'Brien has threatened to institute proceedings for the alleged loss and injury sustained by him by reason of the works aforesaid, which proceedings are proposed to be taken against the said Joan West.

Now hereby it is agreed by the said parties as follows:

1 The said Joan West shall pay to the said Seamus O'Brien the sum of €59,000.

2 In consideration of the payment by the said Joan West of the said sum of €59,000 the said Seamus O'Brien shall:

(a) Stay all further action in respect of complaints hereinbefore referred to against the said Joan West and will accept same in full and final settlement of all actions, costs, claims, demands and loss against the said Joan West.

(b) Will surrender the said lease of the premises set out in the schedule hereto and give vacant possession thereof to the said Joan West.

(c) The said Seamus O'Brien will sign all documentation to implement the terms of this agreement.

In witness whereof the parties have hereunto set their hands and affixed their seals the day and year first herein written.

Signed by the said Seamus O'Brien in the presence of:

"   "   "   "   Joan West   "   "   "   "

SCHEDULE

all that lock-up shop and premises at present in the occupation of the said Seamus O'Brien situated at Munster Street, Mallow in the town and Urban District of Mallow.

(Margin note: Typist enter a page break here. Also double line spacing throughout)

u/c

Personal Letters

Nowadays text messages and e-mail are widely used for personal correspondence; however, the postal service, or 'snail mail', still has its place. Guidelines for setting out personal letters are set out below.

The parts of a personal letter are as follows:

❶ sender's address
❷ date
❸ salutation
❹ body of the letter
❺ complimentary close.

Line space in letters

Leave one clear line between the parts of a letter and between paragraphs in the body of a letter (i.e. press the Return key twice).

▶ Letter 1

Key in the letter below from Helen Fizgerald to Mairéad Kavanagh and save it as Letter 1. Use single-line spacing and left and right margins of 25 cm (1 inch). Ignore the accents in Slí and Mairéad for now.

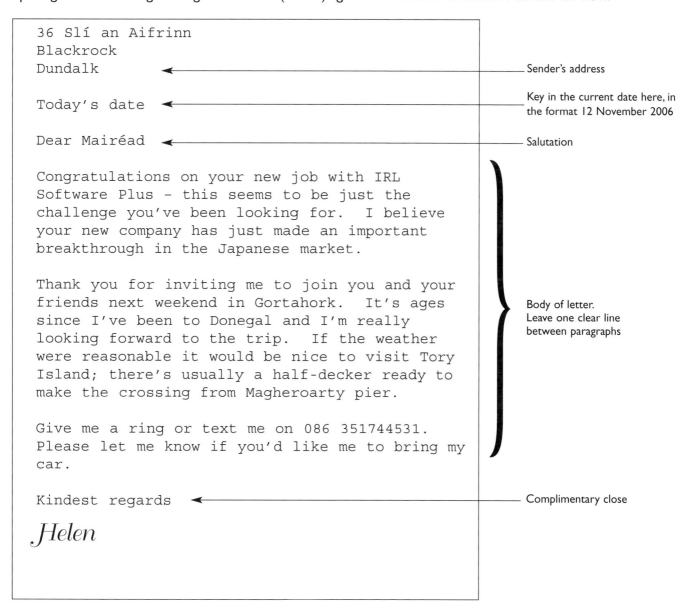

```
36 Slí an Aifrinn
Blackrock
Dundalk                           ←——————————— Sender's address

Today's date   ←——————————————————————— Key in the current date here, in
                                         the format 12 November 2006

Dear Mairéad   ←——————————————————————— Salutation

Congratulations on your new job with IRL
Software Plus - this seems to be just the
challenge you've been looking for.  I believe
your new company has just made an important
breakthrough in the Japanese market.

Thank you for inviting me to join you and your          Body of letter.
friends next weekend in Gortahork.  It's ages          Leave one clear line
since I've been to Donegal and I'm really              between paragraphs
looking forward to the trip.  If the weather
were reasonable it would be nice to visit Tory
Island; there's usually a half-decker ready to
make the crossing from Magheroarty pier.

Give me a ring or text me on 086 351744531.
Please let me know if you'd like me to bring my
car.

Kindest regards   ←——————————————————— Complimentary close

Helen
```

Key in the Endorsement below and save it as Legal 2.

DATED THIS
SECOND DAY OF MAY 2006

SEAMUS O'BRIEN
AND
JOAN WEST

AGREEMENT

GARDENER WALLACE AND CO
SOLICITORS
PRIORY MEWS
WATERFORD

▶ Legal 2

Personal business letters

After personal letters, we move to a more formal situation where a private individual writes to a person or organisation about a business matter. In such letters, it is necessary to add three further letter parts:

❶ If given, a reference that shows the recipient's reference. References appear one clear line below the sender's address.

❷ The INSIDE ADDRESS — the name and address of the person or organisation to whom/which the letter is being sent.

❸ The SIGNATORY — the printed version of the name of the person who signs the letter.

 Note — Between the COMPLIMENTARY CLOSE and the SIGNATORY, leave from four to six clear lines for the signature.

▶ Letter 2

Under **File**, **Page Setup**, set 25 mm margins and A4 paper size. Key in the personal business letter below and save it as Letter 2.

```
197 Douglas Road
Cork

Your ref JOH/AD22

Today's date

Mr John O'Hara
Loan Officer
Bank of Commerce and Finance
27 Molesworth Street
Dublin 2

Dear Sir

On 17 August last, I repaid Loan Number 1794457/2 and requested that
you cancel the direct debit mandate for €785.00, which I signed in
2003.

I note from checking my bank statements that monthly debits are still
being charged to my account.

Please ensure that this direct debit is cancelled forthwith and
refund the amounts that were debited to my account in error.

Yours faithfully
```

```
Timothy McCarthy
```

Inside address

Typed name of signatory

(c) The said Seamus O'Brien will sign all documentation to implement the terms of this agreement.

IN WITNESS whereof the Parties have hereunto set their hands and affixed their seals the day and year first herein Written.

SIGNED by the said

SEAMUS O'BRIEN

in the presence of:

_____

SIGNED by the said

JOAN WEST

in the presence of:

_____

S C H E D U L E

ALL THAT lock-up shop and premises at present in the occupation of the said Seamus O'Brien situated at Munster Street, Mallow in the Town and Urban District of Mallow.

Page 2 of 2

Dates in letters

If no date is given in an exercise, you are expected to use the current date. Go to the **Insert** menu, **select Date and Time** and then click the date format required, e.g. 19 June 2006. It's generally better to tick the Update automatically box.

Personal and impersonal salutations and complimentary closes

No matter what type of letter you are writing, you should distinguish between personal and impersonal salutations and complimentary closes. If a personal salutation is used, a personal complimentary close must also be used.

Personal

Salutation – Hi (very informal but sometimes seen in e-mail), Dear John and Dear Mr Kavanagh
Complimentary close – See you soon, Kind regards, Yours sincerely (the typical personal complimentary close in business letters)

Impersonal

Salutations – Dear Sir or Dear Sirs
Complimentary close – Yours faithfully

Business Letters

Now we move to fully fledged business letters, i.e. letters from one business to another. The main differences between such a letter and a personal business letters are:

❶ Business letters are printed on headed paper, i.e. paper showing the name and address and other details of a company concerned.

❷ A reference is usually included with shows the sender's reference. A recipient's reference may also be included. References appear one clear line below the sender's address. If there is a recipient's reference, this appears one clear line below the sender's reference.

❸ There is usually a SUBJECT HEADING one clear line after the salutation and one clear line before the body of a letter.

❹ The DESIGNATION, or title, of the SIGNATORY is typed directly under the signatory. There is NO CLEAR LINE between the signatory and the designation.

❺ When documents have been enclosed with a letter, this must be indicated by typing Enc (or Encs, if there is more than one enclosure) one clear line below the designation.

Headed paper

Headed paper is paper with the sender's name and other details already printed on it. When printing on headed paper it is necessary to set a larger than usual top margin.

Key in the Agreement below and save it as Legal I.

A G R E E M E N T made the second day of May Two thousand and six BETWEEN SEAMUS O'BRIEN of 46 Munster Street, Mallow in the County of Cork of the One Part and JOAN WEST of The Walk, Dunmore East, Co Waterford of the Other Part.

WHEREAS:

1 Seamus O'Brien holds the premises set out in the Schedule hereto under lease from Joan West for a term of twenty-one years from the first day of January Nineteen Hundred and Ninety.

2 Seamus O'Brien has complained that works carried out on the premises of the said Joan West at 45 Munster Street, Mallow adjoining the shop of Seamus O'Brien have caused disturbance and financial loss to him.

3 The said Seamus O'Brien has threatened to institute proceedings for the alleged loss and injury sustained by him by reason of the works aforesaid, which proceedings are proposed to be taken against the said Joan West.

NOW HEREBY IT IS AGREED by and between the Parties as follows:

1 The said Joan West shall pay to the said Seamus O'Brien the sum of fifty thousand euro (€50,000).

2 In consideration of the payment by the said Joan West of the said sum of fifty thousand euro (€50,000) the said Seamus O'Brien shall:

(a) Stay all further action in respect of the complaints hereinbefore referred to against the said Joan West and will accept same in full and final settlement of all actions, costs, claims, demands and loss against the said Joan West.

(b) Will surrender the said Lease of the premises set out in the Schedule hereto and give vacant possession thereof to the said Joan West.

Page 1 of 2

Now key in the business letter below, centre the heading and save it as Letter 3. As a general rule, remember to allow just one clear line between the different letter parts and between the paragraphs in the body of the letter. However, no space should be allowed between the SIGNATORY and the DESIGNATION.

Kelly Display Units Ltd
10 O'Connell Street
Dublin 1 ← Sender's address (usually on headed paper)
Tel (01) 159050
E-mail kds@eircom.net
Web http://www.kellydisplay.i.e.
Branches: Cork, Limerick, Galway, Dundalk, Athlone

Our ref RLL/LT ← Sender's reference

Your ref MS/JD ← Recipient's reference

28 October 2006 ← Date

Mr Charles Murphy
Murphy Shop Fittings Ltd ← Inside address
Harrington Street
Dublin 7

Dear Sirs ← Salutation

THURLES STORE ← Subject heading

Thank you for your proposals in connection with our Thurles store.

I must admit that I was rather taken aback by your final quotation of nearly €250,000. However, as I am impressed by the flexibility and quality of your display units, I should be grateful if your representatives would call to our Thurles manager as soon as possible to discuss this matter further.

I have now set an upper limit of €175,000 for expenditure on fittings in Thurles and I enclose a breakdown of how I see this sum being allocated.

If you are to have a realistic chance of securing the Thurles contract, your next proposal will have be more competitive and, if necessary, involve a more economic distribution of the display units.

Yours sincerely ← Complimentary close

R L Lohan ← At least four clear lines here

R L Lohan ← Name of signatory
Development Manager ← NO CLEAR LINE HERE

Enc ← Indicates an enclosure

BODY OF LETTER

Key words

Certain key words and terms are emphasised in legal documents by using spaced or closed capitals; the underscore may or may not be used. Listed below is a number of such words and terms.

Agreements

AGREEMENT; BETWEEN; WHEREAS; NOW HEREBY IT IS AGREED; IN WITNESS; ALL THAT; TOGETHER WITH; ALL THAT AND THOSE; SCHEDULE.

Wills

LAST WILL AND TESTAMENT; HEREBY REVOKE; DECLARE; I APPOINT; I LEAVE, DEVISE AND BEQUEATH; ALL THAT; IN WITNESS WHEREOF.

 Remember — WHEN IN DOUBT, TYPE IT OUT!
If doubtful whether to key in words in capitals, a good rule of thumb is to **use** capitals.

Endorsement

Endorsements are printed on the back of the last page of a legal document. The details are centred on the right side of the paper (see example on page 229) so that they are visible when a document is folded vertically in the middle. If '**No Text**' paper is used, the last page is reversed. Endorsements generally show the date, the name(s) of the person(s) involved, the title of the document, e.g. Will, and the name of the firm of solicitors that drew up the document. If a folio number is used, this is also shown.

Copies of letters

In the past carbon copies were taken when additional copies of a letters were required. The letters 'cc' followed by two spaces and the names of those due to receive copies were typed, as per the example below.

```
cc    Ms M Walsh
cc    Mr R McNamara
cc    File
```

The letters 'cc' (standing for carbon copy) are still widely used despite the fact that carbon copies are rarely taken nowadays. The modern style, 'Copy to' or 'Copies to' (as shown below), is used by some companies.

```
Copy to    Ms M Walsh
           Mr R McNamara
           File
```

Routing

Specific copies of letters are directed or 'routed' to a specific individual or to file by ticking or highlighting (by means of a highlighting pen) the names in question. In the example below the first copy has been routed to Ms M Walsh, the second copy to Mr R McNamara and the third copy has been retained for filing.

```
Copies to  Ms M Walsh      Copies to  Ms M Walsh      Copies to  Ms M Walsh
           Mr R McNamara               Mr R McNamara              Mr R McNamara
           File                        File                      File
```

Part 13
Technical Work

▷▷▷▷▷▷▷▷▷▷▷▷▶▷▷▷

This section gives a brief introduction to word processing associated with legal, construction and medical work.

Legal work

When keying in legal work, first of all look for relevant templates. Templates may be created, purchased or downloaded using the Internet. Such templates contain the approved layout of and standard clauses in documents such as **wills**, **contracts**, **letting agreement**s and so on. Legal firms simply key in the information that varies from one document to another; e.g., in the case of a contract, the names and addresses of the contracting parties. It is therefore not necessary for word-processing operators to have a detailed knowledge of the layout of legal documents.

Like all professions, the legal profession uses **terminology** that may be unfamiliar to the layperson, so a legal dictionary is a useful tool. One legal secretary tells how she spent her first day at work merrily keying in the words 'legal council' instead of 'legal counsel'.

In general, A4 paper is used. Sometimes the words 'No Text' are printed on one side to prevent printing on both sides of a sheet of paper.

General guidelines

❶ Template styles may vary from office to office.

❷ Legal documents should be unambiguous to ensure that they stand up in law. The layout style is of secondary importance.

❸ Double-line spacing is usually used.

❹ In the past, no punctuation was used. Nowadays, punctuation is used in the normal way.

❺ In the past, dates were usually keyed in using words. Nowadays, this is not always the case. However, it is probably better to continue keying in dates using words.

❻ In the past, sums of money were keyed in words followed by the corresponding figures in brackets, e.g. one thousand punts (IR£1,000). Nowadays, sums of money are often simply keyed in using figures, e.g. €1,270. However, it is advisable to continue using words and figures.

❼ To facilitate the binding of documents, margins of 3.8 cm (1.5 in) left and 1.3 cm (0.5 in) right are still widely used.

❽ No abbreviation marks should appear in legal documents.

❾ The names of the parties to a legal document are formatted in block capitals when they first appear.

❿ Each page should be numbered in sequential order at the foot of the page, as follows: 1 of 5, 2 of 5, etc.

⓫ Documents must be carefully proofread, as mistakes render legal documents invalid.

⓬ Blank spaces should be kept to a minimum to prevent additional clauses being added. In this context, note that numbered clauses are **not** normally set out as hanging paragraphs (see example on page 227).

▶ Letter 4

Key in the parts of the letter shown below and then drag and drop (see page 8) them into the correct order. If you have access to a printer, print and route the required copies. Save your file as Letter 4.

 Note — Try to complete this task *before* checking with the suggested answer on page 109.

Letter details

❶ Copies of this letter will be sent to T O'Malley, R Walsh and one copy will be retained for filing.

❷ The subject heading is ZUZISSI 890.

❸ The sender's reference is Ref PB/AA.

❹ The letter is being sent to Mr Stephen Walsh, Arden Vale, Castlebar, Co Mayo.

❺ Use a personal salutation and complimentary close.

❻ The designation of the signatory is Customer Relations.

❼ The letter will be signed by Paula Breen.

❽ The body of the letter is set out below:

```
Thank you for your enquiry about the Zuzissi 890, the best selling
small car in Europe.  I have pleasure in enclosing a price list and
colour brochures for all Zuzissi cars and commercial vehicles currently
available on the Irish market.

As national distributors we do not deal directly with the general
public and I would therefore ask you to kindly contact one of our 30
agents spread throughout the country.  Our agents are always happy to
discuss customers' requirements and to arrange test drives.  Most of
our agents are happy to accept trade-ins and, of course, Zuzissi
interest-free loans are available to all suitable applicants.
Remember, too, that our agents also stock a good selection of
guaranteed second-hand Zuzissi models.

Your local Zuzissi agents are Davitt Motors Ltd, Land League Square,
Castlebar.  Davitt Motors are an established firm with a reputation
for helpfulness, courtesy and after-sales service.  Why not give them
a call today or contact Michael Davitt on (093) 85491.
```

❾ The sender's address is:

Zuzissi Motors Ltd
Naas Road
Dublin 12
Ireland

tel: (01) 765012
e-mail: zuzissi_irl@eircom.net
web: http://www.zuzissi_ireland.com

Running a macro

To run the above macro, bring the insertion point to where you want to insert the table. Click **Tools**, **Macro**, **Macros**. Select the macro you wish to use, i.e. BlankTable, and click **Run**.

▶ *Macro 2*

Create a macro to generate the table below. The first row should be formatted with grey-20% shading. Save as RepublicSales.

Sales in the Republic of Ireland	P O'Reilly	J Wilson	M Flynn	Total
	€	€	€	€
Car Parts				
Cameras				
Footwear				
Total				

▶ *Macro 3*

Create a macro to generate the letterhead below. Save as LetterHead.

McCorquodale College of Business
57 Church Street
Tullamore
Co Offaly
Ireland

tel: 0906 795429
e-mail: mmccb7
web: http://mmccb7.ie

▶ *Letter 5*

Now we add a FOR THE ATTENTION OF line to a business letter. This line should be typed in block capitals, one clear line after the date and one clear line above the inside address. This style is sometimes used to direct a letter to a specific person in a company while at the same time addressing the letter to a company in general.

 Note — An impersonal salutation and complimentary close is always used with this style.

Key in the letter below and drag and drop the different letter parts into the correct order. When you have completed this task, check your answer with the suggested answer on page 110. Save this task as Letter 5.

❶ The letter will be signed by Michael Hopkins.

❷ The sender's reference is MH/BK.

❸ The designation of the signatory is Chief Executive.

❹ The letter should be addressed impersonally to the company, Lewis & Co Ltd, Clara Road, Tullamore, Co Offaly and marked for the attention of Michael Lewis, Chief Buyer.

❺ Sender's address:
ALL IRELAND WHOLESALE LTD
DUBLIN ROAD
ATHLONE
IRELAND
tel: 090 7893510
e-mail: aiw@eircom.net
web: http://www.aiw.com

❻ The body of the letter is set out below:

```
As part of our pursuit of excellence we have now completed a customer
survey in the Republic.  From this survey we are delighted to learn
that virtually all of our customers, including Lewis & Co Ltd,
Tullamore are complimentary about our general level of service.

Some customers did, however, mention that they would like to see an
increase in our range of leisure goods, particularly goods like golf
and fishing equipment.

We have now responded by introducing a number of exciting new
products, including Watertex foul weather gear.  Watertex is a fully
waterproof material that actually 'breathes', just like cotton or
other similar fabrics.  We are happy to announce that we have been
appointed sole Irish distributors for this revolutionary new product.

We have pleasure in enclosing a copy of our greatly expanded brochure
and we look forward to hearing from you soon or seeing you in person
in our Athlone showrooms.
```

Other special marks or indications

Apart from FOR THE ATTENTION OF, other special indications such as URGENT, PRIVATE or PERSONAL may be used. All indications are typed in the same way as the FOR THE ATTENTION OF line.

Macros

A Word macro is a mini computer program containing Word commands and actions.

▶ Macro 1 – Creating a simple macro

The simplest way to create a macro is to record a series of actions that you perform while working on a document. First click **Tools** menu, **Macro**, **Record New Macro**. The Record Macro dialog box appears, as shown below.

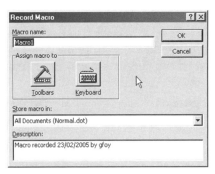

In the Macro name box, type the name of your new macro. Let's call ours 'SalesTable', and click OK. (Please note: No spaces are allowed in a macro name). The mouse pointer changes and now has an icon of a cassette attached to it. Also, a toolbar with Stop Recording and Pause Recording buttons appears. From this point on, Word will record all keystrokes and mouse clicks until the Stop Recording button is clicked.

We are going to create a macro capable of producing the table below.

❶ Click the Tables and Borders button on the Standard toolbar. This will open the Tables and Borders toolbar.

❷ On the Tables and Borders toolbar, click the Insert Table button. In the Insert Table dialog box, type 6 in the columns box and 5 in the rows box, then click OK.

❸ The required table outline appears with the cursor in the first cell. Hold down the Shift key and press the right arrow, ⟶, six times to select the first row. On the Tables and Borders toolbar, click the Shading and Colour down arrow. In the colour palette that appears, click the third box to apply 'Grey-10%' shading. The first row of the table is now formatted with the required shading.

❹ To deselect the shaded column, press the left arrow, ⟵ , once. The insertion point will now appear in the first cell. Type 'Department' in the first cell and use the right and left and up and down arrows to insert the remainder of the text in the table below.

❺ Click the Stop Recording button on the Macro toolbar.

Department	Quarter 1	Quarter 2	Quarter 3	Quarter 4	Total
Gents					
Ladies					
Footwear					
Total					

 Please note — It is not possible to use the mouse pointer to select text, etc. when recording a macro.

Now type and drag and drop the letter parts below into position. When you have finished check your work with the suggested model answer on page 111. Save this letter as Letter 6.

❶ The subject heading is 'hire of grass seed barrow'.

❷ Use a personal salutation and complimentary close.

❸ The designation of the signatory is Director.

❹ The inside address is Mr Rodney Smyth, Pinewood Cottage, South Riding Road, Clonmel.

❺ The sender's reference is POS/AM.

❻ The letter will be signed by Patrick O'Shea.

❼ Mark this letter urgent. (Be careful to use block capital letters for all special marks.)

❽ The body of the letter is set out below:

```
On 15 September last you hired one of our grass seed barrows for two
days.  To date this barrow has not been returned and hire charges
now stand at €523.50.

I therefore regret to inform you that unless hire charges are paid in
full and the barrow returned within three days we shall have to put
this matter in the hands of our solicitors.  Should this become
necessary you will be liable for all legal expenses.

I enclose a copy of the hire docket showing our conditions, your
signature and the date in question.
```

❾ The sender's address is:

CLONMEL TOOL HIRE
DUNGARVAN ROAD
CLONMEL
IRELAND
TEL (0908) 54124
E-MAIL clonmeltoolhire7@eircom.net
WEB http://www.hireclonmel7.com

Key in the exercise below and save it as Pictures 6. The logo may be created as explained on page 220.

ADVANCED WORD PROCESSING COURSE
USING MICROSOFT WORD 2006

Course participants should be familiar with the computer keyboard and have an intermediate knowledge of Microsoft Word. During the course, emphasis will be placed on the production of advanced word processing outputs, which involve sophisticated typographical, formatting and layout presentations.

WHEN AND WHERE

Starting
Friday 29 June 2003, 8.00 – 10.00 pm
Location
McCorquodale College of Business
42 Mardyke Street, Buncrana, Ireland
Duration
2 hours x 3 weeks

COURSE CONTENT

FORMS
Create forms
Form templates[1]
Creating a form template
Inserting fields in a form

MACROS
Tasks
Automating tasks
Administering macros[2]
Toolbars and menus
Creating buttons
Creating custom menus

REFERENCE
Document information
Referencing document information
Inserting bookmarks
Footnotes and endnotes
Inserting footnotes
Inserting endnotes

TIME SAVERS
Time savers within Word
Using time savers
Creating a document using a template

LANGUAGES
Checking spelling and grammar
Changing a word using a thesaurus

DOCUMENTS
Document versions
Creating document versions
Distributing a document

ADVANCED WEB CREATION
HTML pages
Modifying an HTML page
Saving documents as web pages
Editing web pages

PREPARATION
Margins
Setting book margins
Indexing a document

---

[1] A master document that can be used to create other similar documents.
[2] A single Word command that initiates a series of actions.

Page breaks

The amount of text that fits on the first page of a document depends on factors such as paper size, page setup, font and font size. In long documents, text automatically runs onto a second page and a dotted line appears across the bottom of the screen to indicate that a **soft page break** has been created.

When a soft page break comes at an inappropriate place, it may be necessary to insert a **hard page break**. Such a break appears as a continuous line across the screen.

To insert a hard page break, click the Insert menu, then click **Break**. Make sure **Page Break** is selected in the Break dialog box, then click OK.

A quick way to insert a page break is to use the keyboard command **Ctrl+Return**.

Tear-off sections

Tear-off sections usually consist of a short form that the addressee is requested to detach, fill in and then return. To type a tear-off section, proceed as follows:

❶ Leave one clear line after the body a letter.

❷ Insert a straight line that extends from the left to the right margin. Leave one clear line.

❸ Type the straight lines required (see instructions above).

❹ Leave one clear character space between a typed word and a following line and between a line and a following word, as illustrated below:

SURNAME _____ FIRST NAME _____

ADDRESS _____

Insert text boxes from the Drawing toolbar to complete this exercise. Save as Pictures 5.

Irish Association of
Barbershop Singers
**2006
Convention**

```
Athlone
BARBERSHOP
HARMONY
CONCERT
```

Saturday 15 October at 8.00 pm

Dean Crowe Hall

**Tickets €5.00 –
GAP/Students €3.50
Available at
Athlone Chamber of
Commerce
Tel 0902 73173, Fax 0902 73326**

Registration fee: €10.00, which
includes tickets to all events.
Competition entry fee: Quartet –
€15.00, Chorus €30.00.
For more details, tickets, fees, etc.
contact: Siobhan Bigley, Athlone
Chamber of Commerce.

**Irish Barbershop Convention
14–16 October 2006 ATHLONE
Co Westmeath
Ireland**

Programme

<u>FRIDAY</u> – PRINCE OF WALES HOTEL

6.00 pm – Registration & Informal
Get-together

<u>SATURDAY</u> – DEAN CROWE HALL

10.30 am–5.00 pm – Competitions

<u>Categories</u>: National Men's & Women's Quartet
Competitions
International Men's & Women's Quartet Competitions
National & International Chorus Competitions

8.00 pm–10.30 pm – Gala Concert

Featuring Prize Winners & Special Guests
PRINCE OF WALES HOTEL

11.30 pm–till Late – Afterglow

<u>SUNDAY</u> – PRINCE OF WALES HOTEL

1.00 pm – Farewell Get-together

▶ Letter 7

Key in the following circular letter and drag and drop the different letter parts into their correct positions. When you have finished, check your answer with the suggested model answer on page 112. Save as Letter 7.

❶ Tear-off section.

```
--------------------------------------------------------------------------------
     SPECIAL JOURNAL OFFER

     I wish to avail of the special introductory offer from Personal
     Assistant Power and I enclose my cheque for €20.

     Surname _____    First Name  _____

     Address _____

     _____

     Telephone No _____
```

❷ The body of the letter is set out below:

```
We are delighted to introduce Personal Assistant Power, the new
monthly journal for the upwardly mobile secretary and personal
assistant.

For too long secretaries have been unable to highlight the important
role they play in the world of business - a role that has become
increasingly pivotal with every passing year.  Indeed, the secretary
of today should be thought of as working in 'office information
systems' rather than filling the role of the secretary of old.

Personal Assistant Power is your forum, your chance to exchange ideas
and to heighten the profile of the modern PA.  Your complimentary
copy of the first issue is enclosed and we should be delighted to
receive your comments and suggestions for future editions.

Selected secretaries, such as yourself, can now avail of a special
half-price subscription by simply completing the tear-off section
below and returning it to us not later than 30 November 2006.
```

❸ Designation of signatory: Circulation Manager.

❹ Sender's address:

O'Connor Publishing
11 Grafton Street
Dublin 2

❺ Name of signatory: Assumpta Galvin.

❻ Salutation: Dear Reader.

❱ *Pictures 3*

Key in the text below, then insert a ClipArt picture with a number of people in it and reformat the wrapping style to in front of text. Change the picture size to 2 cm height and make two additional copies. Then crop and arrange the pictures as shown below. Save as Pictures 3.

There were five.

Then there were four.

And then there were three.

Print screen

Sometimes you may want to make a copy of something that appears on your computer screen. This is done by pressing the **Print Screen** key and then going to **Edit**, **Paste** to insert a 'picture' of the screen you copied. If you only want to make a copy of an active Word window, i.e. a window with a bright, not dimmed, title bar, hold down the **Alt** key while pressing the **Print Screen** key.

❱ *Pictures 4*

Click the **Help** menu and select **About Microsoft Word**, then make a copy of the active window (the About Microsoft Word window) and close it. Then paste the picture into your document and reformat it using the 'In front of text' wrapping style Crop the picture so that only the logo below remains, then drag the logo into centre of your screen, as shown below. Save this exercise as Pictures 4.

Circular letters

Organisations sometimes send the same letter to many different people, for example the secretary of a camogie club may send a letter to each member of the club. Such letters do not contain an inside address and they are addressed impersonally as 'Dear Member', 'Dear Parent', 'Dear Customer', etc. This style is convenient for the sender but, as it is clear to recipients that the letters are impersonal, it is generally better to personalise correspondence. Circular letters are easily personalised through the use of the mail merge (see page 210).

Note the following procedure may be followed when **not** using mail merge.

❶ If references are required, they should be keyed in as in standard letters.

❷ The date may be keyed in using one of the following styles:
  • 9 December 2006
  • December 2006
  • Date as postmark.

❸ The inside address is often not included. However, space should be left so that it may be added by hand (if required).

❹ Salutations such as Dear Member, Dear Customer, Dear Madam, etc. may be used. Alternatively, just the word 'Dear' is keyed in and the rest of the salutation is added by hand.

❺ If the writer **wishes** to sign a circular letter, the complimentary close, name of signatory and designation should be keyed in the usual way.

❻ If the writer **does not wish** to sign, the complimentary close should be keyed in and followed on the next line by the organisation's name. Then **one** clear line should be left and followed on the next line by the writer's title or designation. See example below:

```
Yours sincerely
Ballinasloe Camogie Club

Breda Mahon
Secretary
```

Resizing objects

Select the object. Position the mouse over one of the resizing handles; it will change to a double arrow. Click and drag to resize the object.

The Picture toolbar

When an object is selected, the Picture toolbar should automatically appear, as shown below. Hold the mouse pointer over each button in turn. After a second, a pop-up label will give the name of the relevant button.

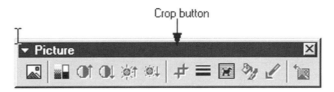

Crop button

Cropping an object/picture

It takes a little practice to crop a picture successfully. First select the picture/object to be cropped and note that the sizing handles appear. Click the crop button on the Picture toolbar. Then place the mouse pointer **exactly over** one of the sizing tools, so that the pointer changes to a ⊢ shape, then click and hold down the left mouse button and drag over the area to be cropped.

Text wrapping

Refer to the Format Picture dialog box on the previous page, and note that text can be wrapped around an object/picture in different ways: **Square**, **Tight**, **Behind text** or **In front of text**. Two other text-wrapping options, **Through** and **Top and bottom**, are available by clicking the **Advanced** button in the Format Picture dialog box. When the **Advanced Layout** dialog box opens, click the **Text Wrapping** tab.

▶ Pictures 1

Key in the text below, then find and insert a suitable ClipArt picture by entering the keyword 'worker' in the **Insert ClipArt** dialog box. Select the required picture and click **Format** menu, **Picture**, and in the **Format Picture** dialog box, click **Layout** and **Tight**. Then click the **Size** tab and enter '3 cm' in the **Height** box. Drag the picture into the text as shown. Save as Pictures 1.

Virtual Help

The Association of Virtual Assistants of Ireland about a further awareness of the profession of overloaded businesspeople to find

A VA is a new breed of home-office worker. who have cut their teeth in big corporations and jam by providing a variety of specialist services

(AVA Ireland) has been established to bring virtual assisting and to make it easier for a virtual assistant (VA) quickly.

They are highly skilled office administrators who offer to get you out of an administrative on a pay-as-you-go basis.

▶ Pictures 2

Retrieve Pictures 1 and add the text below. Reformat the picture with the Square wrapping style and drag the picture into the middle of the three paragraphs. Save this exercise as Pictures 2.

VAs claim to offer a wide rang of services to meet business needs, including everything from travel arrangement to transcription, bookkeeping to desktop publishing, word processing to web design. Because they are freelancers working from their own premises, there is no need to worry about providing equipment or office space. They also do not require pension provision, holiday or sick pay.

▶ Letter 8

Key in the circular letter parts that follow, then drag and drop them into place. Check your work on page 113. Save as Letter 8.

❶ The subject heading is Membership Subscriptions 2006.

❷ Use a personal complimentary close.

❸ The designation of the signatory is Secretary.

❹ The body of the letter is as follows:

```
It's that time of the year again when membership subscriptions are
due.  This year we would like members to make a special effort to
pay fees promptly and thus help to reduce our overdraft interest
charges.

This year fees are as follows:

Family €200
Individual €140
Intermediate €110
Junior €80
```

❺ The sender's address is Littletown Tennis Club, Chestnut Close, Littletown, Co Offaly, Ireland, tel 094 78953, e-mail lttennis@eircom.net.

❻ Mary Lohan will sign the letter.

Part 12
Graphics, Macros, etc.

▷▷▷▷▷▷▷▷▷▷▷▶▷▷▷▷

ClipArt

Microsoft Word includes a large selection of pictures, images, background designs, etc. ClipArt images can be inserted by going to the **Insert** menu, **Picture** and **ClipArt**. You can then select a category or search for an image type by typing a keyword such as 'business' in the **Search for clips** box in the **Insert ClipArt** dialog box, as shown below.

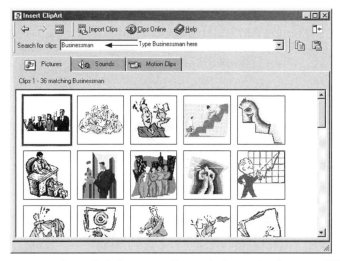

Click the picture you want to use, then click **Insert clip** and close the **Insert ClipArt** dialog box.

Inline objects

When you insert a ClipArt picture it will normally be an 'inline object', i.e. is a picture that is inserted in line with the text at the insertion point. Inline pictures/objects cannot be moved easily around a document. When inline objects are selected, black resizing handles appear.

Floating objects

Floating objects float over or behind text. When such an object is selected, white resizing handles appear. To move a floating object, select it, position the mouse over it and drag the object to its new location.

Changing an inline object to a floating object

Select the object. Go to the **Format** menu, click **Picture** and in the **Format Picture** dialog box, select **In front of text** or any of the options apart from **In line with text** (as shown below).

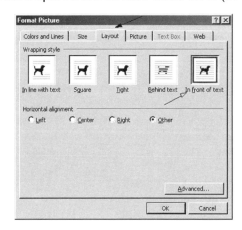

Letter templates

In theory, the quickest way to key in a letter is to use a letter template or the letter wizard. However, as the templates and letter wizard available are Americanised, organisations generally create their own letter templates. To create a template, key in the text that is unlikely to change from letter to letter, such as the sender's address, and in the **Save As** dialog box under **Save as type**, click down to **Document Template** and give your template a suitable name in the **File name** box. Then click **Save**.

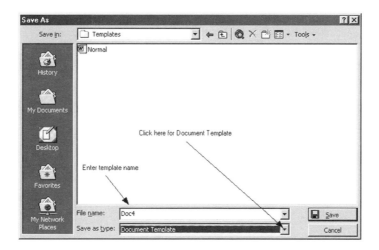

To use the available templates, click the **File menu**, select **New** and click the **Letters and Faxes** tab in the **New** dialog box. A number of letter templates are available, such as Contemporary Letter and Ele.g.ant Letter. Click the different templates and examine them in the **Preview** window, which is on the right side of the New dialog box. Decide which style you wish to use and then click OK. Templates can be thought of as forms onto which details may be added.

> **Note** — Files saved as normal Word documents can also be retrieved and used as templates. However, such templates will not appear in the **New** dialog box when **File, New** is clicked.

▶ Letter 9

❶ Retrieve the Letter 4 file and copy the letter heading to a new document.

❷ Save this new document as a template called Zuzissi Motors.

❸ Close both Letter 4 and the Zuzissi Motors template.

❹ Click **File, New** (and the **General** tab if necessary) and double click the Zuzissi Motors template.

❺ Set out a letter to Charles Lennon, Lennon Motors, Church Street, Tullamore, Co Offaly for signature by Paula Breen. The designation of the signatory is Customer Relations. The body of the letter is:

```
Thank you for your recent enquiry, which is receiving attention.

One of our directors will be in contact with you shortly. In the
meantime, I enclose a number of brochures, which give details of all
Zuzissi models currently available in the Republic of Ireland.
```

❻ Save this letter as Letter 9 and then check your work with the model answer on page 114.

When the Data Form dialog box appears, click **View Source**.

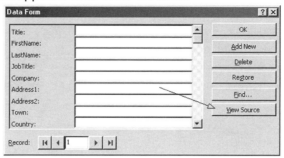

The Mail Merge toolbar changes. Click the Manage Fields button.

In the Manage Fields dialog box, click the **Grade** field and then **Remove**. Type **Date** in the **Field Name** box and then **Add**. Similarly, type **Time** in the Field Name box and then Add. Then click **OK**.

Then click the Data Form button  and in the Data Form dialog box, add the date and time for each candidate. Save this file as MM Data 2 in the Interview folder.

Then go to Section 3 of the Mail Merge Helper and conclude the exercise in the same way you concluded Mail Merge Exercise 1.

Indicating that a letter is a continuation

When a business letter continues onto a second page, it is important to key in a continuation symbol at the bottom of page one and a continuation heading at the top of page two, as shown below.

 Note — As students often forget to indicate that a letter has been continued, this section should be studied carefully.

Letter page 1   Letter page 2

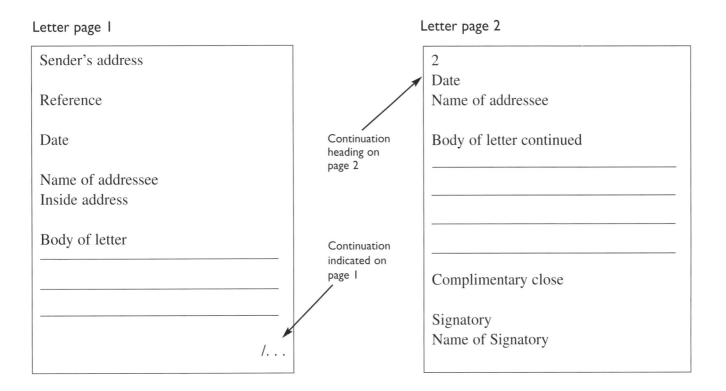

At the bottom of page 1

❶ Key in a continuation symbol, as shown above. This symbol consists of a forward slash followed by three dots. Alternative continuation symbols, or a 'catchword', may be used.

❷ Use the **Right Align** button on the Formatting toolbar to move the continuation symbol to the right margin.

❸ When a letter continues onto a second page, the first page should be arranged so that at least three lines of the letter are continued onto the second page. In no circumstances is it permissible to commence the second page with the complimentary close. If necessary, insert a page break (see page **98**).

At the top of page 2

❶ Key in the page number, the date and the title and name of the addressee, in single spacing, as shown above.

❷ Leave a clear line and continue with the body of the letter, as shown above.

❸ Continuation headings may also be keyed in using double-line spacing. In this case, two clear lines should be left between the heading and the body of the letter.

Continuation paper

❶ The paper used for continuation should be of the same quality and colour as the headed paper. Continuation paper may be blank or printed with the words 'Page number', 'Date' and 'Name of addressee'.

❷ The second and subsequent pages of letters should never be printed on normal headed paper.

Mail Merge Exercise 2

Assume now that the students in the database we created, MM Data1, are in fact applicants for a job with Sharpe Engineering Ltd, Market Street, Mullingar, tel 098 879123, e-mail sengmul@eircom.net. A letter must be sent to each job applicant offering him or her an interview on the date and time shown below.

Ms Mary Loughnane	Mr Patrick Lynch	Mr Mohammad Javed	Ms Sarah O'Reilly	Mr Stephen Waters
Tara Grove	42 Chestnut Walk	Main Street	70 McDermot Terrace	67 North View
Navan	Cork	Youghal	Drogheda	Edgeworthstown
Co Meath	Co Cork	Co Cork	Co Louth	Co Longford
22 November 2006	22 November 2006	22 November 2006	22 November 2006	22 November 2006
10.00 am	11.00 am	12.00 am	2.00 pm	3.00 pm
Ms Anne Fox	Mr Michael Carter	Ms Joan Logan	Mr John Jackson	Ms Caroline Steward
Priory Park	29 Fr Griffin Road	34 High Street	128 Sarsfield Drive	2 Royal Crescent
Moate	Midleton	Ballina	Clonakilty	Martinstown
Co Westmeath	Co Cork	Co Mayo	Co Cork	Co Antrim
23 November 2006	23 November 2006	23 November 2006	23 November 2006	23 November 2006
10.00 am	11.00 am	12.00 am	2.00 pm	3.00 pm

Create a **form letter** that will be signed by Agnes Whelan, Human Resources Department.

The body of the form letter is as follows:

> Thank you for your interest in Sharpe Engineering.
>
> We would like to discuss your application further and accordingly we would like you to attend our offices in Mullingar on   at   .
>
> If you are unable to come for interview at the above time, please contact me at your earliest convenience.

Save the form letter in a folder called Interviews with the file name MM Letter 2. Then go to the **Tools** menu, select **Mail Merge** and click **Create**, **Form Letters**, **Active Window** in Section 1 of the Mail Merge Helper.

Then proceed to Section 2 of the Mail Merge Helper and click **Get Data**, **Open Data Source**. In the Open Data Source window, open the MM Data1 file we created in Mail Merge Exercise 1.

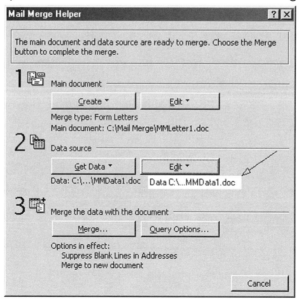

Envelopes and labels

Click the **Tools** menu, click **Envelopes and Labels** and then click the **Envelopes** tab in the Envelopes and Labels dialog box. If a letter file is open, Word automatically selects the inside address; it assumes a number of consecutive, short lines constitute the required address.

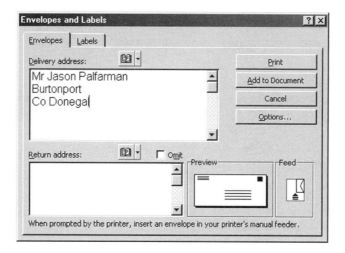

Please note

❶ If Word selects the wrong lines for the inside address, select the correct lines, then click the **Tools** menu again and repeat the steps set out above.

❷ It is generally better to click the **Omit** box, which is above the **Return address** box.

❸ To alter the way an envelope is fed into a printer, click the **Feed** icon.

❹ To vary the position of the **Delivery address** on the envelope, click the envelope icon under **Preview**. The **Envelopes Options** dialog box opens (as shown below). Click the arrows in the **From left** and/or **From top** boxes as necessary.

To print envelopes of a particular size, click the **Options** tab (as shown below), then click the arrow in the **Envelope size** box (as shown below).

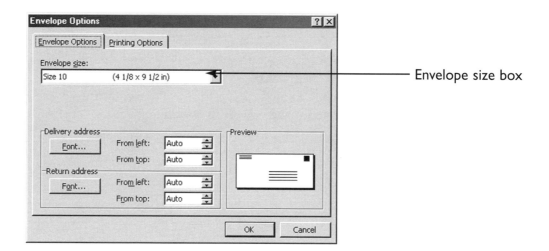

Envelope size box

Merging selected records only

To merge selected records only, click the **From** button in the Merge dialog box and fill in the first and last record required in the **From** and **To** boxes.

Query Options

The Merge window also gives you the option to extract all records that meet certain criteria. Click **Query Options** to open the Query Options dialog box, as shown below.

For example, to create letters only to students that were awarded a Distinction grade, click the down arrow in the **Field** column and select **Grade**, then key in **Distinction** in the **Compare to** column, as shown below. Finally, click **OK**.

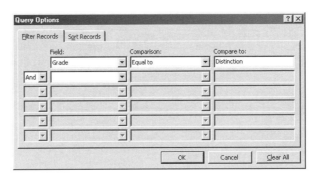

To create letters only to students from Co Cork who were awarded a Distinction grade, click the down arrow in the second row of the field column and select **County**. Then key in Co Cork in the **Compare to** column. Finally, click **OK**.

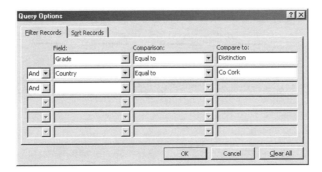

Using and altering an existing database

In the exercise overleaf, Mail Merge Exercise 2, we shall use the database we created, MM Data 1, and alter it so that unwanted fields are deleted and new fields are added.

General notes about envelopes

❶ Envelopes are generally printed in single-line spacing with blocked style layout.

❷ Envelopes should correspond <u>exactly</u> with the inside address section of the relevant letter. For example, if there is a SPECIAL INDICATION such as FOR THE ATTENTION OF, PRIVATE, PERSONAL, CONFIDENTIAL or URGENT in the letter, there should be a similar indication on the envelope.

❸ The address should be printed approximately halfway down an envelope and one-third of the way in from the left-hand edge.

❹ If there is a SPECIAL INDICATION, the address should start two single lines higher than usual.

❺ Particular indications such as AIRMAIL or REGISTERED MAIL should appear in capitals at the top left corner of an envelope.

❻ BY HAND or a similar indication should be printed in the position normally reserved for stamps, i.e. the top right corner.

❼ FREEPOST and POSTE RESTANTE should be printed after the name of the addressee. (POSTE RESTANTE indicates that mail should be kept for collection at the post office that handles mail for the address in question.)

Window envelopes

Window envelopes have a transparent section which allows the inside address to be seen through the envelope. Stationery used with window envelopes is usually marked to indicate where the inside addresses should be printed. Window envelopes are generally only used for impersonal mail such as invoices or statements.

Stick-on labels

To print addresses on labels, click **Tools**, click **Envelopes and Labels** then click **Labels** in the Envelopes and Labels dialog box.

Practice

Practise keying in and then printing the following addresses. Use envelopes and then practise printing on Avery labels, if available. If neither envelopes nor labels are available, print on ordinary A4 paper.

❶ Mrs Mary McGarry, 7 Whitebeam Avenue, Tralee, Co Kerry, Ireland.

❷ Ms Concepta Joyce, 78 Rahoon Drive, Northern Drive, Belfast. Mark this letter 'Urgent'.

❸ Ms M Smyth, c/o Powers Ltd, 1st Floor, 56 Grafton Street, Dublin 2.

❹ Mr John O'Connor, O'Connor & Co Ltd, 9 Devonish Square, Cork. Mark the envelope 'Confidential'.

❺ Ms Bernadette Logan, 4 Summerhill Road, Sligo. Mark this envelope 'By Hand'.

❱ *Letter 10*

Retrieve Letter 5, increase the font to 16 points Times New Roman and display the letter over two pages. Save as Letter 10 and check your work with the model answer on page 115. (Please note that as the model answer is shown on just one page, the font used is less than 16 points.)

Key in the data relating to the first student, Ms Mary Loughnane, then click **Add New** to add details of the next student, and so on. Note — resist the tendency to click **OK** until you have entered the records for **all** students. Save the data file again.

Ms Mary Loughnane	Mr Patrick Lynch	Mr Mohammad Javed	Ms Sarah O'Reilly	Mr Stephen Waters
Tara Grove	42 Chestnut Walk	Main Street	70 McDermot Terrace	67 North View
Navan	Cork	Youghal	Drogheda	Edgeworthstown
Co Meath	Co Cork	Co Cork	Co Louth	Co Longford
Merit	Pass	Distinction	Pass	Merit
Ms Anne Fox	Mr Michael Carter	Ms Joan Logan	Mr John Jackson	Ms Caroline Steward
Priory Park	29 Fr Griffin Road	34 High Street	128 Sarsfield Drive	2 Royal Crescent
Moate	Midleton	Ballina	Clonakilty	Martinstown
Co Westmeath	Co Cork	Co Mayo	Co Cork	Co Antrim
Pass	Distinction	Distinction	Distinction	Merit

Click the **View Merged Data** button ⟪ ⟫ᴬᴮᶜ on the Mail Merge toolbar to check that the first merged record merged correctly.

Now proceed to Section 3 of the Mail Merge Helper and click the **Merge** button.

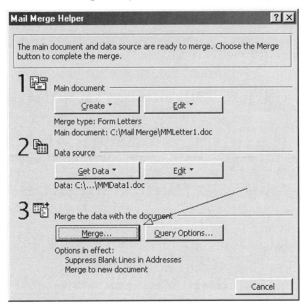

The Merge window appears, as shown below. Click the **Merge** button.

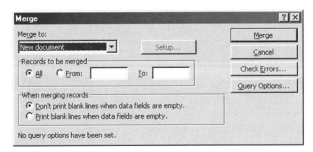

A new document is created that contains a personalised letter to each student, with a page break between each letter. Save this new file in the Mail Merge Exercise folder, using the file name Merge1.

Full punctuation and other letter styles

As some employers still insist on the use of full punctuation, the following notes have been included for reference purposes.

Using full punctuation

❶ Full stops are inserted after abbreviations, for example Ms. S. R. Lynch, B. Comm.

❷ Never insert full stops in the 24-hour clock, e.g. 1750 hours (i.e. ten to six in the evening).

❸ A full stop must be inserted when keying in the 12-hour clock, e.g. 5.50 pm. (This rule also applies when using open punctuation.)

❹ Some abbreviations and acronyms may be keyed in without full stops, such as USA, RTÉ, VDU, NCVA, RTC, NCEA.

❺ **Never** insert full stops when abbreviating metric measurements, e.g. 2 m x 600 mm. Only when **full punctuation** is used should full stops be inserted in the abbreviations used for imperial measurements, e.g. 7 ft. 3 in. x 5 ft. 2 in.

 Note — Acronyms are words that have been made up from the initial letters of other words, e.g. VAT comes from Value Added Tax and PAYE comes from Pay As You Earn.

House style and other letter styles

As stated, the blocked style (with open punctuation) is the layout style recommended in this text. However, though the use of blocked style is now generally accepted, some employers are unwilling to accept the use of open punctuation. (Employees should, of course, be prepared to adopt the house style of their organisation.)

Fully blocked letters with full punctuation

When using the above style (see example overleaf), letters are blocked in the usual way and full punctuation is used. The following points should also be noted:

❶ No full stops should be inserted after the FOR ATTENTION line or after the SUBJECT HEADING.

❷ Commas should be inserted after each line and a full stop should be inserted after the last line of the inside address. Postal codes should not be punctuated.

❸ A comma is inserted after the salutation and after the complimentary close.

Semi-blocked letters with open or full punctuation

The semi-blocked style (see example on page 108) may be used with open or full punctuation. The following points should be noted:

❶ The reference should appear at the left margin and the date should end at the right margin.

❷ The subject heading should be centred.

❸ The first word of each paragraph is indented by approximately one centimetre.

❹ The complimentary close should be centred.

❺ The name and title of the signatory should start at the same point as the complimentary close.

The letter should now appear as shown below:

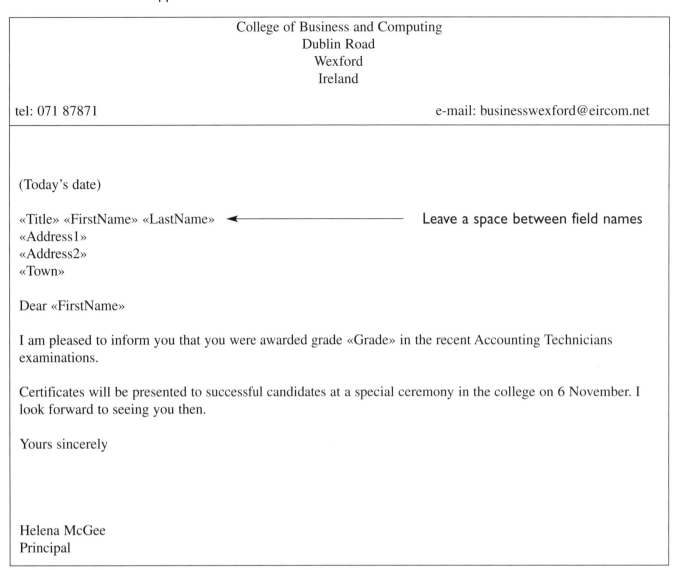

College of Business and Computing
Dublin Road
Wexford
Ireland

tel: 071 87871   e-mail: businesswexford@eircom.net

(Today's date)

«Title» «FirstName» «LastName» ◄———————— Leave a space between field names
«Address1»
«Address2»
«Town»

Dear «FirstName»

I am pleased to inform you that you were awarded grade «Grade» in the recent Accounting Technicians examinations.

Certificates will be presented to successful candidates at a special ceremony in the college on 6 November. I look forward to seeing you then.

Yours sincerely

Helena McGee
Principal

Now that we have worked on the main document, it is time to do more work on the data source. Click the **Mail Merge Helper** 📇 button on the Mail Merge toolbar, or click the **Tools** menu and then click **Mail Merge**. (Remember to keep going back to the Mail Merge Helper as you work through mail merge exercises.)

Click the **Edit** button in Section 2 of the Mail Merge Helper. The Data Form now appears as shown below:

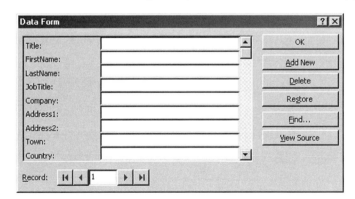

Example of fully blocked letter with full punctuation

SAVILLE SOFTWARE
176 Airport Road,
Belfast
BT6 8DP
UK

tel: 0232 458197
fax: 0232 460881

svw@sssbs.uk
http://www.sssbs.com

Our ref. NVW/AJ

6 October, 2006.

Ballynure Manufacturing Ltd.,
Ballynure Road,
Ballyclare,
Co. Antrim.
BT39 9AG

Dear Sirs,

E-BUSINESS

Further to your enquiry about the relevance of e-business to a company such as yours.

According to an article published in a supplement with *The Sunday Times*, an organisation must do a number of things, including the following, to come to terms with e-business:

1. It must redefine its approach to marketing and no longer simply sell a single product to the world at large. It must focus on specific customers and sell them products and services tailored to their needs.
2. It must exploit its enhanced capacity to analyse data on customers' behaviour and preferences to gain a better understanding of customer needs.
3. It must become more agile and flexible. It must redefine its business around customer needs, refocus capital away from non-core activities and use the Net to establish alliances with business partners that add value up and down the supply chain.
4. Perhaps most important of all, companies that want to succeed in converging industries must be led by courageous decision makers who are on top of their markets, understand their customers and have the vision to know when even a successful business has to change.

I would also refer you to a useful guide called E-BUSINESS ST@RT-UP by Philip Treleaven. It may be ordered online by visiting www.sundaytimes-eshop.co.uk.

When you have had the times to consider the above, I suggest that you contact me again with a view to formulating a comprehensive e-business strategy for Ballynure Manufacturing Ltd.

Yours sincerely,

Samuel V. Wilson
Partner

We now need to add the Town, County and Grade fields by keying them into the **Field Name** box and clicking the **Add Field Name** button after each name. Resist the common tendency to click **OK** until all the required field names have been added and are in the right order.

> **Notes** —
> ❶ No spaces are accepted in a field name.
>
> ❷ To change the position of a field name, select it and use the up or down arrow in the **Create Data Source** dialog box. (You may wish to have field names in the order they will appear in your letter.)

When you have finished working on field names, click **OK**. The **Save As** dialog box appears, as shown below. At this stage it is important to check the **Save As** dialog box to ensure that the correct folder appears in the **Save in** box and the correct file name is entered in the **File name** box. For this exercise, save the file using the file name MM Data1 in the Mail Merge directory you created when saving MM Letter1.

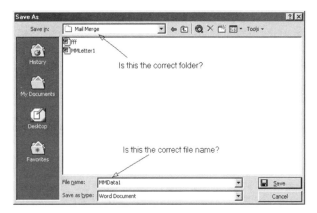

After you have checked that you are saving in the correct folder and with the correct file same, click **Save**. We shall work on the main document.

Click **Edit Main Document** and then click the Insert Merge Field button on the Mail Merge toolbar. Then select and insert the required fields in the correct places. Save the letter again.

Example of semi-blocked letter with full punctuation

SAVILLE SOFTWARE
176 Airport Road,
Belfast
BT6 8DP
UK

tel: 0232 458197
fax: 0232 460881

svw@sssbs.uk
http://www.sssbs.com

Our ref. NVW/AJ   6 October, 2006

Ballynure Manufacturing Ltd.,
Ballynure Road,
Ballyclare,
Co. Antrim.
BT39 9AG

Dear Sirs,

E-BUSINESS

Further to your enquiry about the relevance of e-business to a company such as yours.

According to an article published in a supplement with *The Sunday Times*, an organisation must do a number of things, including the following, to come to terms with e-business:

1. It must redefine its approach to marketing and no longer simply sell a single product to the world at large. It must focus on specific customers and sell them products and services tailored to their needs.
2. It must exploit its enhanced capacity to analyse data on customers' behaviour and preferences to gain a better understanding of customer needs.
3. It must become more agile and flexible. It must redefine its business around customer needs, refocus capital away from non-core activities and use the Net to establish alliances with business partners that add value up and down the supply chain.
4. Perhaps most important of all, companies that want to succeed in converging industries must be led by courageous decision makers who are on top of their markets, understand their customers and have the vision to know when even a successful business has to change.

I would also refer you to a useful guide called E-BUSINESS ST@RT-UP by Philip Treleaven. It may be ordered online by visiting www.sundaytimes-eshop.co.uk.

When you have had the times to consider the above, I suggest that you contact me again with a view to formulating a comprehensive e-business strategy for Ballynure Manufacturing Ltd.

Yours sincerely,

Samuel V. Wilson
Partner

Now click the **Tools** menu and select **Mail Merge**. The dialog box appears. Click **Create** in Section 1 of the **Mail Merge Helper** dialog box that appears (see below) and click **Form Letters** in the drop-down list.

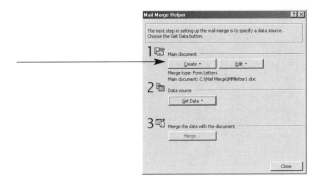

In the dialog box that appears, click **Active Window** (see below). This means that the letter you saved, MM Letter1, will be used in the mail merge process.

Now it's time to progress to Section 2 of the Mail Merge Helper. Click **Get Data** and click **Create Data Source** in the drop-down list.

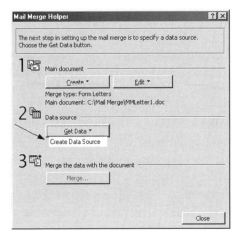

The **Create Data Source** dialog box appears (see below) and common letter field names are automatically added. For the present exercise, you only need to retain the fields Title, FirstName, LastName, Address1, Address2. Therefore, select and then remove other field names by clicking **Remove Field Name**.

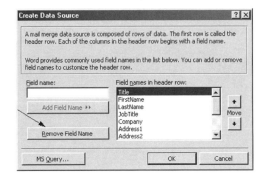

Zuzissi Motors Ltd
Naas Road
Dublin 12
Ireland

tel: (01) 765012
e-mail: zuzissi_irl@eircom.net
web: http://www.zuzissi_ireland.com

Ref PB/AA

Today's date

Mr Stephen Walsh
Arden Vale
Castlebar
Co Mayo

Dear Mr Walsh

ZUZISSI 890

Thank you for your enquiry about the Zuzissi 890, the best selling small car in Europe. I have pleasure in enclosing a price list and colour brochures for all Zuzissi cars and commercial vehicles currently available on the Irish market.

As national distributors we do not deal directly with the general public and I would therefore ask you to kindly contact one of our 30 agents spread throughout the country. Our agents are always happy to discuss customers' requirements and to arrange test drives. Most of our agents are happy to accept trade-ins and, of course, Zuzissi interest-free loans are available to all suitable applicants. Remember, too, that our agents also stock a good selection of guaranteed second-hand Zuzissi models.

Your local Zuzissi agents are Davitt Motors Ltd, Land League Square, Castlebar. Davitt Motors are an established firm with a reputation for helpfulness, courtesy and after-sales service. Why not give them a call today or contact Michael Davitt on (093) 85491.

Yours sincerely

Paula Breen
Customer Relations

Encs

cc T O'Malley
    R Walsh
    File

Part 11
Mail Merge

▷▷▷▷▷▷▷▷▷▷►▷▷▷▷

Mail merge involves merging, or combining, a **main document** (such as a letter) with a **data file** (such as a list of names and addresses). In the example below, a college principal uses mail merge to create letters that give the results of an examination to ten different students. The main document, the letter, is keyed in first, but spaces are left for the information that will vary from one letter to another, i.e. the inside address, the salutation and the exam grade achieved.

Mail Merge Exercise 1

Key in and save the main document below as MM Letter 1 in a directory called Mail Merge Exercise. Do not type the text in brackets.

College of Business and Computing
Dublin Road
Wexford
Ireland

tel: 071 87871   e-mail: businesswexford7@eircom.net

Today's date (Go to the **Insert** menu, click **Date and Time** and select the third date format option in the Date and Time dialog box. Click the **Update automatically** checkbox.)

(Leave four line spaces here for the inside address merge fields.)

Dear (leave space for the first name merge field)

I am pleased to inform you that you were awarded grade (leave space for the grade merge field) in the recent Accounting Technicians examinations.

Certificates will be presented to successful candidates at a special ceremony in the college on 6 November. I look forward to seeing you then.

Yours sincerely

Helena McGee
Principal

 Note — Before proceeding, check that you have saved the exercise exactly as stated above.

ALL IRELAND WHOLESALE LTD   tel (090) 7893510
DUBLIN ROAD   e-mail: aiw@eircom.net
ATHLONE   web: http://www.aiw.com
IRELAND

MH/BK

Today's date

FOR THE ATTENTION OF MICHAEL LEWIS, CHIEF BUYER

Lewis & Co Ltd
Clara Road
Tullamore
Co Offaly

Dear Sirs

As part of our pursuit of excellence we have now completed a customer survey in the Republic. From this survey we are delighted to learn that virtually all of our customers, including Lewis & Co Ltd, Tullamore are complimentary about our general level of service.

Some customers did, however, mention that they would like to see an increase in our range of leisure goods, particularly goods like golf and fishing equipment.

We have now responded by introducing a number of exciting new products, including Watertex foul weather gear. Watertex is a fully waterproof material that actually 'breathes', just like cotton or other similar fabrics. We are happy to announce that we have been appointed sole Irish distributors for this revolutionary new product.

We have pleasure in enclosing a copy of our greatly expanded brochure and we look forward to hearing from you soon or seeing you in person in our Athlone showrooms.

Yours faithfully

Michael Hopkins
Chief Executive

Enc

	Joseph Dolan Glass & Windows Ltd, Lynn Industrial Estate, Mullingar, Ireland
Tel 044 7891276	jdgw7@eircom.net http://www.jdgw7.com

National Sales Conference

Mullingar House Hotel, Austin Friars Street, Mullingar
15 September 2006

Agenda

9.15 am–9.30 am	**Registration**
9.30 am–10.05 am	**Company progress**

Ms Helen Vance, Managing Director, will trace the progress of the company for the year to date, including:
- national market share
- market share in each of the four regions.

Ms Vance will also introduce two new products:
- Sun World Patio Porch Doors
- Martin Mirrors.

10.05 am–10.20 am	**Q Mark and ISO 9000 Certification**

Mr Paul O'Toole, Quality Officer, will congratulate staff on reaching these two important quality standards.

10.20 am–11.00 am	**The company, product by product**

Ms Lisa Hand, Sales Manager, will detail the turnover and profitability of the company's principal products:
- Double Glazing
- Single Glazing
- Aluminium Gutters, Fascia and Soffit.

11.00 am–11.10 am	**Coffee break**
11.10 am–11.50 am	**Company, product by product (continued)**

- Aluminium Windows and Doors
- Emergency Replacement Service
- Mirrors and Mirror Design
- Sandblasting

11.50 am–12.20 pm	**Advertising and the search for new products**

Ms Karen Lynch, Marketing Manager, will report on the following:
- the nature and success of the company's advertising strategy
- the ongoing search for new product lines

12.20 pm–1.20 pm	**Lunch**
1.20 pm–2.00 pm	**Targets for the coming year**

Ms Helen Vance, Managing Director, will conclude the meeting by setting out the company's main targets for the coming year.

CLONMEL TOOL HIRE
DUNGARVAN ROAD
CLONMEL
IRELAND
TEL (0908) 54124
E-MAIL clonmeltoolhire7@eircom.net
WEB http://www.hireclonmel7.com

Our ref POS/AM

15 October 2006

URGENT

Mr Rodney Smyth
Pinewood Cottage
South Riding Road
Clonmel

Dear Mr Smyth

HIRE OF GRASS SEED BARROW

On 15 September last you hired one of our grass seed barrows for two days. To date this barrow has not been returned and hire charges now stand at €523.50.

I therefore regret to inform you that unless hire charges are paid in full and the barrow returned within three days we shall have to put this matter in the hands of our solicitors. Should this become necessary you will be liable for all the legal expenses.

I enclose a copy of the hire docket showing our conditions, your signature and the date in question.

Yours sincerely

Patrick O'Shea
Director

Enc

Display 2.12 continued (ii)

Additional notes for TP operator
❶ Allocate the following times for the different items on the agenda:
- (i) 15 minutes
- (ii) 35 minutes
- (iii) 15 minutes
- (iv) 40 minutes
- (v) 10 minutes
- (vi) 40 minutes
- (vii) 30 minutes
- (viii) 1 hour
- (ix) 40 minutes

❷ The sales conference will commence at 9.15 am and conclude at 2.00 pm.

❸ There should no line spaces between the items on the agenda.

❹ The agenda should be top aligned and fit on one page.

Additional information required for certain agenda items

Q Mark and ISO 9000 Certification
Mr Paul O'Toole, Quality Officer, will congratulate staff on reaching these two important quality standards.

The company, product by product
Ms Lisa Hand, Sales Manager, will detail the turnover and profitability of the company's principal products:
- Double Glazing
- Single Glazing
- Aluminium Gutters, Fascia and Soffit.

The company, product by product (continued)
- Aluminium Windows and Doors
- Emergency Replacement Service
- Mirrors and Mirror Design
- Sandblasting.

Advertising and the search for new products
Ms Karen Lynch, Marketing Manager, will report on the following:
- the nature and success of the company's advertising strategy
- the ongoing search for new product lines.

Targets for the coming year and conclusion
Ms Helen Vance, Managing Director, will conclude the meeting by setting out the company's main targets for the coming year.

O'Connor Publishing
11 Grafton Street
Dublin 2

3 November 2006

Dear Reader

We are delighted to introduce *Personal Assistant Power*, the new monthly journal for the upwardly mobile secretary and personal assistant.

For too long secretaries have been unable to highlight the important role they play in the world of business - a role that has become increasingly pivotal with every passing year. Indeed, the secretary of today should be thought of as working in 'office information systems' rather than filling the role of the secretary of old.

Personal Assistant Power is your forum, your chance to exchange ideas and to heighten the profile of the modern PA. Your complimentary copy of the first issue is enclosed and we should be delighted to receive your comments and suggestions for future editions.

Selected secretaries, such as yourself, can now avail of a special half-price subscription by simply completing the tear-off section below and returning it to us not later than 30 November 2006.

Yours sincerely

Assumpta Galvin
Circulation Manager

- -

SPECIAL JOURNAL OFFER

I wish to avail of the special introductory offer from *Personal Assistant Power* and I enclose my cheque for €20.

Surname _____ First Name _____

Address _____

_____

Telephone No _____

Key in the exercise below and save it as Display 2.12. When you have finished, check your answer with the suggested answer on page 209.

Type an agenda from the information set out below. Use 11 points Times New Roman font throughout, unless indicated otherwise. Centre vertically and set margins of 2.5 cm.

Heading

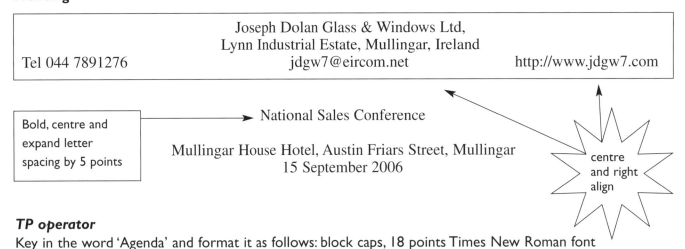

	Joseph Dolan Glass & Windows Ltd,	
	Lynn Industrial Estate, Mullingar, Ireland	
Tel 044 7891276	jdgw7@eircom.net	http://www.jdgw7.com

Bold, centre and expand letter spacing by 5 points

National Sales Conference

Mullingar House Hotel, Austin Friars Street, Mullingar
15 September 2006

centre and right align

TP operator

Key in the word 'Agenda' and format it as follows: block caps, 18 points Times New Roman font and centre. Leave a clear line before and after Agenda.

Type the items on the agenda in the order shown below:

  (i) Registration
 (ii) Company progress
(iii) Q Mark and ISO 9000 certification
 (iv) The company, product by product
  (v) Coffee break
 (vi) The company, product by product (continued)
(vii) Advertising and search for new products
(viii) Lunch
 (ix) Targets for the coming year

Follow the format of the 'Company Progress' item below in order to display all items on the agenda in a consistent manner. Note:

- The times of the start and conclusion of the various items on the agenda should appear at the left margin.
- There should be approximately 2 cm between the column showing the time and the column showing the title of each item, etc.
- The time and the name of each item should be in bold.

9.30 am–10.35 am   **Company progress**
Ms Helen Vance, Managing Director, will trace the progress of the company for the year to date, including:
- national market share
- market share in each of the four regions.

Ms Vance will also introduce two new products:
- Sun World Patio Porch Doors
- Martin Mirrors.   /...

Littletown Tennis Club
Chestnut Close
Littletown
Co Offaly
Ireland

tel 094 78953, e-mail lttennis@eircom.net

March 2006

Dear Member

MEMBERSHIP SUBSCRIPTIONS 2006

It's that time of the year again when membership subscriptions are due. This year we would like members to make a special effort to pay fees promptly and thus help to reduce our overdraft interest charges.

This year fees are as follows:

Family €200
Individual €140
Intermediate €110
Junior €80

Yours sincerely

Mary Lohan
Secretary

page 3 starts here

Access ← *Block caps & bold*

u/c
∅
Entrance to the park is on the cliffen side of Letterfrack village. The park grounds are open all year and the visitors centre is open from May to September. d/

leave two clear lines only

Visiting Groups ← *BLOCK CAPS*

stet
Special arrangements can be made to provide access to the visitor's centre at other times.

←   *Insert After*
FLORA on
page 2

FAUNA ← Block caps

Meadow pipits
Skylarks
Stonechats
Chaffinches
Robins
Wrens
Woodcock
Snipe
Starling
Song thrush
Mistle thrush

Zuzissi Motors Ltd
Naas Road
Dublin 12
Ireland

tel: (01) 765012
e-mail: zuzissi_irl@eircom.net
web: http://www.zuzissi_ireland.com

Today's date

Mr Charles Lennon
Lennon Motors
Church Street
Tullamore
Co Offaly

Dear Mr Lennon

Thank you for your enquiry, which is receiving attention.

One of our directors will be in contact with you shortly. In the meantime, I enclose a number of brochures, which give details of all Zuzissi models currently available in the Republic of Ireland.

Yours sincerely

Paula Breen
Customer Relations

Encs

Retrieve Display 2.10 and make the changes indicated below and on page 206. Save it as Display 2.11. To insert a header, click the **View** menu and then click **Header and Footer**.

Type the following;

justify right margins. Print on 3 pages, inserting page breaks as indicated. Insert a header as shown below:

CONNEMARA   NATIONAL   PARK ← *SPACED CAPS AND CENTRE*

The Visitor's Centre ← *BLOCK CAPS & BOLD*

The development of the Connemara landscape over 10,000 years is explained and illustrated with 3D models and other exhibits. An audiovisual presentation is shown at regular intervals.

Other Facilities ← *BLOCK CAPS*

- PICNIC AREAS
- TEA - ROOM
- NATURE TRAILS
- HERITAGE SITE INFORMATION

Stet *PAGE 2 Starts here* ✓

THE PARK ← *BLOCK CAPS AND BOLD*

APPROXIMATELY 2,000 HECTARES OF MOUNTAIN heath and grassland. Situated in Connemara in the west of Ireland.

FLORA ← *BLOCK CAPS*

Cross-leaved heath and bell heather
Ling
purple moor-grass
Insectivorous plants
  - sundew
  - butterwort
Lousewort,
Bog-cotton
milkwort

ALL IRELAND WHOLESALE LTD tel (090) 7893510
DUBLIN ROAD e-mail: aiw@eircom.net
ATHLONE web: http://www.aiw.com
IRELAND

MH/BK

Today's date

FOR THE ATTENTION OF MICHAEL LEWIS, CHIEF BUYER

Lewis & Co Ltd
Clara Road
Tullamore
Co Offaly

Dear Sirs

As part of our pursuit of excellence we have now completed a customer survey in the Republic. From this survey we are delighted to learn that virtually all of our customers, including Lewis & Co Ltd, Tullamore are complimentary about our general level of service.

Some customers did, however, mention that they would like to see an increase in our range of leisure goods, particularly goods like golf and fishing equipment.

We have now responded by introducing a number of exciting new products, including Watertex foul weather gear. Watertex is a fully waterproof material that actually 'breathes', just like cotton or other similar fabrics. We are happy to announce that we have been

/ . . .

2
Today's date
Lewis & Co Ltd

appointed sole Irish distributors for this revolutionary new product.

We have pleasure in enclosing a copy of our greatly expanded brochure and we look forward to hearing from you soon or seeing you in person in our Athlone showrooms.

Yours faithfully

Michael Hopkins
Chief Executive

Enc

Key in the exercise below and save it as Display 2.10. To insert a page break, click the **Insert** menu, click **Break** and then click the **Page Break** button in the Break dialog box. The keyboard command is **Ctrl+Enter**, i.e. Ctrl + the Return key.

The Visitor's Centre

The development of the Connemara landscape over 10,000 years is explained and illustrated with 3D models and other exhibits. An audiovisual presentation is shown at regular intervals.

WP operator please insert

a   Page break   here

Correct all errors

THE PARK

APPROXIMATELY 2,000 HECTARES OF MOUNTAIN heath and grassland. Situated in Connemara in the west of Ireland.

a   Page break   here

Access

Entrance to the park is on the cliffen side of Letterfrack village. The park grounds are open all year and the visitors centre is open from May to September.

Visiting Groups

Special arrangements can be made to provide access to the visitor's centre at other times.

Part 6
Manuscripts

▷▷▷▷▷▶▷▷▷▷▷▷▷▷

Sometimes text-processing operators have to work from handwritten (manuscript) material or printed text that has been altered by hand. The alterations required may be shown by means of ballooned notes, crossed out text or recognised proofreaders' marks.

Working on Manuscripts

❶ Read the material fully to assess the general content.

❷ Read the material a second time and clarify any unclear instructions or words by marking them. Remember, there may be an instruction on page two that relates to page one and so on. Mark and correct all errors, including spelling errors.

❸ All abbreviations must be keyed in fully, apart from recognised abbreviations and acronyms (see pages 124 and 125).

❹ Work must be consistent. In this regard, special attention should be paid to layout and whether numbers are shown as figures or words (see page 128).

❺ Check and edit the text on screen (the soft copy), use the print preview function and finally, check the printout (the hard copy).

 Tip 1 — In examinations it may be advisable to use a highlighter pen to mark all instructions and all required alterations.

 Tip 2 — Set up the spell checker to **check** spelling as you type (see page 82). Ensure the 'English (Ireland) dictionary' is your Custom Dictionary. Make a deliberate spelling error (erreor) to ensure the spell checker is configured correctly. Don't forget to correct your deliberate erreor!

Collins College, Clonakilty, Spiller's Lane, Clonakilty, Co Cork, Ireland

Press Release

For release on 20 June 2006.

HISTORIC RESEARCH AWARD FOR COLLINS COLLEGE, CLONAKILTY

CCC has been awarded €1.2 million in research funding by ARL Environmental Consultants, Inchydoney, Clonakilty. This landmark award will be used, in part, to fund the provision of additional state-of-the-art facilities at the college.

The research in question will focus on of the effects of pollutants in Clonakilty Bay and will be carried out by three environmental science graduates who are pursuing postgraduate degree programmes at the college.

This is the first major investment by the private sector in CCC and points to the growing recognition of the college as a centre of excellence.

ENDS

For further information contact Susan O'Driscoll, Head of Communications,

tel 021 477980654, mobile 087 67090543, e-mail susanodriscoll7@ccc.ie.

Hyphenation

Line-end word division

Nowadays there is a tendency to ignore the question of dividing words at the end of a line. However, line-end word division improves the uneven or ragged appearance of right-hand margins. Also, when text is justified — that is, when there are flush margins both left and right — line-end word division may mean that fewer blank spaces have to be inserted between words. Line-end word division is especially useful when working with narrow columns, e.g. those used in newspapers. Consider the text below:

Ragged right margin	
Without line-end word division	**With line-end word division**
Total Quality applies to any organisation with people. Total Quality is about motivating people to give of their knowledge, creative ideas and experience to improve continually the way they do things.	Total Quality applies to any organisation with people. Total Quality is about mo-tivating people to give of their knowledge, creative ideas and experience to improve continually the way they do things.

Justified right margin	
Without line-end word division	**With line-end word division**
Total Quality applies to any organisation with people. Total Quality is about motivating people to give of their knowledge, creative ideas and experience to improve continually the way they do things.	Total Quality applies to any organisation with people. Total Quality is about moti-vating people to give of their knowledge, creative ideas and experience to improve continually the way they do things.

 Note — The word-processing operator can choose to have hyphens inserted automatically when keying in, but it is usually more efficient to have hyphens inserted when final text editing is being carried out.

Press Releases

Organisations like to attract positive publicity. One way of achieving this is by issuing press releases to the media or by posting them on their websites. For example, a school may wish it to be known that one of its students achieved seven A's in the Leaving Certificate. However, information such as this will not be published unless it is considered newsworthy. Also, if a press release appears too like an advertisement it will similarly go unpublished as newspapers expect to be paid to publish such material.

The following style may be used to prepare a press release:

❶ Type the name of the organisation responsible for releasing the information. Leave a clear line.
❷ Type the words 'PRESS RELEASE' in bold and leave a clear line.
❸ Give details of when the organisation wishes the information to appear in the press, e.g. 'For release on 20 June 2006'. Leave a clear line.
❹ Type the subject heading in block capitals. Leave a clear line.
❺ Type the body of the text in double-line spacing.
❻ Type the word 'END' in block capitals after the final paragraph. Leave a clear line.
❼ Give details of a person within the organisation who may be contacted to supply further information.

▶ Display 2.9

Prepare a press release from the information below and save it as Display 2.9. After you have completed this task, check your work with the suggested layout overleaf.

Further information may be obtained from Susan O'Driscoll, Head of Communications, tel 021 477980654, mobile 087 67090543, e-mail susanodriscoll7@ccc.ie.

The body of the press release is set out below:

CCC has been awarded €1.2 million in research funding by ARL Environmental Consultants, Inchydoney, Clonakilty. This landmark award will be used, in part, to fund the provision of additional state-of-the-art facilities at the college.

The research in question will focus on of the effects of pollutants in Clonakilty Bay and will be carried out by three environmental science graduates who are pursuing postgraduate degree programmes at the college.

This is the first major investment by the private sector in CCC and points to the growing recognition of the college as a centre of excellence.

The title is as follows: Historic research award for Collins College, Clonakilty.
CCC would like the press release to appear on 20 June 2006.
The name of the organisation issuing the press release is Collins College, Clonakilty, Spiller's Lane, Clonakilty, Co Cork, Ireland.

▶ Display 2.9a

Go to the UCD website, http://www.ucd.ie, and key in 'Press Releases' in the Search box to access the archive of press releases issued by the college.

To hyphenate text automatically, click the **Tools** menu, select **Language** and click **Hyphenation**. In the **Hyphenation zone** box, key in the amount of space to be left between the last word in a line and the right margin. A wider hyphenation zone will mean less hyphens but a more ragged right margin. Ensure **Automatically hyphenate** is activated, as shown below.

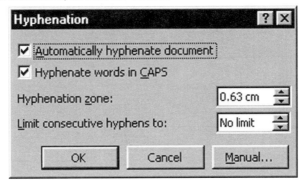

Rules for line-end word division

 Note — Although word-processing software provides for automatic word division, word-processing operators should be aware of the rules governing line-end word division.

As a general rule, do not divide words unnecessarily, because line ends with divided words look untidy. When it is necessary to divide words, observe the following rules:

DO
1. Divide according to syllables, provided this does not result in changing the pronunciation of a word.
2. Divide after a prefix, e.g. un-wise.
3. Divide before a suffix, e.g. commence-ment.
4. Divide between double consonants in the middle of a word, e.g. paral-lel.
5. Divide before 'ing' at the end of a word, except where the final consonant is doubled due to 'ing' being added to the root word, e.g. com-ing, run-ning.
6. Retain a sufficient portion, of the word at the end of a line to make it clear what the complete word is e.g. mahog-any, not ma-hogany.

DO NOT
1. Carry two letters only to the next line, e.g. painted, not paint-ed.
2. Divide on more than two consecutive lines.
3. Divide words of one syllable or their plurals, e.g. does, not do-es.
4. Divide proper names, e.g. McSweeney, not McSwee-ney.
5. Divide amounts of money.
6. Divide the last word of a paragraph.
7. Divide after one letter only, e.g. against, not a-gainst.

Hyphenation exercise
Key in the text below, set left and right margins of 7.5 cm and a hyphenation zone of 0.5 cm. Allow the hyphenation of words in capitals and limit consecutive hyphenation to two lines. Use 11 points Courier New font.

```
Businessmen argue whether
a Top Down or Bottom Up
approach should be ap-
plied to the implementa-
tion of Total Quality
programmes.  Most plump
for a Top Down approach.
```

Viewing the screen

Do not forget to magnify font size on the screen if you suffer from tired eyes. For example, Word 6 users can go to the View menu and select Zoom. Magnifying text to 120% of normal size makes quite a difference and with some fonts does not usually require scrolling to the right to see line ends.

Reflections and glare

Many VDUs can be tilted to reduce reflections and glare. Of course, machines can always be moved if necessary.

Do not forget

Opticians recommend having your eyes examined every two years.

WORKING WITH VDUs

THINGS YOU SHOULD KNOW

Correction signs (proofreaders' marks)

Mark which may be in the margin	Mark in text	Meaning	Corrected text
ONE OF THESE: = or *del*	copies to John Devins ~~and Partick Devine~~	delete	copies to John Devins
lc or ≠	the ʃecretary or Secretary	lower case, i.e. small letter	the secretary
uc or CAPS	in ǥalway or in galway	upper case, i.e. capital letter	in Galway
⌢ ⌣	com ⌢ mon sense ⌣	close up, i.e. leave less space	common sense
#	the Regional⏐College ∧	insert space	the Regional College
trs or ⌐⌐	the new Zuzissi Deluxe, family car	transpose, i.e. change the order of words	Zuzissi Deluxe, the new family car
stet or ✓	the wp operator must ~~proofread~~ work carefully	let it stand, i.e. the word with a dotted line underneath should be retained	the wp operator must proofread work carefully
NP or //	. . . at the beginning. ⌐Further information . . . or . . . at the beginning. ‖Further information . . .	new paragraph	. . . at the beginning. Further information
∧ , Cork	Galway╱and Kerry ∧	insert text	Galway, Cork and Kerry
run on	. . . at an early stage. ⌐Once combined . . .	no new paragraph required	at an early stage. Once combined . . .
‖	‖This is the first . . . ‖ The position . . .	straighten margin	This is the first . . . The position . . .

> **Note** — To clarify the correction required, a correction sign may appear in the margin as well as in the body of the text

VDUs

The letters stand for visual display unit, that is, the electronic means by which information is processed and read. VDUs allow information to be displayed as 'soft copy' before it is printed and made available as 'hard copy'.

Working with VDUs

Care should be taken to ensure that the working environment is suitable for the VDU operator. Factors such as machine height, the operator's distance from the screen and lighting are important.

Do operators need to have their eyes checked?

Opticians normally say that eyes should be examined every two years. However, symptoms such as sore eyes, headaches and general fatigue may well indicate visual problems and the need for an immediate eye examination.

Do VDUs cause eye problems?

Many users complain of visual fatigue when using VDUs. It is therefore important that both employers and employees do their utmost to keep such fatigue to a minimum. Focusing on a screen demands more effort than focusing on objects which are some distance away, so operators should look away from the VDU, out the window if possible, for a few seconds every 20 minutes or so. If possible, operators should spend, say, 10 minutes every hour doing alternative work.

Bifocal lenses

Those wearing bifocal lenses may experience particular difficulties, as it may be that neither the distance nor close-up part of the lenses is suitable for working at VDU distance. Therefore, lenses that correct vision at this distance may be required.

Screen brightness

Some operators find the screen brightness a problem. This can usually be adjusted by altering the brightness or contrast settings on a VDU.

Tinted spectacles and glare-absorbent screen filters are sometimes found useful. However, some people consider such accessories to be no more than gimmicks.

```
++++++
++++
+++
+
```

Key in the manuscript below. Use double-line spacing. Save it as Manuscript 1.

lc   English Language Summer Schools are bracing themselves for a drop in the numbers of teenage students coming to Ireland this summer. The crippling ④ effects of [economic ② recession/ ⑤]

trs -- [political uncertainty] and currency devaluations/ in Spain and Italy

⁹/ are being blamed for what may well signal the end of a boom in educational tourism in Ireland.

                          Second
stet Teaching English as a ~~Foreign~~ Language (TEFL) enjoyed a dramatic

spurt of growth in Ireland and elsewhere in recent years. In 1988, about 47,000 foreign students came to Ireland to study English and

⁹⁷ by 1991/ the number had more than doubled to 100,000. Bord Fáilte estimates that the revenue (TOURISM) generated by educational tourism

million/ was £81/ in 1991.

(Typist: spread this piece 'Difficult times for English Language Industry.")

Folded leaflets

The front cover of a leaflet usually shows important information which is emphasised through the use of block capitals, bold, etc. The back cover contains information that is of less importance. Work on folded leaflets requires some forethought. The procedure below may be followed:

❶ Fold a blank sheet of paper in the required way.

❷ Draw an outline of the required layout. This should show the normal page margins (the outside margins) and the margins on each side of a fold line (the inside margins).

❸ The outside margins should be about 2.5 cm and the inside margins about 1.3 cm.

❹ Click the **File** menu and select **Page Setup**. Select the paper size, orientation and margins required. When four-fold leaflets are required, paper longer than the A4 size may be used.

❺ Click the **Table** menu and select **Insert Table**. In the Insert Table dialog box, enter the number of columns required and just one row. Treat the inside margin as an additional column.

❻ Select the blank table that now appears on screen. Click the **Table** menu and click **Table Properties**. Click the **Column** tab and key in the width of the required columns.

❼ Key in text into the appropriate cells. To achieve a uniform layout, key in the cell which contains the most text first. Try to align the first and last lines in all cells.

❽ Select the table again and click the arrow to the right of the **Border** button on the Formatting toolbar. Select **No Border**.

▶ *Display 2.8*

Key in the leaflet set out on the next two pages as a three-fold leaflet that is folded inward. Save it as Display 2.8.

Key in the manuscript below. Use double-line spacing. Save it as Manuscript 2.

Evidence has been growing over the past two years that the wild west Cork coastline has become a favourite drop-off point for cannabis smugglers.

This quiet and picturesque area with its strings of islands and inlets is a perfect haven for the smugglers as it is almost impossible to patrol it efficiently unless there are unlimited manpower resources.

North Africa is the main source of cannabis and shipments are smuggled into this country through the Netherlands, Spain and Portugal.

A list of seizures by gardaí and customs officers shows most of the cannabis confiscated is uncovered at Rosslare – the principal ferry port from the continent.

[WP operator: hyphen, not dash]

Typist: Please give this piece a suitable heading – use block capitals

Leaflets

Landscape A4 paper is sometimes folded vertically in two or three to produce a folded leaflet. There are a number of possible ways of typing such leaflets, as illustrated below:

1 Two-fold leaflet with fold to left.

page 2	page 3
first inside page	second inside page

Front cover = back of page 2
Back cover = back of page 3

2 Three-fold leaflet folded 'accordion style', with left edge of the paper and second fold to the left.

The front of the folded sheet contains the following pages:

front cover	page 1	page 2

The back of the folded sheet contains the following pages:

back cover	usually blank	usually blank

3 Three-fold leaflet folded inward, with first fold to the left and the right edge of the paper tucked in and touching the first fold.

The front of the folded sheet contains the following pages:

page 1	page 2	page 3

The back of the folded sheet contains the following pages:

page 4	back cover	front cover

Key in the manuscript below. Use double-line spacing and correct all errors. Save it as Manuscript 3.

The internet will make your CD collection redundant

A powerful combination of the digital revolution, which is poised to irrevocably change the way we watch television, and the internet, is in the process of revolutionising the music industry and popular music.

Thanks to innovative new technology, songs are being compressed from CDs, to a tenth of their natural size, into smaller computer files and posted on the internet, effectively turning PCs into virtual jukeboxes. For little more than the price of a phone call you can build a library of electronic music that you can access anytime with a click of the mouse button.

This new technology, which is called MP3, means that if you have an internet connection, a multimedia computer and a fast modem, you can download this music anytime, using free software available on the Net, and play it on your computer at near CD quality. And should you want music on the move, you can now download it directly onto one of the new portable MP3 players, like the Rio MPMan, the first digital equivalent of the Walkman. The Rio can store from 32 minutes of good quality music to hours of lesser quality digital music, and costs about €220.

3.

Each Player should repair a minimum of his own plug mark plus other. Please share our desire to care for the course. By the etiquette of the game, we are all expected to be responsible and caring.

Note: Type this paragraph in the same format as the first paragraph

2"

Golf and Country Club

Centre vertically & horizontally between the lines indicated use caps & Bold

Please finish off the document with the following footnote.

The Dress Code must be strictly adhered to at all times

Proofreading

The aspiring word-processing operator should note that many employment agencies now include a proofreading test as part of their assessment procedure.

Proofreading exercise – can you spot seven errors in the piece below?

Most computer system sold today are based on Microsoft Windows and run on Intel chips or clones (near-copies). However, one out of ten non-business customers opt instead for Apple Macintosh machines. There is little or no difference between the two type of machine, either in price or quality, but many of the more popular CD-ROM titles are not available for both formats. The main difference between the Mac from the PC is simplicity, as multimedia is built directly into the Mac.

The PC user, on the other hand, may encounter imcompatibilities, which mean that some CD-ROM titles are unplayable; Almost all these problems arise with packages that were written for MS-DOS, the former operating system on the PC. Those running Microsoft Windows, the new operating system, may still have problems, since MS-DOS still functions in the background. However, if you buy only Windows multimedia titles, you are unlikley to encounter problems

Key to proofreading exercise

Most computer systems sold today are based on Microsoft Windows and run on Intel chips or clones (near-copies). However, one out of ten non-business customers opts instead for Apple Macintosh machines. There is little or no difference between the two types of machine, either in price or quality, but many of the more popular CD-ROM titles are not available for both formats. The main difference between the Mac and the PC is simplicity, as multimedia is built directly into the Mac.

The PC user, on the other hand, may encounter incompatibilities, which mean that some CD-ROM titles are unplayable. Almost all these problems arise with packages that were written for MS-DOS, the former operating system on the PC. Those running Microsoft Windows, the new operating system, may still have problems, since MS-DOS still functions in the background. However, if you buy only Windows multimedia titles, you are unlikely to encounter problems.

2.

Procedure for Play

Reserve teeing off time in advance.
arrive at clubhouse 15 minutes   prior
to teeing off time.

Sign in at clubhouse Reception.

Proceed to baggage area. Golf ~~shoes~~ &
clubs to be left here and a ~~baggage~~
ticket will be issued.

Proceed to locker rooms for changing
purposes.

No smoking in locker rooms.

all Players are requested to
comply with the following rules.

Note: please number the above points
1 - 6 & type in double line spacing.

Locker Rooms

locker keys may be obtained from the
Golf Shop. a deposit of €5.00 is   required,
this deposit will be refunded on return of   /
the key.

Dress Code*

lc basual wear is acceptable in the
Summit Restaurant and bar. Jeans and
training shoes are not permitted in the
clubhouse ~~or~~ on the course.

Abbreviations

Anyone involved in text processing should be clear about the conventions (rules) governing the use of abbreviations. As these rules are a little involved, time should be spent studying this section.

As a general principle, abbreviations should be keyed in full. However, there are exceptions to this principle as some abbreviations should never be keyed in full and some should, or should not, be typed in full — depending on the context.

Abbreviations **never rendered in full**:

Abbreviation	Meaning	Abbreviation	Meaning
ad lib	at pleasure	Messrs	Messieurs
e.g.	for example	Mrs	title of married woman
Esq	Esquire	Mr	Mister
etc	and others	Ms	title substituted for Mrs or Miss
i.e.	that is	NB	note well

Abbreviations **used in certain cases only**:

Abbreviation	Meaning	Abbreviation used in
& (ampersand)	and	the names of firms and numbers
Bros	Brothers	the names of organisations
c/o	care of	addresses
Co.	company	the names of companies
COD	cash on delivery	invoices
Ltd	limited	the names of private limited companies
PLC or plc	public limited company	the names of such companies
PS	postscript	letters and memos
ref	reference	letters and memos

Abbreviations **used with figures only**:

%	per cent	ft	foot (feet)
am	before noon	g	gram(s)
cm	centimetre(s)	cwt	hundredweight(s)
m	metres	oz	ounce(s)
mm	millimetre(s)	lb	pound(s)
no, nos	number(s)	in	inch(es)
pm	after noon	kg	kilogram(s)

Abbreviations which **may be retained**:

Names of countries such as USA, CIS, UK; names of organisations such as ESB, FÁS, NCEA, RSA; acronyms, i.e. where the initials of words make up new words, such as VAT, PAYE, PRSI.

 Note — The following symbols do not require the addition of 's' in the plural: m, mm, cm, kg, in, oz, cwt.

Key in the exercise below and save it as Display 2.7.

Golf and Country Club ← [caps centre bold]

Note: Use paragraph heading throughout with single line spacing unless otherwise specified

[double line spacing]

Our 18 hole championship standard golf course opened in August 1993. Our Resident Professional is available to offer coaching and advice to all golfers.

Green Fees
Green Fees are payable on day of play. The fees are as follows:

X Hotel Residents   Midweek €13·00
                     Weekends €20·00

Non Residents   Midweek € ?
                     Weekends € ? X

Note: Use your own layout to set out the section dealing with green fees i.e. from X to X

Please note that Non Residents are charged €10 more than Residents.

Tee Times

A Tee Time system is in operation. In order to avoid disappointment, residents should always book their teeing off times in advance by telephoning the Golf Clubhouse. Players should be on the tee 5 minutes in advance of play.

Standard longhand abbreviations

Over the years a type of informal shorthand has developed, particularly in the medical and legal professions, whereby certain commonly used words are given standard abbreviations when written in manuscript form. Study the commonly used abbreviations listed below — these abbreviations should always be keyed in full.

a/c(s)	account(s)	/	the
accom	accommodation	necy	necessary
ack	acknowledge	opp(s)	opportunity/ies
advert(s)	advertisement(s)	or	other
amt	amount	org	organisation
altho'	although	pd	paid
approx	approximate/ly	poss	possible
appt(s)	appointment(s)	p/t	part time
asap	as soon as possible	rec	receive
bel	believe	rec(s)	receipt(s)
bn	been	recd	received
bus	business	recom	recommend
cat(s)	catalogues(s)	ref(s)	reference(s)
co(s)	company/ies	refd	referred
cttee(s)	committee(s)	resp	responsible
def	definite/ly	sec(s)	secretary/ies
ex	exercise	sep	separate
exp	experience	sh	shall
exp(s)	expense(s)	shd	should
f	for	sig(s)	signature(s)
fr	from	suff	sufficient
f/t	full time	temp	temporary
g	ing	th	that
gntee(s)	guarantee(s)	thro	through
gov(s)	government(s)	togh	together
hrs	hours	w	with
immed	immediate/ly	wd	would
incon	inconvenient/ence	wh	which
info	information	wl	will
mfr(s)	manufacturer(s)	yr	your/year
misc	miscellaneous		

 Note — Pay particular attention to the symbol for 'the', ☐ / , as it sometimes catches out text-processing operators.

Blank spaces

It is sometimes necessary to leave spaces in text for the insertion of logos, photographs, etc.

Horizontal space (space across the line)

Assume a space of 4 cm is required, from the 4 cm mark to the 8 cm mark, on the ruler line. To do this, key in text as far as the 4 cm mark, set a left tab at the 8 cm mark, press the Tab key and resume keying in text.

Vertical space (space down a document)

Assume a space of 4 cm is required between two paragraphs. To do this, first of all delete any existing space between the paragraphs and ensure that the cursor is exactly at the end of the first paragraph. Then click the **Format** menu and click **Paragraph**. In the Paragraph dialog box, key in 4 cm in the **Spacing before** box, click **OK** and then press the **Return** key.

Horizontal and vertical space

Assume a horizontal <u>and</u> vertical space of 4 cm is required. One way to do this is as follows:

❶ If the Drawing toolbar is not showing, click **View**, **Toolbars** and **Drawing**. Click the **Text Box** icon on the Drawing toolbar.

❷ Key in all the text in the document in the usual way.

❸ On the next line, draw a text box of any size.

❹ Select the text box and click the **Format** menu and select **Text Box**.

❺ In the Format Text Box dialog box, click the **Size** tab and key in 4 cm in the **Height** and **Width** boxes.

❻ Click the **Wrapping** tab and click **Tight**.

❼ If a line is not required around the blank space, click the **Colors and Lines** tab. In the **Line Color** box, select **White** (on the assumption that white paper is being used for printing).

❽ Drag the text box to the required position.

Key in the manuscript below. Use double-line spacing. Revise the distinction between a hyphen and a dash – see page 35. Save it as Manuscript 4.

Please head this piece "Re-correction of Leaving Certificate" – use Block CAPS.

ᴄᴛ Almost one in ~~ten~~ 10 of the applications for re-correction of the Leaving Certificate results last year succeeded, according to official department of education statistics – this is double the ⬡ number in previous years.

It's worth bearing in mind, of course, that the numbers who apply for a recheck are relatively small – last year 3,243 candidates of the 66,000 who (sit) for the exam sought a re-check.

The Department is anxious that (applications) should only be made for genuine reasons. APPLICANTS

(✓) ~~In applying they have~~ to pay a fee of
€25 per subject and their school has to testify that the result in a particular
subject is seriously out of line with what

NORMALLY | the school would have expected from that student.

It is also worth bearing in mind that the ~~huge~~ HUGE increase in successful applications last year has to do with the introduction of the new grading system.

/...

Special Interests: Ind. is soccer + playing the guitar.

Referees: Mr Brenden Woldean, Director, O'Shea
Construction, Clash Road, Tralee

Principal

Sister Philomena, St Fribugg Community College, TRALEE

Now prepare your own CV

▶ Display 2.6a

Key in the following and save it as Display 2.6a

Some interview checkpoints

■ Check out the website of your target company. Get as much
information as possible and use it to formulate at least three
intelligent questions.

■ Do not arrive late.

■ Remember, appearance is vital. Avoid excessive make-up or strong
perfume/cologne.

■ Smile, give a firm handshake and make eye contact. Place your
hands on your lap and avoid fidgeting.

■ Be as honest and accurate about your accomplishments as possible.
Be positive, but avoid appearing too sure of yourself.

■ Do not appear humble or self-effacing.

■ Never interrupt the interviewer.

■ Be careful to answer the questions asked.

■ Avoid being negative about your last job or former colleagues.

■ Be firm in expressing your interest in the job in question.

■ When the interview is over, thank the interviewers for their time
and for considering your application.

2

(WP OPERATOR) → Be sure to check the spelling of the words that have been circled.

Yes   Parents and pupils are not the only people suffering from pre-exam
NERVES
nerves; (officials) from the Department of Education face long, [sleepless]
Yes
.. nights and [worrying days] hoping that everything will go without a
major problem — minor hitches they have come to expect.

It's easy to see why they are anxious, as there will be over
130,000 candidates sitting for
\|4,000 various tests in over 14,000
centres around the country.
Between them the candidates will prepare 1.4m scripts and other
EXERCISES worked excercises which will
all have to be transported to
the examination centre in Athlone
for marking.

Secrecy and security are the hallmarks
of the planning process for the operation
which (begins) a full year before the
excams.

Key in the sample CV below and save it as Display 2.6.

Name

Christine O'Sullivan
7 Maple Court
Dingle Road
Tralee
Co Kerry

Date of Birth - 27 August 1970
Marital Status - Single   Nationality. Irish

Education
                    1982   1988

St. Finbar's
Community College
Tralee

[BARDONS] Bardon Business Academy, West St, Tralee   SEPTEMBER ↓ 1988 - 1989 JUNE

QUALIFICATIONS

1/c   Leaving Certificate with Honours in Geography
       and Home Economics

       Certificate i Secretarial Studies with [50 words]
       per minute i Typewriting + [Word Perfect 5.1.]

EXPERIENCE

July 1989 - to date . Secretary with O'Shea
Contraction, Clash Road, Tralee . Duties include:
word processing using Microsoft Word for Windows
a computerised Accounting using Pegasus.

AVAILABLE FOR
EMPLOYMENT   one Month.

Measurements

The imperial system of measurement is gradually giving way to the metric system. For example, metres and kilos are increasingly used instead of yards and pounds.

The following points should be noted:

❶ There are recognised abbreviations for both metric and imperial measures. These may be retained when keying in manuscript work. (See 'Abbreviations' on page 124.)

❷ Leave one space between numbers and related units of measurement, e.g. 4 m for 4 metres.

❸ Most abbreviations indicating measurement do not require the addition of 's' in the plural, e.g. 4 m (not 4 ms) stands for 4 metres.

❹ Lower case 'x' is often used to indicate 'by' or 'multiplied by'. One space should be left before and after the 'x'. For example, 4 metres by 2 metres may be keyed in as 4 x 2 metres or 4 m x 2 m.

❺ Never use full stops in abbreviations indicating metric measurements, unless such abbreviations come at the end of a sentence — even when using full punctuation.

Numbers — figures or words

It is sometimes difficult to decide whether to show numbers as words or figures. As a consistent approach is essential, it is advisable to follow a set of guidelines, such as those set out below.

Words should be used in the following cases:

❶ For the numbers one to ten inclusive, e.g. 'He offered her ten red roses.'

❷ At the start of a sentence (see note below).

❸ For single fractions in a sentence, e.g. 'There was a prize for about a quarter of those who attended.'

❹ For time when followed by 'o'clock', e.g. 'He left at nine o'clock in the morning.'

Figures should be used in the following cases:

❶ For the numbers 11 and above.

❷ For dates.

❸ For time, except when followed by the words 'o'clock', e.g. 'He left at 4 am.'

❹ For property numbers.

❺ For measurements.

 Note — It is usually better to reconstruct sentences which begin with large numbers. For example, '999 delegates attended the conference' would be better phrased, 'The conference was attended by 999 delegates.'

```
2

HONORARY POSITIONS

1989/90                                 President of the UCG German Society
1985/86                                 Class representative for 5B in St Catherine's
                                        College


INTERESTS                               Languages, foreign travel, reading and voluntary
                                        work


REFEREES                                Mr Gerald Walsh
                                        Marketing Manager
                                        Balladur Teo
                                        Roundstone
                                        Co Galway
                                        tel (091) 73424

                                        Sister Bernadette
                                        St Catherine's College
                                        Spiddal Road
                                        Galway
                                        tel (091) 88854
```

Interview techniques and CV preparation

There is a wealth of information on the web giving guidance on matters such as interview technique and the preparation of CVs and covering letters. One approach is to go to the websites of third-level colleges and follow relevant links. In the case of the author's college, go to http://www.ait.ie, Facilities, Student Services, Careers and Appointments Services, Students, Compiling CVs. Another useful site is http://www.alec.co.uk.

Job hunting

Try websites such as the following: monster.ie, recruitireland.com, irishjobs.ie, grafton-group.com, irishtimesjobs.ie, craigslist.org (go to the Dublin link), summerjobs.com. Don't forget to key in http://www. before each part of the address.

▶ *Display 2.5a*

Go to the web and copy a sample CV into a Word document, then fill in your details in place of the sample details. Save as Display 2.5a.

Key in the manuscript below. Use double-line spacing. Save it as Manuscript 5.

CAREERS IN ACCOUNTANCY / Spaced Caps & underscore

A WIDE CHOICE IN QUALIFICATIONS / Caps & underscore

With such a wide variety [*choice* crossed out] of careers and job opportunities available to members of the

lc / Accountancy Profession – and at such attractive salaries – it is no surprise that qualifications for posts can also vary.

Write in full / The Institute of Chartered accountants / uc is the predominant accountancy institute. They have APPROX. ↑ 6,000 members, half of which are [PREDOMINENT]

lc / in practice; [*and* crossed out] the other half working work in Industry and Commerce. Members

of the ICA are heavily [heavily] represented in financial services, with the exception of

trs uc / the associated banks, where many members ② of the institute of Chartered / Certified

NP / Accountants are employed. [Qualifications for chartered Accountancy are determined by the Institute of Chartered Accountants.

NP [There are a number of Routes [Routes] to

① / becoming a chartered Accountant, including

[New] a ↑ pilot training scheme with connections to a small number of ↑ industrial or commercial organisations.

/...

Key in the exercise below and save it as Display 2.5.

CURRICULUM VITAE

PERSONAL DETAILS

Name	Georgina B Malone 6 Maple Court Galway Ireland
Telephone	Home (091) 78041 Work (091) 72647 e-mail: gbmalone@btr.ie
Date of Birth	25 June 1970
Marital Status	Single
Driving Licence	Class C

FULL-TIME EDUCATION

St Catherine's College, Galway	1982-87
University College Galway	1987-90
University of Lille, France	1991

QUALIFICATIONS

Leaving Certificate	1987
BA degree in Marketing and Languages	1990
Certificate in Commercial French, University of Lille	1991

LANGUAGE ABILITY

French	Fluent
German	Fluent
Irish	Fluent

EXPERIENCE

1991 to date	Trainee marketing assistant with Balladur Teo, Roundstone, Co Galway
Summer holidays while in UCG	Voluntary work helping old people through 'Les Petits Frères des Pauvres' in France

/...

NP/ [For graduates, the normal term of the
stet
training contract (in which ~~they~~ usually work in
Write
in
words/ a practice) is 3½ years, or three years
in the case of students who have completed
close
up/ some post-graduate programmes. Holders
of business degrees and other qualifications
~~eligible~~
stet
are ~~liable~~ for a number of training and
examination exemptions, including the 1st part/write
out
of the Institute examination known as
Professional One.
run
on/
But, in order to be fully qualified, the
student must have successfully completed
write
in
words/ the Professional 2 and Three and final
auditing examinations.

There are three core areas of training in
accountancy – auditing, accountancy and
taxation, and all accountants, whether they
have qualified with the ICA or with the
other professional institutes, should have a
good
for grounding in these areas. [Certain /NP
qualifications seem to direct accountants
into certain careers, as the list below
suggests:

/ ...

Key in the footnote exercise below and save it as Display 2.4.

<u>Bus tour of Belleek Pottery</u>

'It is a joy to visit Belleek and the island and inlets of Lough Erne at any time of year.' [1]

This tour includes Belleek Pottery, where the intricate techniques used by the craftsmen who made the first pieces are still used today. Visitors can enjoy a video presentation which goes through the production process from beginning to end.

----

[1] From *Ireland Visited* by Seathrún O'Meara, published by Little Guides Ltd, Belfast.

Curriculum Vitae (CV)

CVs generally run to one or two pages. They are laid out in different ways. The following details should be included:

❶ Name, address and phone number.
❷ Date of birth.
❸ Education, training and awards received.
❹ Experience.
❺ Interests.
❻ Date on which available for work.
❼ The name and address of two referees.

Positive achievements should be emphasised and less noteworthy events played down. For example, evidence of leadership qualities or entrepreneurial flair should be highlighted. On the other hand, if one just scraped through Junior Certificate, what's the point of listing results in every subject?

In America, potential employers look for a one-page résumé rather than a CV. A number of résumé templates come with Word. To access them, click **File** and **New**. In the New dialog box click the **Other Documents** tab and then click **Resume Wizard**, **Contemporary Resume**, **Elegant Resume**, etc. Resume Wizard is probably the most useful of these for Irish job applicants.

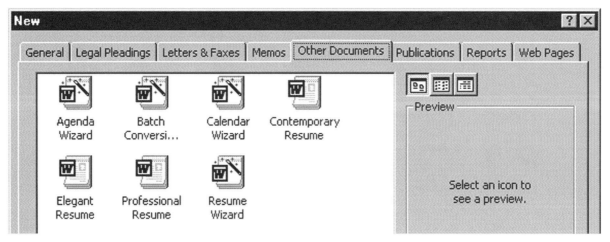

Wizards

Wizards are interactive templates which allow the user to fill in appropriate details.

All headings to be typed as paragraph headings

Auditing: ACA training is ideally suited to this speciality.

(use small 's')

Insolvency: ACAs [and] and ACCAs are both ideally qualified for this kind of work.

Corporate Finance:

ACAs tend to be more strongly represented because of the auditing/financial experience they would have received while with larger practices.

Tax: Tax work is mainly done by ACAs in practice (ideally with legal qualifications and Institute of Taxation Exams).

quite in full

field

✓ Computer Auditing: A specialist field area which suits ACAs (who receive intense training) and accountants with computer science degrees and backgrounds.

intensive

The Public Service:

Though job prospects are quite limited in the public service, it is an area in ; however / which many ACCAs have been trained / it is l/c Not a career preferred by ACAs. / del

Footnotes and endnotes

Footnotes are inserted at the bottom of a page and endnotes at the end of a document. Such notes are used to explain matters arising or to give the source of a quotation or a reference used in the text.

Click the **Insert** menu and then click **Footnote**. As footnotes are not visible in Normal view, click the **View** menu and **Print Layout** to check your work.

 Note — Footnotes should be distinguished from footers. Footers allow for the repetition of information at the bottom of a number of pages, e.g. a chapter title or an author's name.

▶ Display 2.3

Key in the footnote exercise below and save it as Display 2.3.

Walking tour of Kilkenny City

'Kilkenny, a charming little city in the south-east of Ireland, offers the visitor many insights into the history of medieval Ireland.'*

This tour offers the visitor many sights, such as St Canice's Cathedral, from which Kilkenny takes its name, and the Black Abbey, which was founded by the Dominicans.

---

* From *Ireland Visited* by Seathrún O'Meara, published by Little Guides Ltd, Belfast.

Part 7
Memos

▷▷▷▷▷▷▶▷▷▷▷▷▷▷

Written communication between members of the same organisation is still sometimes in the form of a memorandum (memo). Memorandums (or memoranda) are generally brief and to the point.

E-mail (electronic mail) systems
Memos are now usually sent as e-mail attachments, and in many cases they have been replaced by simple e-mail messages.

Memo styles and house style
Different layouts are used, but many organisations have their own house style that must be followed.

Memo templates
The quickest way to key in a memo is to use a memo template. Templates can be thought of as reuseable forms.

Click **File** and **New**. In the New dialog box, click the **Memos** tab, then click **Contemporary Memo**. Look at this template in the Preview window on the right side of the dialog box, then click OK to open it. Repeat the above procedure to open the **Elegant Memo** and the **Professional Memo**, then decide which template you wish to use.

The Contemporary Memo template is illustrated below.

```
Memorandum

To:      [Click here and type name]
CC:      [Click here and type name]
From:    [Click here and type name]
Date:    05/11/06
Re:      [Click here and type subject]

The body of the memo is keyed in here.
```

 Note — CC: above refers to carbon copy. The names of those to whom copies are sent are filled in at this point.

Memo wizard
Apart from templates, the memo wizard may be used to create a memo. Click **File**, **New**. In the New dialog box, click the **Memos** tab, then click **Memo Wizard** and follow the steps outlined.

▶ Display 2.1

Key in the data below, which contains subscripts and superscripts. Save it as Display 2.1.

100°C	Water = H_2O	Vinegar (acetic acid) = CH_3COOH
Sulphuric acid = H_2SO_4	Chloride ion = Cl^-	Ammonia = NH_3
Nitric acid = HNO_3	Hydroxyl ion = OH^-	Bread soda (sodium hydrogen carbonate) = $NaHCO_3$
Sulphate ion = SO_4^{2-}	Ammonium ion = NH_4^+	$\dfrac{1}{u} + \dfrac{1}{v} = \dfrac{1}{f}$

Note — As a general rule, there should be a space before and after the symbols +, -, x and =. However, if - or + form part of a number, there is no such space, e.g. -a + -b, -y - x^2. See also the examples below.

For more complex equations, such as square roots and matrices, click the **Insert** menu, select **Object**, click the **Create New** tab in the Object dialog box and select **Microsoft Equations 3.0**.

▶ Display 2.2

Use Equations Editor 3.0 to key in the following data. Save it as Display 2.2.

The product rule for differentiation: If y = uv $\dfrac{dy}{dx} = u\dfrac{dv}{dx} + v\dfrac{du}{dx}$	Rule to solve quadratic equation of form: $ax^2 + bx + c = 0$ $x = \dfrac{-b \pm \sqrt{b^2 - 4ac}}{2a}$	A matrix: $\begin{bmatrix} 2 & 5 & 8 \\ 0 & 1 & 2 \\ 1 & 4 & 12 \end{bmatrix}$
$y = \dfrac{1}{\sqrt[3]{x}} + \dfrac{1}{\sqrt{x}}$	$Cos^2x + Sin^2x = 1$	4^4 x 5^5 6^6 x 7^7

Check it out — In the above exercises, ensure that you did not confuse the letter O with the number 0.

Creating your own memo template

Key in the memo design you require and click **File**, **Save As**. In the **Save as** dialog box, click the down arrow in the **Save as type** box and select **Document Template**. Double click the **Memos** folder, key in a suitable template name in the **File name** box and click **Save**.

Suggested memo style

There are a number of recognised memo styles. In this book we suggest using the style set out below. Please note the words in bold.

```
                            MEMORANDUM

SPECIAL MARK (if required)


To:
From:
Ref:      (if required)
Date:     (use today's date, if no date given)


SUBJECT HEADING

Body of memo    _____


_____


_____


Enc (if required)


Copy to (if required)
```

Keying in a memo

❶ Work with A4 paper setup, portrait style.

❷ Set margins of 25 mm.

❸ Use single-line spacing and open punctuation

❹ Embolden and centre the word MEMORANDUM. Leave a clear line.

❺ If there is a special mark (such as URGENT, CONFIDENTIAL, PERSONAL, PRIVATE, FOR THE ATTENTION OF), it should be keyed in using block capitals and bold. Do not type the words 'Special Mark'. Leave a clear line.

❻ Key in the lines To:, From:, Ref: and Date: in single-line spacing, then select these lines and set a left-aligned tab half a centimetre to the right of the 'm' in From. (For instructions on setting tabs, refer to page 139.) Tab in after **To** and key in the name of the receiver, tab in after **From** and key in the name of the sender, etc. Leave a clear line.

❼ Key in the subject heading in upper case. Do not embolden the subject heading. Leave a clear line.

❽ Key in the body of the memorandum.

❾ If the body of a memo refers to an enclosure or an attachment, leave a further clear line and key in Enc (or Encs, if there is more than one enclosure) at the left margin.

❿ If copies of a memo are required, type 'Copy to:' and set a left-aligned tab half a centimetre to the right of the 'o' in 'to', then fill in the details as shown above. Use the same technique as at point 6 above.

For example, 36 points font size means there are 36 points between an ascender (top of a capital) and a descender (bottom of a lower-case letter). The second 'May' below is in 36 points, i.e. the capital 'M' extends 24 points above the baseline, and the 'y' descends 12 points below the baseline.

Examples — the word May is shown in 12 points, 36 points and 72 points size.

Picas

The word 'pica' (also called em, or pica em) means a unit of measurement equal to 12 points or 0.166 in. There are six picas to the inch.

Fractions

Fractions may be keyed in as sloping fractions, i.e. by using an oblique symbol (also known as a solidus, a diagonal or forward slash). When the AutoFormat function is set appropriately, some sloping fractions are automatically reformatted as superscript fractions. For example, 1/2 becomes $\frac{1}{2}$, 1/4 becomes $\frac{1}{4}$, 3/4 becomes $\frac{3}{4}$.

 Note — There should be no space between a whole number and a related superscript fraction, e.g. $7\frac{1}{4}$. However, there should be a space between a whole number and a related sloping fraction, e.g. 7 1/4.

To set the AutoFormat function, click the **Format** menu, click **AutoFormat**, click **Options** in the Auto Correct dialog box, click the **AutoFormat As You Type** tab and click the **Fractions (1/2) with fraction character ($\frac{1}{2}$)** checkbox (if it has not already been ticked).

Superscripts and subscripts

Superscripts appear above the normal text line and are used in text to refer to footnotes, for the degree symbol (°) and in mathematics. Subscripts appear below the line and are used in chemistry, electronics, etc.

• Press Ctrl+Shift+= for superscripts.
• Press Ctrl+= for subscripts.

Continuation sheets

In the unlikely event of a memo continuing on to a second page, type the continuation symbol (/...) at the right margin at the foot of the first page. Key in the continuation heading on the second page, showing the page number, the date and the name of the person being written to, as shown below:

```
2
20 November 2006
Ms Susan O'Brien
```

 Note — A continuation heading can save a lot of confusion if the second sheet becomes detached.

▶ Memo 1

Key in the memo below and save it as Memo 1.

```
                        MEMORANDUM

URGENT

To:        All Kitchen Staff
From:      Kitchen Manager
Ref:       JOH/08
Date:      7 October 2006

SANDWICH TOASTERS

It has come to my notice that some staff members are not complying
with regulations regarding the use of toasters.

I attach a copy of the relevant extract from our procedures manual.
I wish to bring the following sentence to your particular attention:
'When removing bread or sandwiches from toasters use the plastic spat-
ulas provided; never use metal implements such as knives or forks.'

In the interest of safety it is important that all staff comply with
this instruction.

Enc

Copy to    J Dillon
           P Walsh
           File
```

 Note — In this book some memo headings show FROM before TO rather than TO before FROM. Either style is acceptable.

 Tip — If an enclosure or attachment is mentioned in a memo or letter, immediately key in Enc or Encs at the bottom of the document, otherwise you may forget to include this important indication.

Part 10
Display Work, Stage Two

▷▷▷▷▷▷▷▷▶▷▷▷▷

Aligning text

To align text with the right margin, click the **Align Right** button on the Formatting toolbar. To align some text to the left and some text to the right on the same line, set a right-aligned tab at the right margin.

To key in the framed line below, proceed as follows:

❶ Key in 'Tel 01-7865992 Fax 01-7865991' at the left margin.

❷ Set a right-aligned tab at the right margin.

❸ After 'Tel 01-7865992', press the Tab key.

Tel 01-7865992	Fax 01-7865991

For more about tabs, see page 139.

Proportional spacing

Proportional spacing, as opposed to monospacing, means that more space is allocated to some characters than others, depending on the natural size of the character in question. For example, the character ⃞M is allocated more space than the character ⃞i.

Do not use the space bar to align text

> ***Don't do it!*** — Do not use the Space Bar in order to move text in from the left margin. Due to proportional spacing, 'tapped in' text is unlikely to align evenly. Set a tab stop and press the Tab key!

In the example below, the Space Bar was used in an effort to align the columns. The columns do not align evenly as the font used, Times New Roman, is in proportional spacing. To ensure that the lines in a column align (start at the same point), it is necessary to set a tab stop and then to tab in to the start of each line.

Month.........Leading Salesperson....Department
January........Fox......................Insurance
February.......O'Meara.................Office Furniture
March..........Manning.................Motor Accessories

Points

In printing and word processing, 'points' form the basic units of measurement. Each point measures approximately 0.01384 inch and there are approximately 72 points to the inch (whether measured vertically or horizontally).

▶ Memo 2

Set out a memo from the information below and save it as Memo 2. When you have finished, check your work with the suggested model answer on page 137.

The subject heading is 'Internet Surfing And Use of E-Mail' and the memo is from B Keyes to S Keane. The body of the memo is as follows:

```
It has come to my attention that unproductive and inappropriate use is being
made of the both the Web and e-mail.

Please draft guidelines covering the use of the Web and e-mail within the comp-
any.  Staff should be informed that we have recently purchased software that
allows our computer controller to monitor what websites employees visit.
Furthermore, they should be told that it is now possible to see how long each
site was visited, on what day it was visited and what each employee did when at
a particular site.

On a cautionary note, I enclose a copy of a statement issued by IMPACT, the
union that represents public service clerical workers.  You will note that they
consider that e-mail should be afforded the same privacy as normal post.
```

B Keyes is the Chief Executive and S Keane is the Office Manager. The sender's reference is BK/SM, the memo should be marked 'Personal' and copies should be prepared for C Russell, P O'Brien and File.

▶ Memo 3

The information below concerns the opening hours of a shopping centre. **Correct all errors** and set out a memo with a suitable subject heading. When you have finished, check your work with the suggested answer on page 138, then save the file as Memo 3. The body of the memo is as follows:

```
The following arangements apply until further notice:

1  The centre will open each morning at 7.50 am. 'News and Views' opens at
   8.00 am; if it is late opening, please remain on duty in the shopping mall.
2  The centre will close at 6.30 pm on Monday, Tuesday, Wednesday and Saturday
   nights.
3  The centre will close at 9.30 pm on Thursday and Friday nights and on late
   shopping nights before Christmas.
4  Additional late shopping nights this Christmas have been agreed with the
   tenants as follows:

Monday 10 December
Tuesday 11 December
Wednesday 12 December
Monday 17 December
Tuesday 18 December
Wednesday 19 December

Please note that I shall be unable to attend our usual Monday morning meeting
next week.
```

The memo is from R Perkins to All Security Staff. It should be marked 'Urgent' and copies should be prepared for P Hynes, L Lynch and File.

Key in the chart below and save it as Chart 12.

MCSL
McCorquodale School of Languages
Black Friars' Street
Kilkenny
Ireland

tel 094-76583
fax 094-76588

FRENCH LANGUAGE COURSES - SEPTEMBER 2005 TO JUNE 2006

Course	Entry Level	Days	Time	Fee €	Course elements include:
Junior Certificate		Tuesday	4.00 to 5.30 pm	95	Oral, aural, writing and grammar
Junior Certificate		Thursday	5.30 to 7.00 pm	95	Oral, aural, writing and grammar
Transition Year	Junior Certificate	Wednesday	4.00 to 5.30 pm	95	Role play, using the phone
Fifth Year	Junior Certificate	Monday	5.30 to 7.00 pm	115	Oral, aural, writing and grammar
Leaving Certificate	Junior Certificate	Monday	4.00 to 5.30 pm	155	Leaving Certificate syllabus
Leaving Certificate	Junior Certificate	Saturday	10.00 to 11.30 am	155	Leaving Certificate syllabus
Adult Beginners		Tuesday	7.00 to 8.30 pm	180	Basic conversation
Adult Intermediate	Junior Certificate	Wednesday	7.00 to 8.30 pm	180	Intermediate conversation
Adult Advanced	Leaving Certificate	Monday	7.00 to 8.30 pm	180	Development of fluency
Business French	Leaving Certificate	Thursday	7.00 to 8.30 pm	210	Commercial exercises, using the phone

We're on the Web at http://www.mcsl.com

▶ Memo 4

Now do Memo 3 using the Contemporary Memo template and save it as Memo 4.

▶ Memo 5

From the information below set out a memo to all office staff from Helen Foley, Office Systems Controller. Mark it 'Important' and prepare a copy for June Watson, Human Resources Manager. Use the reference HF/23 and save this task as Memo 5. The body of the memo is as follows:

in full
stet
hrs
&

~

, ,

#

NP, lc

Run
on

I'm pleased to confirm that I have arranged a series of two - hour
tutorials, lectures + demonstrations f office staff. F your info, I enclose I enclose an outline of / topics that wl be covered.

As you wl see lectures are scheduled to begin on the first Tuesday of next month or run f a total of eight sessions. The First Session deal with / use of styles + templates in word Processing. This Promises to be a particularly interesting lecture.

Key in the organisation chart below and save it as Chart 11.

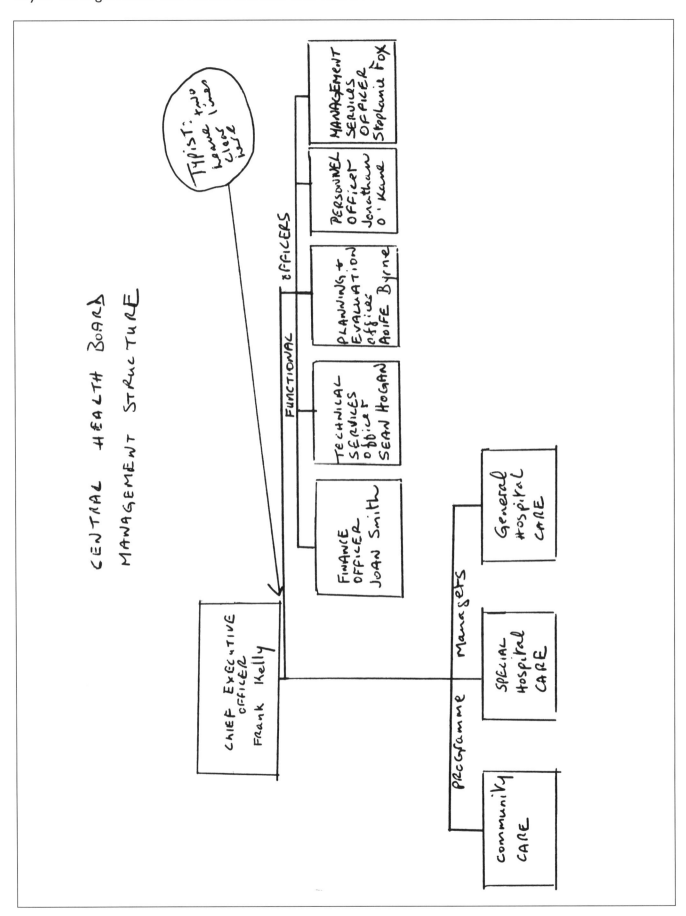

Suggested model answer for Memo 2

```
                        MEMORANDUM

PERSONAL

To:      S Keane, Office Manager
From:    B Keyes, Chief Executive
Ref:     BK/SM
Date:    Today's date

INTERNET SURFING AND USE OF E-MAIL

It has come to my attention that unproductive and inappropriate use
is being made of the both the Web and e-mail.

Please draft guidelines covering the use of the Web and e-mail within
the company.  Staff should be informed that we have recently pur-
chased software that allows our computer controller to monitor what
websites employee visit.  Furthermore, they should be told that it is
now possible to see how long each site was visited, on what day it
was visited and what each employee did when they were at a particular
site.

On a cautionary note, I enclose a copy of a statement issued by
IMPACT, the union that represents public service clerical workers.
You will note that they consider that e-mail should be afforded the
same privacy as normal post.

Encs

Copies to C Russel
         P O'Brien
         File
```

► *Chart 10*

Key in the chart below and save it as Chart 10.

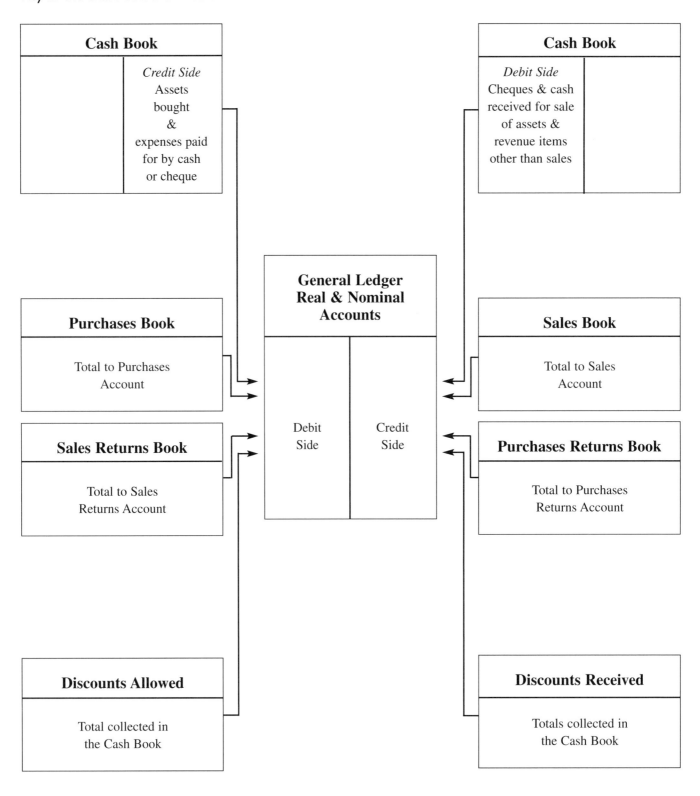

Source: *Business Accounting 1*, Frank Wood, London: Pitman 1990.

Part 9

182

Forms, Business Documents and Charts

Suggested model answer for Memo 3

MEMORANDUM

URGENT

To: All Security Staff
From: R Perkins
Date: Today's date

OPENING HOURS

The following arrangements apply until further notice:

1 The centre will open each morning at 7.50 am. 'News and Views'
   opens at 8.00 am; if it is late opening, please remain on duty in
   the shopping mall.
2 The centre will close at 6.30 pm on Monday, Tuesday, Wednesday and
   Saturday nights.
3 The centre will close at 9.30 pm on Thursday and Friday nights and
   on late shopping nights before Christmas.
4 Additional late shopping nights this Christmas have been agreed
   with the tenants as follows:

   Monday 10 December
   Tuesday 11 December
   Wednesday 12 December
   Monday 17 December
   Tuesday 18 December
   Wednesday 19 December

Please note that I shall be unable to attend our usual Monday morning
meeting next week.

Copies to P Hynes
           L Lynch
           File.

) **Chart 9**

Key in the chart below and save it as Chart 9.

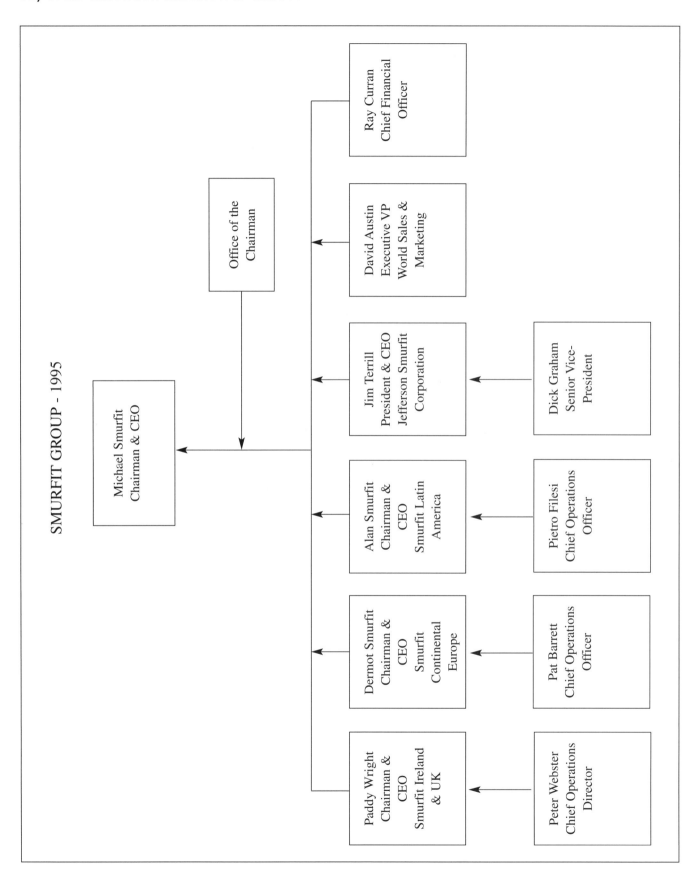

Part 8
Tabs and Tables

▷▷▷▷▷▷▷ ▶ ▷▷▷▷▷▷▷

It is often necessary to arrange text and/or figures in columns. Such work is referred to as tabulation. Work may be conveniently set out in columns by using the table features of Microsoft Word (see page 148). However, we shall postpone discussing the use of tables for the moment.

Using Tabs

Tabs require the use of:

❶ The Tab key, which is located to the left of Q on the keyboard.

❷ Tab stops, i.e. points on the ruler line to which the cursor moves when the Tab key is pressed.

Default or standard tab stops

In Word there are pre-set tab stops, i.e. default tab stops, every 1.27 centimetres (½ inch). Therefore, when the Tab key is pressed the cursor moves to the next 1.27 increment on the ruler line. To see how this works, key in the numbers below, followed by a tab character.

1   2   3   4   5

▶ Tab 1

Copy and save the text below using 12 points Times New Roman font. Use the default tab stops, i.e. do not set tab stops. To separate and align the columns, press the Tab key once or twice, as necessary.

January	April	July	October
February	May	August	November
March	June	September	December

We now have a tabular statement with four clear columns.

Are the spaces between the columns equal?

As with all tabs, we need to ask ourselves if Tab 1 looks all right. As consistency is the hallmark of good word-processing work, we need to ask ourselves if the spaces between the columns are reasonably even.

Look at the space between the longest word in the first column, February, and the second column. Now look at the space between the longest word in the second column, April, and the third column and between the longest word in the third column, September, and the fourth column.

Are these three spaces reasonably even? I'm afraid not. It's time to set our very own tab stops.

▶ Chart 7

Key in the flow diagram below and save it as Chart 7.

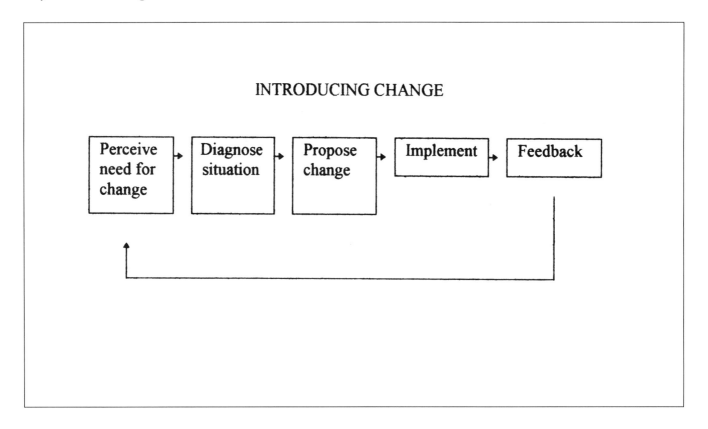

▶ Chart 8

Key in the chart below and save it as Chart 8. This chart may be keyed in using an eight-column table. Decrease the size of the left and right margins, if necessary. (The layout may be based on the position of the entries in the fourth line.)

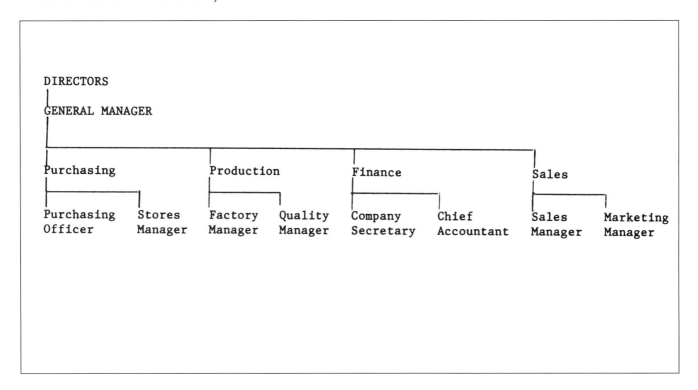

Different types of tab stops

Place the mouse pointer over the tab control on the extreme left of the horizontal ruler line. Note — a box pops up to tell us that this is the **left tab** control. Click this control and note that it changes in succession to **centre tab**, **right tab** and **decimal tab**. For now, we shall confine ourselves to using the left tab, so ensure that the left tab control is showing.

Setting tab stops

With the left tab control showing, click the points on the ruler line at which tab stops are required.

▶ *Tab 2*

Retrieve Tab 1. As the spaces between the columns are unequal, we need to set our own tab stops. Proceed as follows:

❶ Click the Show/Hide button in order to see the tab characters.

❷ If there is more than one tab character between columns on any line, delete it.

❸ Select all three lines.

❹ Set left tabs by clicking the ruler line at the 3 cm, 6 cm and 9 cm marks.

The result is as shown below:

January	April	July	October
February	May	August	November
March	June	September	December

▶ *Tab 3*

Retrieve Tab 2. As the spaces between the columns are still not even, we need to adjust our tab stops. Select all three lines and click on the 9 cm tab stop, hold down the mouse button and drag this tab stop to the 9.5 cm mark. The result is shown below.

January	April	July	October
February	May	August	November
March	June	September	December

Save this altered version of Tab 2 as Tab 3.

▶ *Tab 4*

Retrieve Tab 3. Now try to improve the consistency of the spacing between the columns even more by dragging the tab stops to the left or right as necessary. Save it as Tab 4.

 Important Note — When changing tab stops, it is important that all the relevant lines are selected, otherwise different tab stops will be set on different lines.

Tip — To insert arrows, select the **View** menu, click **Toolbars**, then select the **Drawing** toolbar. On the Drawing toolbar, click on the **Line Style** button and select the type of arrow required. Note that arrows are visible on screen only in Print Layout View or when Print Preview is used.

▶ Chart 5

Key in the chart below and save it as Chart 5.

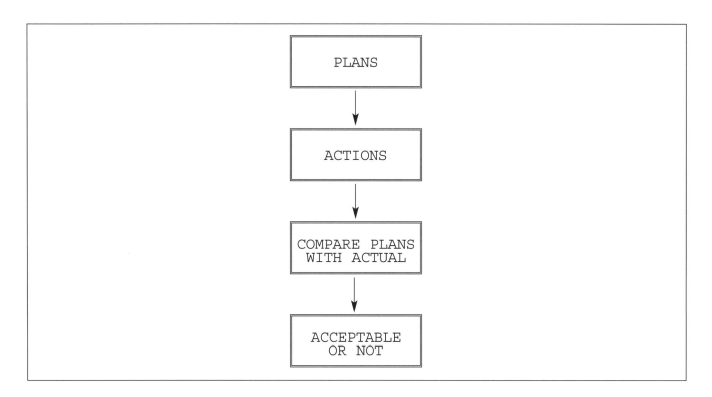

▶ Chart 6

Key in the organisation chart below and save it as Chart 6.

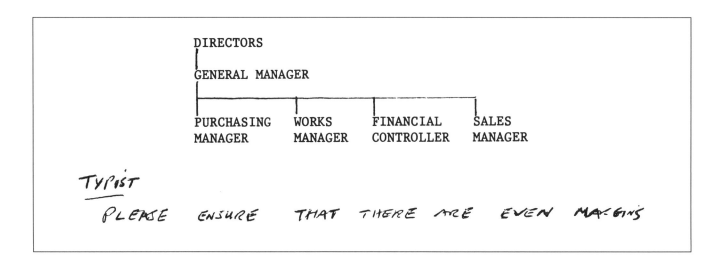

Tab 5

Copy the text below, using only the default tab stops and one tab character between the columns.

SOME PLACES TO VISIT IN COUNTY WEXFORD

Tara Hill Gorey	Dunbrody Abbey	Tacumshane Windmill
Mount Leinster	Tintern Abbey Johnstown Castle	
Enniscorthy Castle	Hook Lighthouse	National Heritage Park
John F Kennedy Park	Saltee Islands Wildfowl Reserve	

Now set left tab stops at points which will ensure that there is a space of about 1 cm between columns. The result should be as shown below. Save it as Tab 5.

SOME PLACES TO VISIT IN COUNTY WEXFORD

Tara Hill Gorey	Dunbrody Abbey	Tacumshane Windmill
Mount Leinster	Tintern Abbey	Johnstown Castle
Enniscorthy Castle	Hook Lighthouse	National Heritage Park
John F Kennedy Park	Saltee Islands	Wildfowl Reserve

Tab 6

Key in the text below. Set left tab stops at points which will ensure that there is a space of approximately 1 cm between the columns. Save it as Tab 6.

SERVICES AVAILABLE AT THE O'SULLIVAN CENTRE

Key Cutting	Carpet Fitting	Gardening
Clothing Repairs	Car Valeting	Massage
Auctioneering	Denture Repairs	Photocopying

Centring tabular statements horizontally, i.e. across the line
Up to now you have probably been keying in tabs which align to the left margin. For display purposes you may need to centre a tabular statement horizontally. It is possible to use the Centre button on the Formatting toolbar. However, this will have the effect of not only centring the tab but also the data in each column. Remember — the tab stop positions will also have to be altered.

Tab 7

Retrieve Tab 6. Centre it using the **Centre** button on the Formatting toolbar, as shown below. Save it as Tab 7.

SERVICES AVAILABLE AT THE O'SULLIVAN CENTRE

Key Cutting	Carpet Fitting	Gardening
Clothing Repairs	Car Valeting	Massage
Auctioneering	Denture Repairs	Photocopying

▶ Chart 3

Use the Drawing toolbar to produce the objects below. The drawing objects should be bottom aligned and there should be equal space between them. Save it as Chart 3.

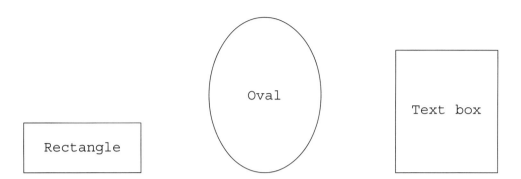

▶ Chart 4

Key in the chart below and save it as Chart 4.

MASLOW'S HIERARCHY OF NEEDS
SELF-ACTUALISATION NEEDS (FULFILMENT)
ESTEEM NEEDS
AFFECTION (OR SOCIAL NEEDS)
SAFETY NEEDS
PHYSIOLOGICAL NEEDS, E.G. FOOD AND SHELTER

▶ Tab 8

Key in the tabs below and save it as Tab 8.

EDUCATIONAL SITES ON THE WORLD WIDE WEB

Ref	Site	Content
1	www.basic-skills.co.uk	help with literacy problems
2	www.funology.com	attempts to make learning fun
3	abc.net.au	a fun experience for children

Centring tabular statements with left-aligned columns

When the **Centre** button was used in Tab 7, each line was centred independently. This is unsatisfactory, as we generally require left-aligned columns in tabular statements.

To centre the above tabular statement and retain left-aligned columns, one approach is as follows:

❶ Make an extra copy of the longest line and centre it using the **Centre** button on the Formatting toolbar. (This line may be used as a guide as to where the tab should start and end.)

❷ Copy, select and centre the heading using the **Centre** button.

❸ Copy and select the tab (excluding the heading) and drag the **Left Indent** control on the ruler line. Keep dragging until the left edge of the tab is in line with the start of the centred copy of the longest line.

❹ Adjust the tab stops until the spaces between the columns are reasonably even. Then, ensure that the right edge of the tab is in line with the end of the extra copy of the longest line.

▶ Tab 9

Retrieve Tab 8 and centre it. Save it as Tab 9. The result should be as shown below. Don't forget to delete the extra copy of the longest line, which was used only as a guide.

    2   www.funology.com   attempts to make learning fun

EDUCATIONAL SITES ON THE WORLD WIDE WEB

Ref	Site	Content
1	www.basic-skills.co.uk	help with literacy problems
2	www.funology.com	attempts to make learning fun
3	abc.net.au	a fun experience for children

Seeing drawing objects on screen

In Normal view, drawing objects are not visible on screen. Click the **View** menu and **Print Layout** to see drawing objects on screen.

Flowcharts

Flowchart symbols can be used to illustrate the flow of documentation through an organisation, the stages of a job, the elements of a system or a sequence of events.

Organisation charts

Word comes complete with standard organisation charts that can be changed as necessary. Click the **Insert** menu, click **Object** and then click the **Create New** tab in the Object dialog box. In the **Object type** box, click **Ms Organisation Chart** 2.0, or later version.

▶ *Chart 1*

Draw the objects below. Ensure that there is equal space between them. Save it as Chart 1.

▶ *Chart 2*

Draw the objects below. Click **AutoShapes** on the Drawing toolbar, then click **Flowcharts** to produce the symbols. Save it as Chart 2.

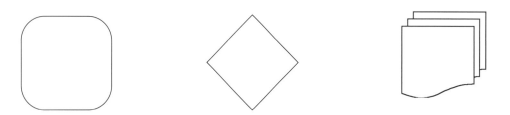

Adding text to objects (other than text boxes)

Select the object. Hold the mouse pointer over the object, right click the mouse and select **Add Text**.

▶ Tab 10

Key in the text below and save it as Tab 10. Set a tab stop at the centre point for the second column, and centre vertically and horizontally.

                S T U D E N T   E N R O L M E N T   R E C O R D
                                2 0 0 6

                                CONFIDENTIAL

Name: Helen Barry

Address: 25 Riverside Road
                                Mallow
                                Co Cork

Student Number: 98884/2

Course Preference: History of Art

Level:*   2

Fees: €800 per annum

Paid   Yes/~~No~~

Important Notes

1 Acceptance subject to results of the Leaving Certificate Examination.
2 Payment must be made within one week of acceptance.
_____

* State number only as follows:

        1 = Advanced
        2 = Ordinary
        3 = Beginners

 Note — To strike through 'No', click the **Format** menu, click **Font**, click the **Font** tab, then click the **Strikethrough** checkbox, which is found under **Effects**.

Charts

Candidates sitting examinations in word processing are sometimes called upon to key in charts. The following may be useful: the Drawing toolbar, the Tables and Borders toolbar and the Table menu.

As with all word-processing work, consistency is important. Therefore, strive for consistent horizontal and vertical spacing when laying out charts.

Using the Drawing toolbar

To show the Drawing toolbar in the Word window, do one of the following:

• click the **Drawing** icon on the Standard Toolbar

• click the **View** menu, click **Toolbars** and then click **Drawing**.

Selecting a number of drawing objects

Method 1 — Click the **Select Objects** button (the pointer arrow) on the Drawing toolbar. Move the mouse pointer arrow above and to the left of the three objects. Hold down the mouse button and trace a rectangle shape that covers the three objects.

Method 2 — Click on the first object, hold down the Shift key and click on the second and then the other objects.

Align and distribute

It is possible to automatically align and distribute drawing objects evenly. To do this, select the relevant drawing objects. Click the **Draw** button on the Drawing toolbar and click **Align and Distribute,** then select the alignment or distribution required.

The draw grid

The draw grid may be thought of as an invisible grid that lies beneath Word documents. Drawing objects, e.g. text boxes, and AutoShapes, e.g. flowchart symbols, 'stars and banners', can be aligned with, or 'snapped to', the lines of this grid. Also, objects of a fixed size can be drawn using this function.

Using the draw grid

Click the Draw button on the Drawing toolbar and click **Grid**.

Adjust the spaces between the cells of the grid, if necessary. For example, if cells of 2.5 cm square are required, key in 2.5 cm into both the **Horizontal spacing** and the **Vertical spacing** boxes in the **Snap to grid** dialog box.

The **Snap to grid** and **Snap to shapes** boxes in the Grid dialog box should be activated or deactivated as required.

The **Horizontal origin** and **Vertical origin** boxes are used to tell Word where gridlines should commence, i.e. how far in from the edge of the Word screen.

Copy drawing objects

When a number of text boxes or other drawing objects of the same size are required, drag and copy the first object as often as necessary.

Leader characters (or leader dots)

When data is presented in tabular format, a series of dots is sometimes used to lead the eye from one column to the next. The three different styles available are shown below.

CULTURAL EVENTS

Jersey .... Jazz Festival .... Leader Style 1
Paris --------------- Fashion Week ------------------------ Leader Style 2
London _____ Picasso: Sculptor and Painter_____ Leader Style 3

Inserting leader characters

Select the lines in which you want to include leader characters. Click the **Format** menu, then click **Tabs**. In the **Tab stop position** box, key in the position of a new tab or select an existing tab. Under **Leader,** click a style and then click **Set**.

▶ *Tab 11*

Retrieve Tab 9 and add Style I leader characters to the tab stops. Save it as Tab II.

▶ *Tab 12*

Retrieve Tab 6 and add Style 2 leader characters to the tab stops. Save it as Tab 12.

▶ *Tab 13*

Retrieve Tab II and change the leader characters to Style 3. Centre vertically and horizontally. Save it as Tab 13.

Key in the account below and save it as Bus Doc 3.

SEAMUS ENNIS — SOLE TRADER

Trading and Profit and Loss Account for the Year Ended 31 December 2006

	€		€
Opening Stock	25,261	Sales	49,800
Add Purchases	10,642		
	35,903		
Less Closing Stock	6,499		
Cost of Goods Sold	29,404		
Gross Profit c/d	20,396		
	49,800		49,800
Wages & Salaries	1,200	Gross Profit b/d	20,396
Rent, Rates & Salaries	5,600		
Bad Debts	1,000		
Depreciation	100		
Net Profit	12,496		
	20,396		20,396

Balance Sheet as at 31 December 2006

	€	€		€
Capital			Fixed Assets	
Balance 1/1/06		3,100	Fixtures & Fittings	750
Add Net Profit		12,496	Less Depreciation	100
for year		15,596		650
Less Drawings		10,000	Current Assets	
		5,596	Stock	6,499
Current Liabilities			Debtors	947
Creditors	500			
Bank Overdraft	2,000	2,500		
		8,096		8,096

▶ Tab 14

Key in the report below and save it as Tab 14.

EXAMINATIONS REPORT

CONTENTS

TYPIST
Block this column and leave one space only after leader dots

Page

INTRODUCTION	1
Audio-Typewriting	2
Book-keeping and Accounts	4
Commerce	5
Cost and Management Accounting	5
English	6
English for Business Communications	9
English for Office Skills	10
English for the Secretary	13
Keyboarding	20
Office Practice	21
Practical Data Processing	23
Retailing and Distribution	24
Secretarial Practice	25
Shorthand Speed	26
Shorthand Theory	28
Shorthand-Typewriting	29
Typewriting	30
Typewriting Speed Test	32
Understanding Computers	36
Word Processing (Practical)	36
Word Processing (Theory)	38
CONCLUSION	40

*TYPIST - I mean the number 1 should come under the 'a' in page and the number 10 should come under the 'P' in page etc

Financial statements

Financial statements may be keyed in using tables or tabs.

If using tabs to complete the task overleaf (Business Document 3), proceed as follows:

❶ Use A4 paper setup with left and right margins of 2.5 cm.

❷ Set a **decimal tab** at 7.5 cm.

❸ Set a **left tab** at 8.5 cm.

❹ Set a **right tab** at the right margin.

❺ Set left tabs on lines where the € symbol appears.

❻ If there are additional columns on either side, set appropriate tabs.

Working out the mid-point in a document:

❶ Remember, we print on A4 paper, which is 21 cm wide.

❷ We set up with 2.5 cm margins on the left and right, i.e. we allocated a total of 5 cm to margins.

❸ Therefore, there is a total of 16 cm of available space.

❹ The mid-point in a document is therefore 8 cm.

Centre tab, right tab and decimal tab

Up to this point, we have confined ourselves to using left tabs. We now need to use other types of tabs. Position the mouse pointer over the left tab control on the ruler line and click it a number of times. You will note that it changes in succession to **centre tab**, **right tab** and **decimal tab**.

In the examples below, each tab has been set at the 8 cm mark:

Left tab   The book cost €20.75
Centre tab   The book cost €20.75
Right tab   The book cost €20.75
Decimal tab   The book cost €20.75

When the Tab key was pressed, the different tab settings had the following effects:

❶ Left tab — the second column started at the 8 cm mark.
❷ Centre tab — the second column was centred each side of the 8 cm mark.
❸ Right tab — the second column finished at the 8 cm mark.
❹ Decimal tab — the decimal point was in line with the 8 cm mark.

▶ Tab 15A

Key in the tabular statement below, using left tabs. Save it as Tab 15A.

	February	March	April	May
	€	€	€	€
R Walsh	5.50	99.50	2,690.00	.50
N Murphy	125.00	2,000.00	20.17	2.75
T Egan	1,750.00	9.50	2.95	1,560.50

▶ Tab 15B

Retrieve Tab 15A, select it and set decimal tabs as explained below. Save it as Tab 15B.

Select the lines which contain figures. Click the **Format** menu, click **Tabs** and in the Tabs dialog box, click **Clear All**. Now set and drag the decimal tabs into position so that the highest-value figure in each column aligns with the € sign, as shown below.

	February	March	April	May
	€	€	€	€
R Walsh	5.50	99.50	2,690.00	.50
N Murphy	125.00	2,000.00	20.17	12.75
T Egan	1,750.00	9.50	2.95	1,560.50

Check your work

Bus Doc 2 should appear similar to the invoice shown below.

VAT REG NO IE Q/57483337L	INVOICE NO 8767391	Tel (059) 74555 Fax (059) 74978

MURPHY AND O'LEARY WHOLESALE LTD
CHAPEL STREET
CLONAKILTY
CO CORK
IRELAND

In account with:

Byrne Hardware Baltimore Road Skibbereen Co Cork	**Date** 21 09 06

Order No 83147 | **Terms: 2¹/₂% 30 days, otherwise strictly net.**

QUANTITY	DESCRIPTION	UNIT PRICE	VAT	TOTAL
		€	€	€
500	NO 67 light bulbs	0.20		100.00
10	Door knockers	2.75		27.50
10	Kingfisher bells	3.35		33.50
50	Yacht varnish (small)	1.95		97.50
				258.50
	Add VAT at		21%	54.28
	Total			312.78

▶ Tab 15C

Retrieve Tab 15B, select it and set right tabs as explained below. Save it as Tab 15C.

Select the entire tabular statement. Click the **Format** menu, click **Tabs** and in the Tabs dialog box, click **Clear All**. Now set and drag the right tabs into position so that the spaces between the columns are reasonably even, as shown below:

	February	March	April	May
	€	€	€	€
R Walsh	5.50	99.50	2,690.00	.50
N Murphy	125.00	2,000.00	20.17	12.75
T Egan	1,750.00	9.50	2.95	1,560.50

▶ Tab 15D

Retrieve 15C, select it and set centred tabs, as explained below. Save it as Tab 15D.

Select the entire tabular statement. Click the **Format** menu, click **Tabs** and in the Tabs dialog box, click **Clear All**. Now set the centre tabs so that the spaces between the columns are reasonably even, as shown below.

	February	March	April	May
	€	€	€	€
R Walsh	5.50	99.50	2,690.00	.50
N Murphy	125.00	2,000.00	20.17	12.75
T Egan	1,750.00	9.50	2.95	1,560.50

 Note — For most purposes it is better to block columns in tabular work, i.e. data in columns should align to the left. When figures are used, the largest figure should align to the left and smaller figures should align so that units are under units, tens under tens and so on.

▶ Business Document 2

Retrieve Bus Doc TP1. Include the details that have been circled. Save it as Bus Doc 2.

Underlining totals

Totals may be underlined using either Style A or Style B, as shown below.

```
Style A                              Style B

€                                    €
5,600                                5,600
  750                                  750
   89                                   89
1,950        no return               1,950        no return
             two returns                          two returns
8,389                                8,389         one return


```

Double underline — Style A

❶ Select 8,389 and press Ctrl+Shift+D.

Double underline — Style B

❶ Ensure the cursor is in the line in question.

❷ Set a left tab where the underline should start and another left tab where it should finish.

❸ Press Ctrl+Tab to move the cursor to the first tab position.

❹ Press Shift+Ctrl+D to activate the double underline function.

❺ Press Ctrl+Tab to double underline as far as the second tab stop.

In both *Style A* and *Style B* press Shift+Ctrl+D again to deactivate the double underline function.

Using Tables

Now that we have served our apprenticeship handling tabs, it's time to move onto tables. The table function in Microsoft Word makes handling tabular work easy. Click the **Table** menu, select **Insert Table** and specify the number of rows and columns required. The space between the margins is automatically divided into equal column widths.

The Tab key in tables

In tables, the Tab key moves the cursor to the next cell. To move the insertion point to a tab stop within a cell, it is necessary to hold down Ctrl while pressing the Tab key.

▶ Table 1

Key in the heading in the exercise below. Then insert a table with four columns and six rows. Save it as Table 1.

EXECUTIVE CARS

MODEL	CC	MPH	MPG
Audi 100 2.6	2,598	130	23
BMW 525	2,494	140	23
Ford Granada 2.9I	2,933	124	19
Mercedes C280	2,799	143	20
Volvo 850 GLT	2,435	131	22

▶ Table 2

Key in the heading in the exercise below. Then insert a table with five rows and four columns. Use 12 points Times New Roman font. Save it as Table 2.

EXPENDITURE ON TELEPHONE CALLS

Category	2003	2004	2005
	€	€	€
Local Calls	75,060	79,171	60,127
National Calls	36,615	38,124	35,147
International Calls	10,126	11,746	11,388

 Note — Rows go across and and columns go down.

Business Documents

▶ Business Document 1

Create an invoice template from the details below (ignore the circled items for the moment) and save it as Bus Doc TP1.

Use the **Tables and Borders** button ⊞ on the Formatting toolbar to create the required lines. To key in a double underline, hold down Shift+Ctrl and the 'd' key.

VAT REG NO	**INVOICE**	Tel (059) 74555
IE Q/57483337L	NO 8767391	Fax (059) 74978

MURPHY AND O'LEARY WHOLESALE LTD
CHAPEL STREET
CLONAKILTY
CO CORK
IRELAND

In account with:

Byrne Hardware
Baltimore Road
Skibbereen
Co Cork

Date 21 09 06

Order No 83147   Terms: 2½% 30 days, otherwise strictly net.

QUANTITY	DESCRIPTION	UNIT PRICE	VAT	TOTAL
		€		€
500	NO 67 light bulbs	0.20		100.00
10	Door knockers	2.75		27.50
10	Kingfisher bells	3.35		33.50
50	Yacht varnish (small)	1.95		97.50
				258.50
	Add VAT at		21%	54.28
	Total			312.78

WP OPERATOR, PLEASE:

1 Set a decimal tab to ensure that figures align correctly in the Total column & THE QUANTITY COLUMN.

2 Ensure the spaces before and after the total ARE equal.

3 Ensure the ½ in 2½% aligns correctly. Just type the sloping fraction 1/2 and tap the space bar. The fraction character ½ will appear if "AutoFormat As You Type" HAS BEEN SET TO MAKE THIS CHANGE.

▶ Table 3

Key in the table below and save it as Table 3.

IRISH CORAL CONVENTION TARIFF SHEET

HOTEL	B & B	B & B AND EVENING MEAL	FULL BOARD
	€	€	€
Shamrock Lodge	30.00	40.00	45.00
Tara Inn	40.00	55.00	60.00
Abbey House	50.00	70.00	80.00
The Lakeside	65.00	85.00	95.00

Columns, rows and cells

Columns are the vertical divisions and rows are the horizontal divisions in a table. For example, in the table above hotel names appear down the first column and details relating to Abbey House appear across the fifth row. Cells are the individual boxes in a table. For example, we can say that the figure 70.00 is in the fifth cell in the third column, or the third cell in the fifth row.

▶ Table 4

Key in the table below and save it as Table 4.

TAKE THE FAMILY TO FRANCE

DATES	MOBILE HOMES		SUPER TENTS	
	10 nights	12 nights	10 nights	12 nights
	€	€	€	€
June	650	700	450	500
July	750	750	500	525
August	850	800	550	580

Merging cells

As the heading MOBILE HOMES refers to information in both the second and third columns, we need to merge the second and third cells in the first row. To do this, select both cells, go to the **Table** menu and click on **Merge Cells**.

▶ Table 5

Retrieve Table 4 and merge the second and third cells in the first row, as shown below. Save it as Table 5.

DATES	MOBILE HOMES		SUPER TENTS	
	10 nights	12 nights	10 nights	12 nights
	€	€	€	€
June	650	700	450	500
July	750	750	500	525
August	850	800	550	580

Forms should be easy to understand and complete

❶ Allow adequate space for responses to questions.

❷ Use multiple-choice rather than open-ended questions where possible.

❸ Leave a space between words and lines, as shown below:

```
Name _____  Date of Birth  _____
```

▶ Form 6

Use the Draw Table and Erase buttons on the Form toolbar to key in the form below. You should also use the Tables and Borders toolbar to align text and distribute rows and columns evenly. Protect the table and save as Form 6.

<table>
<tr><td colspan="6" align="center">**Morning Star Financial Services**
Application Form</td></tr>
<tr><td>Surname</td><td></td><td>First Name</td><td></td></tr>
<tr><td colspan="6">Address</td></tr>
<tr><td>Telephone</td><td>Mobile</td><td></td><td>Work</td><td></td></tr>
<tr><td>Date of Birth</td><td></td><td>E-mail</td><td></td></tr>
<tr><td colspan="6">I wish to invest in the following funds (please tick)

Income and Growth   ☐

Secure Bond Fund   ☐

Euro Growth Bond   ☐</td></tr>
<tr><td colspan="6">Please enter the amount you wish to invest monthly or annually.</td></tr>
<tr><td>Amount Payable</td><td>Monthly</td><td></td><td>Annually</td><td></td></tr>
<tr><td colspan="6">I/we appoint Morning Star Financial Services as Investment Advisors to exercise fund switches on my/our behalf. I/we accept the above named will have full authority to decide and effect changes to the asset mix of the above funds.

I/we further undertake to advise Morning Star Financial Services in writing immediately if I/we wish to revoke the above appointment.</td></tr>
<tr><td>Signature of proposer</td><td></td><td>Date</td><td></td></tr>
</table>

Changing the height of a row

Never key in extra line returns to increase the height of rows in a table. Instead, use one of the methods listed below:

❶ Click the **View** menu and select **Print Layout**. (This method only works when in Print Layout view.) Hold the mouse pointer on the bottom border of a row and drag the border to the required position.

❷ If a precise row height is required, click in the row. Then click the **Table** menu, **Table Properties**, the **Row** tab, the **Specify height** box and enter the required height.

❸ Select the table and press Ctrl+2 for double-line spacing.

▶ Table 6

Retrieve Table 1. Embolden the first row and format the table in double-line spacing, as shown below. Save it as Table 6.

EXECUTIVE CARS

MODEL	CC	MPH	MPG
Audi 100 2.6	2,598	130	23
BMW 525	2,494	140	23
Ford Granada 2.9I	2,933	124	19
Mercedes C280	2,799	143	20
Volvo 850 GLT	2,435	131	22

Adjusting the space between columns

When working with **tabs**, we mentioned that it's generally better to have reasonably equal space between columns (see page 139). Remember, we looked at the space between the longest word in the first column and the start of the second column. Then we looked at the space between the longest word in the second column and the start of the third column and so on. In Table 6 you will see that the space between the first and second columns is less than the space between the other columns.

Question — Why are the spaces between the columns unequal?

Answer — We asked Word to insert a table with four columns and six rows. Word then divided the spaces between the margins into four equal lengths. Word had no way of knowing that we were about to key in columns of different lengths.

▶ *Form 5*

Key in the lines below using method 2, referred to on the previous page, and save as Form 5. Proceed as follows:

❶ Set left tabs at the 2 cm and 8 cm marks on the ruler line.

❷ Tab to the first tab stop.

❸ Click the Underline button on the Formatting toolbar.

❹ Tab to the second tab stop.

❺ Press the Return key twice.

❻ Select the first line.

❼ Hold down the Control key and drag a copy of the first line to the second line, then to the third line.

    _____

    _____

    _____

It is suggested that 6 points spacing should be allowed before and after the lines in a form. To do this, click the **Format** menu, then click **Paragraph**. Click the **Indents and Spacing** tab in the Paragraph dialog box. Key in '6 pt' in both the **Before** and **After** boxes under Spacing.

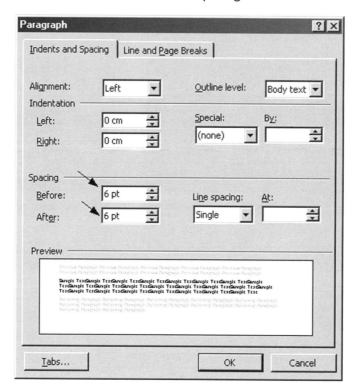

How do we solve the problem of unequal spaces between the columns?

❶ Move the mouse pointer to the edge of a column. When the pointer changes to a left-and-right arrow, drag its border.

❷ If a precise column width is required, click in a column. Then click the **Table** menu, **Table Properties**, the **Column** tab and enter the required width.

Using AutoFit

▶ *Table 7*

Retrieve Table 6. Use AutoFit to adjust the spaces between the columns, as shown below. To do this, click the **Table** menu, then click **AutoFit to Contents**. Save it as Table 7.

EXECUTIVE CARS

MODEL	CC	MPH	MPG
Audi 100 2.6	2,598	130	23
BMW 525	2,494	140	23
Ford Granada 2.9I	2,933	124	19
Mercedes C280	2,799	143	20
Volvo 850 GLT	2,435	131	22

Dragging to move table columns' edges on the ruler line

▶ *Table 8*

Retrieve Table 6 and drag the column border to allow 1.5 cm between the columns, as shown below. Save it as Table 8.

EXECUTIVE CARS

MODEL	CC	MPH	MPG
Audi 100 2.6	2,598	130	23
BMW 525	2,494	140	23
Ford Granada 2.9I	2,933	124	19
Mercedes C280	2,799	143	20
Volvo 850 GLT	2,435	131	22

▶ Form 4

Retrieve Form 3, enter the details shown below and save as Form 4.

❶ The first field should be a text form field and the date type should be **Current Date**.

❷ The arrival date is 17/8/06 and the departure date is 20/8/06.

❸ Answer 'Usually' to statement 1 and 4 and 'Always' to statements 2 and 3.

❹ The excursions/events particularly enjoyed were Galway Races and Hill Walking.

❺ For 'Other – please specify', key in 'Listening to the Irish language being spoken in Connemara'.

❻ For suggestions, key in 'The hotel would benefit greatly from the addition of a sea-facing conservatory.'

Manual forms

In addition to computerised forms, it may be necessary to prepare forms that can be filled in manually. Apart from the Forms toolbar, the Drawing toolbar is useful for this purpose. Click the **View** menu, **Toolbars** and ensure the Forms and Drawing toolbars are selected, i.e. ticked.

Lines in forms

Lines may be drawn in different ways, as set out below. The first way is particularly convenient.

❶ Use the Draw Table and Eraser buttons on the Forms toolbar.

❷ Click the mouse where the line is required. Set a tab at the point where the line should end, click the **Underline** button on the Formatting toolbar and press the Tab key.

❸ Click the **View** menu, **Toolbars**, **Drawing**, **Line** button. The I-beam changes to a cross (crosshair). Click the mouse again at the point where the line should start and drag, while holding down the Shift key, to where the line should end.

❹ Key in continuous hyphens.

Centring a table across the page

Click anywhere in the table, then click **Table Properties**, the **Table** tab and **Centre.**

▶ *Table 9*

Retrieve Table 7 and centre the heading first, then centre the table, as shown below. Save it as Table 9.

EXECUTIVE CARS

MODEL	CC	MPH	MPG
Audi 100 2.6	2,598	130	23
BMW 525	2,494	140	23
Ford Granada 2.9I	2,933	124	19
Mercedes C280	2,799	143	20
Volvo 850 GLT	2,435	131	22

Lines in tables

When a table is inserted in Word, lines automatically appear between the cells. If you do not require lines, select the relevant cells. Then click the down arrow to the right of the **Outside Border** button on the Formatting toolbar and click the **No Border** button.

Alternative method: Select the relevant cells. Click the **Format** menu, **Borders and Shading**, the **Borders** tab and then click **None.**

▶ *Table 10*

Retrieve Table 5 and delete all the lines. Save it as Table 10.

▶ *Table 11*

Retrieve Table 10 and reinsert the lines around and between the cells in the first row only, as shown below. Save it as Table 11.

TAKE THE FAMILY TO FRANCE

DATES	MOBILE HOMES		SUPER TENTS	
	10 nights	12 nights	10 nights	12 nights
	€	€	€	€
June	650	700	450	500
July	750	750	500	525
August	850	800	550	580

▶ Form 3

Complete, protect and test the survey form below and save it as Form 3.

CUSTOMER SURVEY
Cré Dubh Hotel
Connemara
Co Galway
Ireland
http://www.cdhcdh.ie

Date ▨ (text form field, data type: Current Date)

Dear Customer

Thank you for staying with us here in Connemara. We hope we will have the pleasure of welcoming you again in the not too distant future. To help us to improve the experience we offer our guests, we would ask you to kindly complete the following brief survey.

When did you stay with us?   Arrival date ▨ (text form field, data type: Date)
Departure date ▨ (text form field, data type: Date)

Please click the arrow in the shaded areas after the statements below to reveal the words **Always**, **Usually** and **Rarely**. Please select the word that best describes your experience in the Cré Dubh Hotel.

1. Reception personnel were friendly and efficient
    (This section requires drop-down form fields Always, Usually and Rarely) | Always ± |

2. Bedrooms were well cleaned and maintained | Always ± |

3. The standard of food served was good | Always ± |

4. Dining room service was good | Always ± |

Which areas or events did you particularly enjoy (please tick)?
(This section requires check box form fields)

Connemara	☐	The Burren	☐	Aran Islands	☐
Swimming	☐	Angling	☐	Hill Walking	☐
Galway Oyster Festival	☐	Galway Arts Festival	☐	Galway Races	☐
Galway Film Festival	☐				

Other – please specify ▨ (text form field)

Have you any suggestions as to how we can improve the experience we offer our guests?
Please write your suggestions here: ▨ (text form field)

Inserting rows

If an additional row is required, click where the new row is to go, then click the **Table** menu, **Insert** and **Rows Above** or **Rows Below**.

▶ *Table 12*

Retrieve Table 11 and insert the additional row, as shown below. Delete all grid lines and then insert lines around the outside of the table only. Save it as Table 12.

DATES	MOBILE HOMES		SUPER TENTS	
	10 nights	12 nights	10 nights	12 nights
	€	€	€	€
May	550	600	350	455
June	650	700	450	500
July	750	750	500	525
August	850	800	550	580

Inserting columns

If an additional column is required, click where the column is to go, then click the **Table** menu, **Insert** and **Columns to the Left** or **Columns to the Right**.

▶ *Table 13*

Retrieve Table 3 and insert an additional column, as shown. Use AutoFit, delete all lines and then reinstate the lines shown. Save it as Table 13.

IRISH CORAL CONVENTION TARIFF SHEET

HOTEL	ROOM ONLY	B & B	B & B AND EVENING MEAL	FULL BOARD
	€	€	€	€
Shamrock Lodge	20.00	30.00	40.00	45.00
Tara Inn	30.00	40.00	55.00	60.00
Abbey House	40.00	50.00	70.00	80.00
The Lakeside	50.00	65.00	85.00	95.00

Now retrieve the Form I template, enter the details shown below and save as Form 2.

Please note:
❶ Click a check box form field to select it, i.e. cross it.
❷ Form field shading may be cancelled by clicking the Form Field Shading button.
❸ Your form should have the current date, not the date below (which was the date when this text was written).

Halpin's·Hotel·Registration·Form¶

¶
Surname·Flynn → First·Name·Helen¶
Address·6·Church·Street¶
City/Town·Midleton¶
Country·Ireland¶
Postal·or·Zip·Code·None¶
¶
Phone·Number· → 217396522¶
E-mail·Address·→ hflynn66@eircom.net¶
¶
Method·of·Payment¶
Visa· → ☒ → Master·Card· → ☐ → American·Express· → ☐¶
Cash· → ☐ → Cheque·   →   ☐ → Traveller's·Cheque· → ☐¶
¶
How·long·do·you·intend·to·stay?·Please·enter·number·and·click·the·down·arrow·to·select·
Days,·Weeks·or·Months.··5··Day(s)¶
¶
¶
Date·11/08/2004¶

▶ Table 14

Refer to the notes that follow and then key in the table shown below. Save it as Table 14.

CAR HIRE IN LONDON

Self-drive packages are arranged in association with AVIS, who offer a wide range of vehicles at excellent rates. All prices are in £ sterling per day.

Vehicle Group	Capacity	Vehicle Type	Consecutive Days		
			7-13	14-20	21+
A	5-Door (seats 4)	Toyota Corolla	32	30	28
C	4-Door (seats 4)	Toyota Camry	35	33	31
E	4-Door (seats 5)	Ford Falcon	39	38	35
G	4-Door (seats 5)	Ford Mondeo	48	46	44
F	5-Door (seats 5)	Nissan Primera	50	48	46
J	5-Door (seats 5)	Mazda	52	50	48

[handwritten note pointing to top-right of table:] ✱ TYPIST - SEE BELOW

Included in your hire:

* One transfer from airport or city to depot or vice/versa
* Government taxes and stamp duties

Not included in your hire:

* Vehicle insurance, personal accident plan
* Petrol and traffic fines

[handwritten note:] Typist ✱ Insert the £ symbol over the figure columns. Leave a clear line before and after the symbols.

To produce the grid in the above table, proceed as follows:

Method 1 — For the first three columns, delete the line between the first and second rows (use the Borders button on the Formatting toolbar), then **merge** the last three cells of the first row.

Double click the text form field you entered after Phone Number and in the **Text Form Field Options** dialog box, click the **Type** down arrow, click **Number** and then click **OK**. Repeat these steps for the text form field you entered after Days, Weeks or Months.

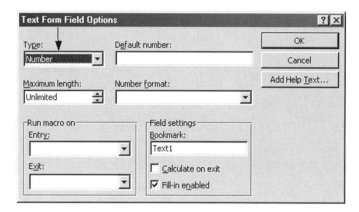

Double click the text form field you entered after Date and in the **Text Form Field Options** dialog box, click the **Type** down arrow, click **Current Date** and then click **OK**.

Entering check box form fields

Click the Check Box Form Field button after Visa, Master Card, American Express, Cash, Cheque and Traveller's Cheque.

Entering the drop-down form fields

Click the Drop-Down Form Field button, one clear space **after** the text field you entered for Days, Weeks or Months. In the Drop-Down Form Field Options dialog box, enter Day(s), click the **Add** button and enter Week(s) and Month(s) in the same way, click **OK**.

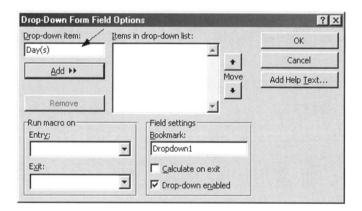

Protecting a form

Before a form can function as a template, it must be protected, by pressing the Protect Form button . In this way the form layout is not changed when it is filled in.

Testing a form

When a form has been designed and protected, it should be tested by entering relevant data into each field. For example, drop-down form fields should function correctly and it should not be possible to enter text into a number form field.

Method 2 — Click **Table**, **Draw Table**, then draw the required table outline, as shown below. To adjust the outline, click the mouse pointer on a vertical or horizontal line and drag when a double-headed arrow appears.

The result of using Draw Table

▶ **Table 15**

Key in the table below and save it as Table 15.

O'BRIEN   FINANCIAL SERVICES

<u>Current Base and Compound Interest Rates</u>
(Rates subject to fluctuation)

TYPE OF INVESTMENT	Interest Rate		MINIMUM INVESTMENT
	Base % X	CAR % X	
			€
Plus Fund	8.25	7.55	20,000
Extra Fund	6.25	7.30	10,000
Euro Fund	7.50	8.25	15,000
Plus Cash Flow	7.25	8.15	250
Cash Flow no 7	7.50	8.30	5,000
Cash Flow no 14	7.75	8.50	10,000
Cash Flow No 21	8.00	9.25	20,000
Monthly Savings	7.55	7.90	€5 per month
Deposits	6.00	6.05	100
Subscription Shares X	7.00	7.12	1,000
Convertible Shares	9.15	9.36	2,000

equal spaces between columns AT ✗

Part 9
Forms, Business Documents
and Charts

▷▷▷▷▷▷▷▶▷▷▷▷▷

Forms
The Form toolbar
Word provides a form toolbar with buttons for creating form fields, as shown below.

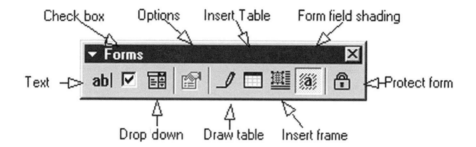

▶ Form 1

Refer to the instructions below and overleaf and create a form template by keying in the text and form fields shown in the Halpin's Hotel Registration Form that follows. Save this exercise as a template, called Form 1.

Halpin's·Hotel·Registration·Form¶

¶
Surname·ooooo → First·Name·ooooo¶
Address·ooooo¶
City/Town·ooooo¶
Country·ooooo¶
Postal·or·Zip·Code·ooooo¶
¶
Phone·Number· → ooooo¶
E-mail·Address·→ ooooo¶
¶
Method·of·Payment¶
Visa· → ☐ → Master·Card· → ☐ → American·Express· → ☐¶
Cash· → ☐ → Cheque· → ☐ → Traveller's·Cheque· → ☐¶
¶
How·long·do·you·intend·to·stay?·Please·enter·number·and·click·the·down·arrow·to·select·
Days,·Weeks·or·Months.·ooooo··Day(s) ±
¶   Day(s)
∥   Week(s)
Date·ooooo¶   Month(s)

Entering text form fields
Leave one space after Surname and click the Text Form Field button on the Form Toolbar. Now enter a text form field after First Name, Address, City/Town, Country and Postal or Zip code, Phone Number, E-mail Address, Days, Weeks or Months and Date. (Use drag and copy to quickly carry out this task.)

Leader characters in tables

It is usually unnecessary to insert leader characters in tables. However, if they are required, proceed as follows:

Select the column in which the leader characters are required and click the ruler line at the point where the leader characters should end. Click **Format** and **Tabs**. In the Tabs dialog box, click the type of leader characters required, click **Set** and click **OK**. Finally, press CTRL+Tab after the text that is to be followed by the leader characters.

Refer to page 144 for more information on leader characters.

 Remember — To move to a tab stop in a table, hold down the Control key (Ctrl) while pressing the Tab key, i.e. Ctrl+Tab.

Changing the lines in tables

Select the cells around which different lines are required, click the **Format** menu, then click **Borders and Shading**. In the Borders and Shading dialog box, click the **Borders** tab, then under **Setting** and **Style** select the type of line required, then click **OK**.

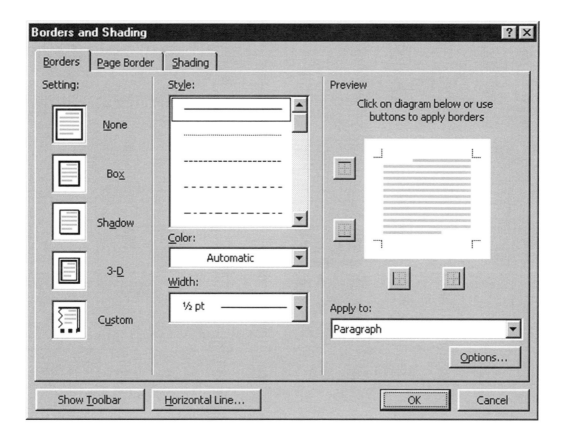

▶ Table 23

Key in the table below. Use Style 2, referred to on page 161. Save it as Table 23.

Insert Turn up twice

Bank/Building Society Mortgage Rates as of 4th July 2005

Turn up 1 before 2 after

Lender	Variable Rates	APR	€ per '000	1 yr Fixed Rates
ACC Bank	7.25	7.45	7.88	6.75
AIB Bank	7.25	7.44	7.87	6.25
Bank of Ireland	7.45	7.8	8.00	6.5
National Irish Bank	6.7	6.9	7.57	–
TSB	~~6.75~~ 7.0	~~7.0~~ 7.2	7.75	–
Ulster Bank	6.75	7.0	7.71	–
EBS	7.1	7.6	7.93	5.90
First National	7.69	8.3	8.29	–
~~ICS~~	~~7.25~~	~~7.7~~	~~8.01~~	~~–~~
Irish Life	6.99	7.2	7.75	–
Irish Permanent	7.0	7.3	7.75	6.75

Key in the table below and save it as Table 16. Insert double lines and leader characters where shown. As usual, align all data in the columns to the left.

NORTHERN INDUSTRIES PLC

> LEAVE A SPACE HERE AT LEAST 51 'm ACROSS AND 25 'm DOWN

TP Operator — Delete this line & Block "Number employed"

Type of Labour	Number Employed		
	31 December	31 December	Increase or Decrease*
Production			
Raw Materials ····	1,120	1,210	(90)
Production Lines	2,835	3,032	(197)
Assembly Lines···	1,725	2,026	(301)
Finishing Lines..	601	727	(126)
	6,281	6,995	(714)
Administration			
Clerical........·	140	152	(12)
Finance . ..·..···	70	100	(30)
Personnel Welfare	14	14	–
Medical . . ..··	18	18	–
Legal..·.......·	10	11	(1)
Warehousing ····	120	140	(20)
Cleaning. . .:···.	30	36	(6)
	402	471	(69)
Total	6,683	7,466	(783)

* Minus figures are shown in brackets.

Although the total manpower dropped by 783, production rose by 5.9%, which was a considerable achievement. Provisional figures for 2006 show an even more remarkable result.

TP Operator — under PRODUCTION and Administration. REARRANGE details in Alphabetical order

Key in the table below. Use heading Style 2, referred to on page 161. Save it as Table 22.

O'BRIEN FINANCIAL SERVICES ← BLOCK & BOLD

CURRENT BASE AND COMPOUND ~~INSURANCES~~ INTEREST RATES ARE SUBJECT TO FLUCTUATION — INITIAL CAPITALS

TYPE OF INVESTMENT	BASE INTEREST RATE %	COMPOUND RATE %	MINIMUM INVESTMENT
			£
FUND 105	5.2	7.1	20,000
FUND 106	5.0	6.8	18,000
FUND 107	5.0	6.8	17,000
FUND 108	4.9	6.7	16,000
FUND 109	4.8	6.6	15,000
FUND 110	4.5	6.2	10,000
FUND 111	4.3	5.9	5,000
FUND 112	4.1	5.2	2,000

← ALIGN THESE HEADING TO THE LEFT IN EACH COLUMN

CENTRE THE TABLE HORIZONTALLY & THE WHOLE EXERCISE VERTICALLY

EACH COLUMN SHOULD BE ALIGNED TO THE LEFT

Aligning figures

As a general rule, figures should align to the left. However, as stated on page 147, units must come under units, e.g. tens under tens, hundreds under hundreds. This alignment is achieved in tabular work and tables through the use of decimal tabs.

▶ *Table 17*

Key in the table below and save it as Table 17.

WHO OWNS CUNNINGHAM AND McGRATH LTD? ← BLOCK CAPS

INITIAL CAPS → BREAKDOWN OF ISSUED CAPITAL by class of Shareholder

(INCREASE SPACE HERE)

	1998	1999	2000		2001	2002
	%	%	%		%	%
INDIVIDUALS	34.6	38.4	30.7	29.7		23.1
NOMINEES	28.7	32.0	32.0	40.9		37.0
INSURANCE COMPANIES	16.1	16.5	18.3	11.9		12.3
OTHER COMPANIES	10.6	12.2	6.1	5.6		14.5
PENSION FUNDS						

(Delete this column)

CALCULATE THE FIGURES THAT SHOULD GO IN THE LAST ROW BY ADDING THE FIGURES FOR EACH YEAR + SUBTRACTING FROM 100%.

— PLACE THE CURSOR IN THE REQUIRED CELL, CLICK THE TABLE MENU, Select Formula + ENTER THE FORMULA =100-SUM(ABOVE)

Vertical column headings — Style 1

Occasionally tabulation headings are keyed in with vertical headings. One way of doing this is to key in one letter under the other. Let us call this vertical heading, Style 1. Note — the height of the row containing the column headings will adjust automatically with each line return.

Vertical column headings — Style 2

These headings are formatted to read sideways. To insert such headings, click the **Format** menu, click **Text Direction**, click the orientation required in the **Text Direction** dialog box, then click **OK**.

Bottom-to-top style

June	July	August	September

Top-to-bottom style

June	July	August	September

Changing the position of a row or columns

To do this, select the row(s) or column(s) to be moved, place the mouse pointer over the selected area and drag to the new location.

▶ Table 18

Retrieve Table 17. Move the columns to show the years in reverse order, i.e. 2002 first, 2001 second. Then position the 'Pension Funds' row before the 'Individuals' row. Save it as Table 18.

▶ Table 19

Key in the table below. Format it with the exact grid lines shown. Save it as Table 19.

ATALAYA APARTMENTS

RESORT	PRAIA DA ROCHA			
ACCOM. BASIS	ACCOMMODATION ONLY			
ACCOMMODATION	STUDIO	1 BEDROOM		
NO OF PERSONS	2	4	3	2
NO OF WEEKS	2	2	2	2
	€	€	€	€
May 1, 8	259	239	259	289
May 15	269	249	269	299
May 22, 29	299	269	273	310
June 5, 12	319	289	284	325
June 19	329	301	295	335
June 26	339	320	300	340
July 3, 10	359	330	310	350
July 17, 24	379	340	325	370
July 31	399	350	340	380
Aug 7	389	340	325	370
Aug 14	379	330	310	350
Aug 21	369	300	310	340

▶ Table 20

Retrieve Table 19 and arrange the rows containing dates in reverse chronological order, i.e. reverse date order. Then place the three columns that come under '1 Bedroom' to the left of the 'Studio' column. Save it as Table 20.

Key in the tables below and save them as Table 21. To complete this task, insert a table with four rows and five columns, click in the third row, then click the **Table** menu and **Split Table**.

Survey of Remuneration – O'Rahilly and Byrne

stet / Average Salaries by Region ~~Location~~

REMUNERATION

Typist – insert € signs: (REMAIN ABBREVIATIONS) uc/

	Function Head	Dept Head	Staff	Manager
Dublin City	34,686	27,852	22,891	18,749
North East	31,234	22,802	20,645	18,181
South East	32,155	22,630	25,874	20,075
Midlands	30,600	23,868	19,804	18,124
Cork City	32,155	25,874	22,630	18,855
Shannon area	31,844	25,620	22,807	17,976
West	30,920	22,321	20,314	14,124
North West	29,840	20,400	16,820	16,021

← Typist: leave 3 clear lines here

Average Salaries by Qualification

	Function Head	Dept Head	Manager	Staff
Post grad	33,932	28,027	23,977	20,458
Degree	33,605	27,004	23,023	18,760
Leaving Cert	29,874	24,500	22,818	18,196
None	24,642	21,714	18,202	15,660